The Contemporary Printmaker

Intaglio-Type
&
Acrylic Resist Etching

By Keith Howard

Contributions from:
Friedhard Kiekeben
David Jay Reed
Elizabeth Dove
Monona Rossel

Acknowledgements

To my partner Bernice for her love and support.

To Bernice Cross, my publisher and born printmaker, for her dedication, research, patience and help in demonstrating the techniques for this book.

To Alan Koval, from Thomas J. Liptons Inc., who was the primary force behind the corporate sponsorship of my first book *Safe Photo Etching for Photographers and Artists.*

To Dr. Harold and Joan Wynne of Wynne Resources for their love and support when publishing my first book.

To Dr. Joan Stone and faculty at the Rochester Institute of Technology who have supported Contemporary (Non-Toxic) Printmaking research and education as an important component of the School of Art course offerings.

Special thanks to Alan Singer, Anna Sears for their friendship and loving support.

To Dr. Tom Lightfoot for collaborating in our dream to make R.I.T. a leading institution in the world for Contemporary (Non-Toxic) Printmaking education.

To Elizabeth Dove, a tireless and brilliant printmaker who was instrumental in helping me with my last publication.

To the following people and companies:
1. Susan Rostow, President of Akua Color, for her friendship, brilliance and unique research contribution.
2. Pavel Rapisky, President of Atlantic Papers, for his friendship and unending support.
3. Vince Libire, from Artek Imaging the Marketing Manager for ImagOn.
4. Steve Quindlin, Tiz Guerra from Du Pont who were instrumental in bringing ImagOn to market. To Ellen Pressley for her background support.

To Rosemary Simmons (former editor) and Roger Farrand (former editor & publisher), of *Printmaking Today* who's support and friendship were there when I needed it most.

To the following Contemporary (Non-Toxic) Printmaking leaders who have contributed to the history of printmaking by facilitating the spread of knowledge:
1. To Doreen Nault who spent many months organizing my workshop and lecture tour in Japan in 1993.

2. To Sally Reed who spent many selfless months coordinating and organizing a 2 month lecture tour in the UK in 1994.

3. To Anneli Martin for her extraordinary efforts in organizing an extensive lecture tour in Sweden in 1995.

4. To Christie Nuell from Middle Tennessee State University for contributing her time and expertise in developing my printmaking page for the Internet.

5. To Pauline Muir and Laurel MacKenzie who have spent many hours promoting my Contemporary (Non-Toxic) Intaglio Printmaking tour in Australia, in 1998.

6. To Joan Isaac, former Program Director from Fairview College, who was the organizational force behind the Canadian summer Non-toxic Printmaking Masters Workshops series.

7. To Lucretia Urbana and Andrea Juan, for organizing my workshop and lectures in Buenos Aires in 2001 and who were instrumental in introducing non-toxic printmaking to Argentina.

8. To Jennifer Shaw, Dawn Henderby, Rebecca Coggins, Lesley Tate and Friedhard Kiekeben who started the Innovative Intaglio Summer workshop series in 1998, at the Gracefield Arts Centre, in Dumfries, Scotland.

9. To my friend Henrik Bøegh who has become a major force in propagating and education of non-toxic printmaking methodology in Europe.

10. To Friedhard Kiekeben, my dear friend, who has contributed his genius to this ever expanding discipline.

11. To Haydee Landing and Consuelo Gotay for your friendship and dedication in organizing my workshop and lecture series in Puerto Rico in 2000

12. To my friend Don Messec, for his tireless efforts in organizing non-toxic printmaking summer courses at the College of Santa Fe.

To my friend Hugh Bryden for his friendship and support.

To my good friend David Jay Reed for his own unique brand of genius and overwhelming support.

To my friend Hugo Bos, President of Polymetaal in the Netherlands, who is an extraordinary engineer with a passion for printmaking. Also to Marit for her help.

To Monona Rossol for her insight, expertise time invested in writing the chapter on Health and Safety for this book.

To my primary proof readers, Linda Thompson and Carrie Clingan. To others who have helped in this task; Joe Thompson, Bernice Cross, Chetna Sappa and Nancy Flemm. To Michael Riorden and Robert Fleck, great colleagues, who's help was greatly appreciated.

To Rachel Farber-Kaiser for your loyalty, friendship and research assistance.

To Marnix Everaert my friend and inspirational colleague from Belgium.

To my friend Johann Feught aided by Rita Hemoltz and Sven Wohlgemuth who have been instrumental in exposing Contemporary Intaglio Printmaking to Germany.

To all others who have helped and supported me over the span of my professional life.

-I cherish my family and friends and I never forget a kindness-

CONTENTS

CONTENTS

CONTENTS

ALPHABETICAL LISTING OF THE NEW PRINTMAKING TERMINOLOGY

ACRYLIC AQUATINT - First documented in by Keith Howard in his 1991 publication "Safe Photo Etching for Photographers and Artists" where Speedball Screen Filler is airbrushed onto a copper plate and etched.

AERATION - A method, using a fish tank aerator, for circulating ferric chloride, or any etchant in a vertical etching tank, developed by Keith Howard in 1997.

AKUA INKS - Water-based inks made with gum-based binders, developed by printmakers Susan Rostow & William Jung. Rostow & Jung offer 2 types of inks. The original, Akua Kolor was developed for monotype in 1996. Akua Intaglio, developed in 2001, is thicker and tackier than Akua Kolor. Akua Oil converter medium will convert Akua Intaglio into a stiffer oil ink, that still cleans up with soap and water.

AQUATINT SCREEN - A transparent screen with opaque random dots, generally made through an imagesetter, which is used to simulate the effect of a traditional intaglio aquatint.

AQUATINT INTAGLIO-TYPE - Techniques, developed by Keith Howard in 2003, to utilize airbrush stencils to create tonal variations with the Intaglio-Type non-etch technique.

INK-EMBOSS WITH INTAGLIO-TYPE - Refers to the thickness of the ink on the final print.

BADGER ACRYLIC AQUATINT SOLUTION FOR PRINTMAKERS - An acrylic aquatint solution developed by Keith Howard and Elizabeth Dove in 1997 in collaboration with the Badger Airbrush Company, as a high quality airbrushed acrylic aquatint.

BORDEAUX ETCH - First introduced into printmaking by Cedric Green, is a copper sulphate solution designed for etching zinc plates quickly and safely.

COMBINATION TECHNIQUES - Refers to combining different printmaking techniques to achieve unique results.

INTAGLIO PRINTING - Is a method of inking a plate whereby the ink is forced into lines and textures in a plate, after which the top surface of the plate is wiped clean leaving the ink in the recessed areas. This ink is then pressed onto printing or intaglio paper though the use of an etching press.

CONTEMPORARY PRINTMAKING - A new philosophical approach of knowledge sharing and enthusiasm for safer printmaking practices and innovation. It is not just about non-toxic printmaking practices but also the integration of computer imagery and technology with traditional painting and drawing skills. It is a user friendly approach to printmaking that offers the intaglio printmaker a totally new realm of creative image making. It is fundamentally a new printmaking discipline that integrates technology, unbridled enthusiasm, dynamic creative potential, and health and environmental awareness.

CRACKLE INTAGLIO-TYPE - A non-exposure technique, developed by Keith Howard in 2001, where a raw unexposed ImagOn plate is heated on a hot-plate and then painted with Gum Arabic. As the Gum dries it cracks. The plate is developed in the soda ash developer and then printed.

DESTRUCTION-GROUND - An etch resist technique, first developed by Keith Howard in 1991, where Speedball Screen Filler is diluted and painted onto a copper plate. It is then etched in ferric chloride and printed revealing a corresponding tonal value to the thickness that the screen filler was applied to the plate.

DIGITAL HALFTONE - A halftone is an image created with a series of large and small dots to facilitate photo reproduction plate making techniques. A digital halftone is made through computer technology and printed from laser or inkjet printers onto clear film.

DIRECT INTAGLIO-TYPE - A technique, developed by Keith Howard in 2000, where the top Mylar of an Intaglio-Type plate is used to carry the image prior to exposing the plate in the exposure unit.

DUO-TONE INTAGLIO-TYPE - Intaglio-Type made from two plates with two different tonal values of one color.

EDINBURGH ETCH - A mixture of ferric chloride and citric acid, invented by Friedhard Kiekeben in 1997, which offers a superior etchant for printmakers.

ETCHED INTAGLIO-TYPE - Developed by Keith Howard in 1996, where an ImagOn plate emulsion is thinned by placing it in a developing/thinning solution for 8 minutes. The plate is then dried and exposed to a halftone image, redeveloped, etched and then printed.

EXPOSURE SYSTEM - Refers to an exposure unit or plate maker for exposing ImagOn ULTRA plates to an image.

FLASH EXPOSURE - This refers to a burst of light to a naked ImagOn plate. The duration of the light is such that the tonal range of the image on the plate is increased.

FLOW COATING - A hard-ground plate coating technique where Future or Klear acrylic floor finish is poured onto a clean etching plate.

4-COLOR INTAGLIO-TYPE - A technique developed by Elizabeth Dove in 2002, where a full color Intaglio-Type print are made in conjunction with, process colors, full density digital halftones and Aquatinted ImagOn plates.

IMAGON DEVELOPER - Is made from soda ash or anhydrous sodium carbonate. It is a soft-water solution comprising of 10 gms of soda ash and 1 litre of pH 7 water.

IMAGON ULTRA- Du Pont made, high resolution, dry, photopolymer film, used for intaglio printmaking.

INTAGLIO-TYPE - A name coined by Keith Howard to describe the range of intaglio printmaking techniques utilize photopolymer film for intaglio plate making.

INTAGLIO-TYPE PLATES - Intaglio plates with ImagOn film laminated on one side.

LAYERED INTAGLIO-TYPE - Technique, developed by Keith Howard in 1996, where a plate is comprised of two or more layers of ImagOn . Where each layer has the potential to be imaged which is uncovered in the developing technique.

Forward

By Friedhard Kiekeben

professional print studio in the UK to embrace water based screen printing. I had just completed a program of research at the RCA in London, and was then invited by Edinburgh Printmakers to become their dedicated research consultant for 'Safe Etching'. When I first met Keith Howard during a workshop in Northern England there was a real buzz amongst the participating group. In his enthusiastic Australian manner Howard demonstrated an intaglio method which looked so alien to the usual acid etching approach that I was simply stunned.

Two weeks earlier he had been introduced to an etching resist called 'Riston', a product from the circuit board industry. Instead of using this to etch metal Howard simply exposed the photo-polymer emulsion to a random dot screen and then to a tonal positive, which could be hand drawn or photographic. He then developed the plate in soft water, and produced printed images of stunning clarity directly from the film surface. This was the birth of the 'non-etch etching'. Arguably, non-etch photo polymer printmaking, or Intaglio-Type as this medium is now called, is one of the great innovations in 20th century intaglio printmaking. This safe and straightforward process greatly expands the creative possibilities of intaglio, and is now used by many artists who are working with photo reproductive and digital approaches, or indeed with direct drawing techniques. Photographic imagery acquires a new dimension through the depth given to it by this new intaglio process.

In my own research program I was aiming to extend the range of acrylic resist mark-making and etching methods, and in collaboration with Keith Howard the generic term 'Acrylic Resist Etching' was coined. I was looking for processes that would allow the various intaglio metals to be etched without the hazards of strong acids. Keith Howard had already improved the usability of ferric chloride as an etchant for copper by using agitated tanks. In 1997 I invented the Edinburgh Etch which solved the sedimentation issue that

normally hinders this electrochemical process. Publications in Printmaking Today and in Keith Howard's seminal manual 'Non-toxic Intaglio Printmaking' in 1998 aided the rapid dissemination of the Edinburgh Etch throughout the printmaking world.

Around that time the electro etching expert Cedric Green started to promote a copper sulphate based process, 'The Bordeaux Etch', for etching zinc and steel on his web site, and Bader and Semenoff published similar research in 1998. A new copper sulphate based solution, the 'Saline Sulphate Etch' is described in this book. The complete system of innovative etching solutions is now called 'Metal Salt Etching' and is recommended by the Rochester Institute of Technology chemistry professors Dr Paul Craig and Dr Paul Rosenberg as a contemporary alternative to Acid Etching.

While the acrylic resist etching methodology started as a safer alternative to the traditional methods - which it rivals in terms of quality - it is now widely recognized as a field which actually offers a whole range of new creative possibilities not previously thought possible. This includes a wealth of painterly and textural processes, modulated aquatint and the unique combined intaglio and collagraph approaches. Acrylic resists facilitate a more painterly pictorial language than their oil based counterparts, while also satisfying the needs of line based etchers. Rather than losing some of the essential imaging possibilities of etching, as was initially feared by some printmakers, the new approach has been shown to fully retain the unique vocabulary of intaglio, while extending it and making it a viable option for 21st century art.

The need for non-toxic etching materials has also been recognized by the art materials industry, and a number of paint and ink manufacturers are now offering acrylic resist etching grounds. The traditional oil based inks are very suitable for acrylic resist etching but still require sweat and

Forward

By Friedhard Kiekeben

patience in the inking and wiping process. The New York artist Susan Rostow was recently awarded a Krasner Pollock award for her innovative ink developments. Her soft, gum based inks allow intaglio plates to be inked and printed with much greater ease than conventional inks.

Innovation can be costly but non-toxic developments have proved to be economically viable too. The initial investment in new or refurbished facilities for acrylic resist etching is often quickly recouped by reduced running costs. An expenditure calculation carried out at EPW in 1996 (after the change to non-toxic processes) showed a 40 % reduction in the annual consumable cost of the print studio, amounting to thousands of pounds worth of savings. Non-toxic practice can also attract new sources of funding; Prof. Susan Groce at the University of Maine received a major increase to her printmaking budget in support of her efforts to reduce health hazards.

Perhaps the most resistance to healthy innovation has come in lithography, but now acrylic resist etching and water based screen printing have shown that the aesthetic qualities of lithography can be easily emulated. The comparative slowness of non-toxic developments in lithography caused many workshops to eliminate Senefelder's printing chemistry from their program. However, a number of recent innovations now make it possible to practice lithographic printing safely. In 1991 Nik Semenoff refined 'Waterless Lithography' in which silicone is used as an ink repelling substrate, but the process required acetone as a solvent. In the spring issue of Printmaking Today 2000 the Tamarind master printer Ross Zirkle reported that waterless lithography used in conjunction with a new kind of water based ink can now be practiced as a non-toxic medium in which no organic solvents are used.

George Roberts, a lithographic artist and university professor, pursued a different line of investigation in the mid 1990s. Roberts was

intrigued by the polyester plate process widely used in India as a low cost commercial printing option. He managed to develop a system in which polyester plates are used as the matrix in a new lithographic medium he called polyester plate lithography. This process is characterized by three main factors: it is much safer to use than conventional lithography, it fully incorporates the various mark making options typical for the medium, (such as ink washes, lines, and crayon marks), and is much easier to master. It also integrates effortlessly with photography and digital imaging as plates can be produced straight from any laser or inkjet printer. George Roberts summarized his ground-breaking research in his book 'Polyester Plate Lithography' in 2001, but sadly died of cancer soon after its publication. A major international exhibition of non-toxic prints 'Re-Imaging the Multiple' is currently touring the world in honor of George Roberts.

Keith Howard realized early on that new knowledge would have to be shared and communicated as widely as possible for the non-toxic approach to gather momentum. The publication of books, magazine articles, and web sites are all important, but nothing is as effective or persuasive as the practical knowledge gained from hands on demonstrations and teaching sessions.

Encouraged by the success of his travelling workshop sessions Howard set up a professional summer school in, Alberta, canada, in 1993. (This was also the location of his academic program at the Canadian School for Non-Toxic Printmaking). At the same time I created a UK based program of educational events in collaboration with Robert Adam, then director of Edinburgh Printmakers. Both these programs were well subscribed and proved pivotal in attracting key printmaking educators from around the world to the new methodology. Many participants subsequently changed over their home printmaking departments and became ambassadors for the new approach.

LIGHT INTEGRATOR - This is a device generally attached to the vacuum frame that measures UV light out put from the lamp of the exposure unit.

LINE INTAGLIO-TYPE - A technique for working with line and the Intaglio-Type plate making.

LIQUID AQUATINT
A technique first developed by Henri Goetz in France about 30 years ago where carborundum is added to a binder and painted onto a plate. When dry the plate is inked and the resulting *liquid aquatint* has the potential to hold a large quantity of ink.

LIQUID STENCIL WITH AQUATINT - Temporary liquid stencils developed by Keith Howard in 1997 for preventing the spray from the spray acrylic aquatint from landing on the plate.

MEZZO0 INTAGLIO-TYPE - An Intaglio-Type technique, developed by Keith Howard in 1996, commences with a developed aquatinted ImagOn plate which is then painted on with Speedball Screen Filler to create the image. The thicker the Screen Filler the whiter the resultant print.

MULTI-PLATE WASH-DRAWING INTAGLIO-TYPE - Technique, developed by Keith Howard in 1997, whereby several toner-wash drawing are exposed to several ImagOn plates to create a multi-plate non-etch Intaglio-Type print.

MYLAR® - A type of plastic that can be completely transparent or frosted.

OPEN-BITE - Open-Bite occurs when the ImagOn emulsion is developed or abraded from the surface of an ImagOn plate to the degree that ink will not hold in the open-bite area.

ORONO-GROUND - A fortified Graphic Chemical water-based relief ink-ground jointly developed by Friedhard Kiekeben and Susan Gross in 1999. Can be used as a soft or hard-ground.

PASTEL INTAGLIO-TYPE - An Intaglio-Type technique, developed by Erin Holsher and Amy Williams in 2003, where drafting Mylar is worked with wet or dry pastel.

TONER-WASH - Refers to photocopy toner mixed with an acrylic binder such as Future or Klear along with rubbing alcohol and a wetting solution to create a kind of ink-wash.This is then painted onto drafting Mylar to create a wash-drawing-painting.

P.E.T.G. - PETG / Spectar® and (Vivak®)
PETG / Spectar® (Polyethylene Terephthalate) Co-polyester sheet is a thermoplastic sheet used in engineering applications. Distributed by <www.Lairdplastics.com>

PHOTOCELL - The photocell is the actual component of the light integrator that reacts to the UV light exposure which then is converted into a digital numeric read-out.

PHOTOPOLYMER FILMS - Dry laminate films originally designed for imaging computer chips.

PROCESS COLOR INTAGLIO-TYPE - A technique, developed by David Jay Reed in 2002, where the process colors of cyan, magenta, yellow and black are used with corresponding non-etch Intaglio-Type plates to create full color Intaglio-Type prints.

SCREEN FILLER AND LIQUID AQUATINT - Liquid Aquatint is a mixture of Speedball Screen Filler and carborundum which is painted onto an intaglio plate, dried and inked up. The Liquid Aquatint creates a an instant tooth on the plate that will print a rich black.

PROGRESSIVE ETCH - Where an image being etched into a plate receives different lengths of etching time to fully realize the image. Shorter etching times will be represented in light lines or tones in an an image and darker tones will have received longer etching times.

ROLL-COATING - A hard and soft-ground plate coating technique where a charged brayer deposits an acrylic ground to a etching plate.

STANDARD DEVELOPMENT - Refers to the 9 minute standard development time needed for an ImagOn plate.

SALINE SULPHATE ETCH FOR ZINC - A unique etchant, developed by Friedhard Kiekeben in 2002, where salt is added to the Bordeaux Etch to improve the etching properties.

STENCIL INTAGLIO-TYPE - An Intaglio-Type technique, developed by Keith Howard in 2000, where the top Mylar coating on the ImagOn plate is used as part of the plate making process. The top Mylar is used in a similar manner as a hand-cut stencil to divide Intaglio-Type techniques between the Mezzo and Spit-Bite Intaglio-Type.

WASH-DRAWING INTAGLIO-TYPE - Technique, developed by Keith Howard in 1994, whereby a toner-wash drawing is exposed to the ImagOn plate to create a non-etch Intaglio-Type print

SUBMERSION LAMINATION - Refers to a method of ImagOn plate lamination, developed by Keith Howard, where ImagOn film and the receiving plate first come together in a bath of water. It is the first stage of the wet lamination process.

TONER - Refers to the polymer particles used in photocopiers to create photocopies.

VACUUM FRAME - Most exposure units have a glass-toped vacuum bed where art work is placed on top of the ImagOn plate and when the vacuum is engaged perfect contact between the art work and plate is achieved. Thus when being exposed to the UV light source of the exposure unit a high resolution plate can be achieved.

VERTICAL ETCHING TANK - A etching tank, first employed for printmaking by Keith Howard in 1997, for etching plates vertically.

WATER/ALCOHOL RESIST - Developed by McLain (Meg) Zylwitis in 2003, a mixture of water and alcohol as a spray aquatint stencil. The acrylic aquatint spray is sprayed onto the resist solution and allowed to merge with the spray screen filler aquatint and dry onto the plate. The plate is then etched and printed revealing unique clam-shell like marks because of this resist.

Forward

By Friedhard Kiekeben

A Healthy Fusion of Art and Invention

Printmaking involves processes. And where there are processes there are always inventors. Printmaking involves technology and where there is technology there is always room for improvement. The history of printmaking is a history of aesthetics, invention, and perfection - not only in technical terms but also conceptually. Whereas a canvas is always a canvas and the actual practice of painting has changed very little in many centuries the practice of printmaking has been accompanied by continuous development, and more recently by major re-invention.

When Rembrandt wanted to etch crisper lines he invented his own mordant. When Goya wanted tonal richness in a print he perfected aquatint. Andy Warhol was innovative not only by choosing a contemporary medium, silk screen printing, but by centering his entire art around the notion of the reproduced image.

Although fusing art and invention, until recently the art of printmaking had an unhealthy association with a whole range of potentially harmful materials and processes. The powerful fumes of acids, varnishes and solvents were the unfortunate byproduct of this artform. Most technical innovations in intaglio printmaking originated in the 16th and 17th century, when Rembrandt, Goya and their contemporaries researched and established the traditional etching materials and processes from resources available to them at the time. These basic ingredients were used in recipes that went unchallenged until the late twentieth century.

Other major forms of printmaking which were devised and developed, including fine art lithography and screen printing, expanded the creative scope of the medium but also contributed more chemical hazards to an already extensive list. The hydrocarbon solvents introduced into printmaking in the mid 19th century as general cleaning and thinning agents became a new and potent health risk. The only real option for safety conscious artist printmakers and professional workshops was to attempt to control the various hazards by using protective equipment such as vapor masks and fume extraction systems.

The first significant breakthrough came in the mid-eighties when a Swiss manufacturer of artist paints developed a screen printing system based entirely on water based acrylic materials which no longer necessitated the use of any organic solvents, whilst producing quality results. Soon other manufacturers offered similar systems, and in the following decade water based screen printing found widespread acceptance in art education. A healthy fusion of art and invention.

Keith Howard was the first artist to systematically investigate alternative methods in intaglio printmaking in the late eighties. After suffering from ill health (attributed to printmaking hazards), Howard realized that Rembrandt's print medium was in urgent need of modernization. Initially he developed a gelatine based alternative to toxic photo etching which gave photo reproductive quality whilst being safe to use. But Keith Howard was aiming to find a comprehensive set of all intaglio methods, including manual etching, which would eliminate the airborne fumes and other hazards of the old system. He started with the basic assumption that acrylics might make a suitable alternative to the solvent based varnishes of traditional intaglio. After experimenting with a range of acrylic products Howard found ways to use these as etching resists for all major processes, such as hard ground, stop out, and aquatint. In 1991 he published his first book 'Safe Photo Etching for Photographers and Artists' and embarked on a world wide workshop and lecturing program to outline his innovations.

Keith Howard demonstrated the potential of his non-toxic intaglio approach to the Edinburgh Printmakers staff during a workshop in 1994. The EPW already had a history in non-toxic developments, as they had been the first

Until one is committed, there is hesitancy, the chance to draw back, always ineffectiveness, concerning all acts of initiative (and creation). There is one elementary truth the ignorance of which kills countless ideas and splendid plans: that the moment one definitely commits oneself, then providence moves too. All sorts of things occur to help one that would never otherwise have occurred. A whole stream of events issues from the decision, raising in one's favor all manner of unforeseen incidents and meetings and material assistance which no man could have dreamed would have come his way. Whatever you can do or dream you can, begin it. Boldness has genius, power and magic in it. Begin it now.

- Goethe

A Book written for the printmaking world.
Keith Howard designed and took all the photographs for this book.

Published by: Write-Cross Press
eMail < KeithHoward@KeithHoward.org
Web: <www.KeithHoward.org>
Library of Congress Control Number: 2003106700

The Contemporary Printmaker :
Intaglio-Type and Acrylic Resist Etching

ISBN 0-9741946-0-3

1. Etching--Technique. 2. Photo Etching. 3. Photography. 4. Prints--Technique. 5. Intaglio--Printmaking. 6. Non-toxic Printmaking. 7. Intaglio-type. 8. ImagOn. 9. Riston. 10.ImagOnULRA. 11. Photopolymer Film. 12. Art Process. 13. Art Teaching. 14. History of Contemporary Printmaking. 15 Contemporary Printmaking Process.

Bernice A. Cross, **Proofs**, 2003, at left first state Intaglio-Type and right, 4-Color Intaglio-Type, 9" x 6". See more of Bernice Cross's work at: **www.KeithHoward.org**

Forward

By Friedhard Kiekeben

The Danish Printmaker Henrik Boegh attended both the Scottish and the Canadian programs, published a book, and soon became instrumental in the rapid introduction of acrylic resist etching in Scandinavia, where there is strong awareness of the health issues surrounding traditional printmaking. This dissemination process was very much helped by a conference-cum-workshop series staged by Boegh for Scandinavian printmaking professionals in 1998. In 2000 I established a new international summer school program 'Innovative Intaglio' at Gracefield Arts Centre in South West Scotland, which is taught collaboratively with Keith Howard, and many other institutes around the world now offer training in non-toxic printmaking, both in the form of short courses and as part of a university curriculum.

Today many educational print departments in the UK have adopted intaglio type methods and water based screen printing, and an estimated 50% have replaced traditional etching with acrylic resist etching. A recent survey carried out by the Tamarind Workshop shows that 89% of art departments in the US have adopted non-toxic processes, while 33% also state that over the past five years one or more conventional print processes were abandoned due to health concerns.

Keith Howard now heads printmaking research at the Rochester Institute of Technology in upstate New York. Arguably this geographical move from the fringes to the center is analogous to the arrival of the method that he founded in the mainstream of international printmaking.

After over a decade of technical innovation and with the help of many artists, inventors and educators, non-toxic printmaking is now flourishing as an exciting and mature medium, which offers a wealth of creative possibilities. The new incarnation of printmaking now needs today's generation of artists and educators to harness its enormous aesthetic potential.

Friedhard Kiekeben RCA,   April 2003

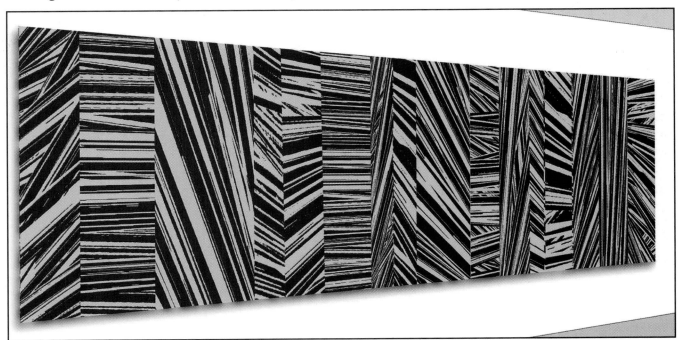

Friedhard Kiekeben, **"Shatter"**, 2003, 14 ft x height 4 ft 3in, Large wall aluminum sculpture etched in Saline Sulphate Etch.

Author's Introduction

Non-Toxic to Contemporary Intaglio

My first sojourns into intaglio research revolved around replacing toxic traditional intaglio techniques with non-toxic. In the beginning 'non-toxic' replacement techniques were my primary focus. Sine then Non-Toxic Intaglio has evolved far beyond its inspired beginnings. It encapsulates a new philosophy of sharing and enthusiasm. It embraces digital and new technologies while making full use of hand drawn skills. It is more user friendly, more cost effective and, in many instances, has a more accessible methodology. This new body of knowledge will allow printmakers to be vastly more productive without the deadly assault of toxic acids and solvents. It has become essentially a new discipline with a new terminology and above all a new creative potential. What began as 'Non-Toxic Printmaking" has essentially become 'Contemporary Printmaking'.

Fear of Change

It was discovered, at the turn of the 19th century, that mercury, in the hat making profession, had caused madness amongst its workers. When safer methods were developed to replace the toxic traditional hat making processes, there were those "Mad Hatters" who threw their arms up in anger at the thought of changing the way that hats had been made for centuries.

They had spent decades mastering their craft, becoming experts in this particular way of making hats. They were worried that hat making would die out and that a great tradition would be lost. Although they were "mad", they were probably fearful about change without considering the positive impact that change would have on the hat making industry. We still have hats today and the toxic tradition of the hat maker is but a part of the history of that craft. This was technical evolution fueled by the necessity to work in a safer manner. This is progress.

 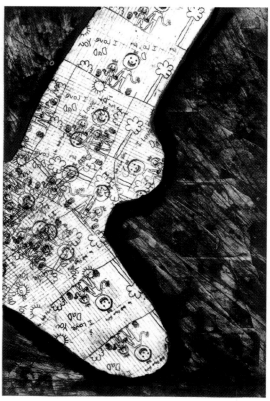

Keith Howard, **Unaccompanied Minor**, 2002, Intaglio-Type (Construction Intaglio-Type with Digital Halftone Intaglio-Type), 36" x 48". Inspired by my daughter Holly's drawing.

Author's Introduction

It is easy for us to step back as 21 century spectators and ridicule the "mad hatters" of the past for their folly. Yet if you consider traditional printmaking, as it is still practiced all around the world today, there are many more dangerous techniques and materials involved.

Resistance to a Healthier Way
It is difficult to understand why there is any resistance to 'non-toxic' printmaking as it presents superior technical alternatives to traditional techniques. It is much like comparing the qualities of an old mechanical typewriter to that of the latest Macintosh computer. It is also, in most instances, more cost effective while employing safer techniques that will not impose the negative health consequences suffered from traditional printmaking techniques.

Contemporary printmaking is far more user friendly, making artists more productive while saving them lots of money on materials and medical bills. Educational institutions are being sued for millions of dollars because of adverse health effects suffered by faculty and students.

Exposure to the harmful effects of acids, grounds and solvents used in traditional intaglio printmaking is not a matter of 'if' you are doing damage to your health but rather 'how much' damage. Back in the early 1980's the how much damage was of ultimate concern to me as I had fallen prey to the toxic effects of acids and solvents used in traditional printmaking studios.

Evolution
The evolution of Contemporary (non-toxic) Intaglio Printmaking started in 1991 with my first book "Safe Photo Etching for Photographers and Artists". This became a precedent setting publication as it was the first and most comprehensive research publication on a safer intaglio methodology. It became the catalyst for artists from all over the world to re-think and re-invent printmaking in a unconventional, innovative, and safer manner.

The original intent behind my first book was to find safer ways of pursuing photo intaglio

printmaking. While developing a gelatin based photo intaglio emulsion, known as the "Howard Process" I decided to look at presenting alternative safer techniques commonly used in intaglio printmaking. There was a natural transition from the more complicated photo generated techniques to simple hand etching methods that was also presented in this first publication.

During the latter decade of the 20th century there became a flurry of new research activity in printmaking. Innovative ideas in electrolytic etching, Polyester Plate Lithography, new mordants, unique acrylic grounds, water-based ink technology and more modern plate making methods. It has been a fascinating and dynamic period for what was universally known as 'Non-Toxic Printmaking'.

There evolved a dedicated and highly motivated group of printmakers, around the world, that contributed unique facets to 'non-toxic' printmaking. This group of individuals, for the most part, have kept good lines of communication open, thus infusing printmaking with a new kind of "sharing philosophy". There is a bond of friendship and passion for the survival of printmaking that has created a very strong worldwide contemporary printmaking community.

The greatest contributing factor to the entrenchment of contemporary printmaking has been education. This has been done both formally through the university and college system but also through publication and workshops. There have been extraordinary individuals that have taken on the challenge and commitment of directing printmaking history through their contributions.

Although my first book in 1991 presented alternative techniques to traditional intaglio there needed to be a lot more individuals involved in technical innovation for printmaking to undergo more rapid change.

Author's Introduction

The best motivation for encouraging technical change is to offer printmakers user friendly technology and methods that promise greater creative freedom. Printmaking needed to undergo greater change than what was made possible with my 1991 book.

Photopolymer Film
Early in 1994 I received a call from Mark Zaffron, who informed me of a photopolymer film called Riston® (a Du Pont Registered Trade Mark) that was manufactured by Du Pont for the printed circuit board industry. He told me that it made a photo etching resist and that I should obtain some and try it. My first experiment with Riston was not in *any way* related to how Zaffron was using this film, but towards the non-etch concept.

Zaffron wrote an article entitled "Photopolymer Films; A Safer and More Versatile Photo-Resist for Intaglio" for the April 1995 issue of **California Printmaker**. He wrote as follows,"*the techniques presented here reflect the contributions of colleagues to whom I've introduced the process. Primary among them is Keith Howard, who while adding the intriguing aspect of **the non-etch techniques**, has further discovered a pre-developing stage which increases the films resolution two-times that which had been possible. With Mr. Howard's permission I include his contribution to the most current incarnations of the technique.*"

Further to Zaffron's article, in the Spring 1996 issue of **Printmaking Today,** on page 27 he writes the following,
"*Once I recognized its potential, I introduced the discovery to colleagues including Keith Howard. Not only did Mr. Howard immediately master it, but he ingeniously added to its potential. Through workshops and contributions to various periodicals, use of this film has spread throughout the world.*"
By 1996, I had introduced the Riston photopolymer film techniques to printmakers all over the world through International Printmaking Workshops in Canada, and with major workshop tours in the UK, and Sweden.

The contents of this book are "*the most current incarnations.*" There are a host of techniques that I have invented since 1995, when Zaffron wrote the above. This is the second book published to explain the *intriguing aspect*, as Zaffron noted, of the *of the non-etch technique*. This has been enlarged with the invention of the Spit-Bite Intaglio-Type, Construction Intaglio-Type, Crackle Intaglio-Type, and Photo Intaglio-Type.

It was not until I started uncovering the creative potential of a Du Pont printed circuit board photopolymer film, that non-toxic intaglio printmaking came of age. Before I worked with this particular type of photopolymer film Zaffron and other printmakers used it exclusively as an etch resist for photo etched plates, a use that was very much in line with how the film was used in the electronics industry. While this presented a greater level of safety for printmakers it never pushed the creative potential of this film beyond that of a number of historically toxic photo-etch methods. Hence, even today, some printmakers believe that ImagOn is only good for reproducing photo imagery. As this book amply demonstrates this could not be further from the truth. *When ImagOn is used, in the Intaglio-Type range of techniques, a totally unique visual intaglio language emerges.*

With the introduction of my second runaway best selling book, "Non-Toxic Intaglio Printmaking", the knowledge of how to explore the creative potential of this exciting new intaglio medium was accessible to many printmakers. This book, not only described how to utilize the Intaglio-Type techniques, but also, presented printmakers with the latest research into other aspects of acrylic resists etching especially those by Friedhard Kiekeben, the inventor of the Edinburgh Etch, the Saline Sulphate Etch and other acrylic resist techniques.

ImagOn ULTRA
Shortly after my last book sold out in 2000 I began researching the next generation of photopolymer film from Du Pont called ImagOn ULTRA. This film proved to be far superior to its predecessor. The working properties of this film

Author's Introduction

were so different that I needed to re-invent the entire ImagOn methodology.

In September 2001 ImagOn ULTRA was launched on an unprepared market. This was unavoidable as the old ImagOn film was being replaced by the new. I needed to come up with an educating method that would fill the gap between this present book and my last. The most expedient way to do this was through a video production. Consequently in September of 2001 I completed *Keith Howard's Non-Toxic Intaglio Instructional Video Series One: Using Du Pont's ImagOn ULTRA Photopolymer Film.*

This video proved to be a good teaching resource as it demonstrated the most important principles and techniques involved in using the new ImagOn Ultra film. It is still available and ordering information can be seen at the back of this book under Sources and Supplies.

Between October, 2001 and May, 2002 I have been further researching and mastering the ImagOn ULTRA film. By this time I had introduced this film to printmakers from Argentina, Brazil, Spain, Belgium, Holland, Germany, England, Scandinavia, Scotland, Canada and the United States.

In the beginning of the development of ImagOn ULTRA techniques I was entranced by the technical predictability and ease with which I could work with this film. However, as I travelled and taught workshops on ImagOn ULTRA I realized that there were factors that made this film under-perform. This was related to local situations such as how hard or soft the tap water was and if a anhydrous or hydrated form of soda ash was used to make the ImagOn developer. This is something I will address in the trouble shooting segments of this book. After working with such a diversity of countries and printmakers I felt confident that most problems were addressed to the point where this book could be completed.

The Non-Toxic Journey
The non-toxic printmaking journey for me is now in its fifteenth year and it seems that I have come

a long way, but in comparison to the length of printmaking history we are just at the beginning.

It is interesting to note that beginning printmakers/artists, who learn how to effectively use contemporary (non-toxic) printmaking technology, would rarely venture into the toxic traditional approach. It would be like expecting us to give up all automobiles and go back to riding to work on horseback. Furthermore, most seasoned printmakers, who are not shackled by fear of change, easily make the transition into contemporary (non-toxic) printmaking. They have become like the hard-core non-smokers of the contemporary printmaking world.

New Printmaking Terminology
Of primary concern in the propagation of Intaglio-Type and Acrylic Resist Etching techniques is terminology. As a printmaking educator I stress the importance of terminology, so that my students and I can have a discourse about these new intaglio techniques. It no longer serves the purpose to just be continually be talking about "that red stuff with that other stuff in it" or "that blue film" or whatever. Terminology must also be accurate. I never allow any of my students to call ferric chloride "the acid". It is Ferric chloride or ferric. When Intaglio-Type prints are exhibited it is professionally responsible to 'properly' name the technique used. To simply use old terminology such as, *etching,* when in fact a Non-Etch Intaglio-Type was used is not only unprofessional, but also, misleading.

New techniques have little value unless they are explored by printmakers. By uncovering the dynamics of these new printmaking techniques and exhibiting wonderful prints you will be contributing to the history of printmaking. Contemporary Printmaking will thrive if great printmakers make great prints with this technology.

Contemporary Printmaking Survey
In 2001, Erin Maurelli and Phil Sanders, from the Tamarind Institute, complied a survey in an attempt to better understand contemporary issues

Author's Introduction

and future directions for printmaking. This survey indicated that 89% of the schools, who responded to the surveyed, have adopted non-toxic printmaking processes. That "33% of schools surveyed have eliminated one or more courses in the past 5 years due to health concerns" is a startling fact. This survey also indicated that "steps are being taken to ensure a healthy working environment for students and faculty." This survey concluded with; "There is evidence to suggest an inclination to adopt non-toxic processes in all print media, and a clear trend towards adding new computers, improved ventilation and better facilities."

A Contemporary Printmaking Renaissance

Over the past decade or so, printmaking in general has undergone a distinctive renaissance. It has moved forward into the 21 century with a momentum generated by safer methodologies and more user friendly technologies. The alchemy and total disdain for personal health and environmental consciousness has been replaced by the next generation of Contemporary Printmakers who want to become part of printmaking history. They want printmaking to not only survive but also to thrive. They want to clean up printmaking and make it a more vital art form which is totally unencumbered by the limitations of its inherited toxic history.

Participate in this 'New Age of Printmaking' by sharing your technical printmaking experiences and your knowledge. Take every opportunity to inform and educate anyone who will listen. Most importantly exercise the highest standards of integrity by acknowledging sources and inventors of this new technology. Cross artistic boundaries by encouraging painters, ceramists, sculptors, photographers, digital artists and artists of any discipline to use these new technologies. Our battle is not only for the survival of printmakers but also for printmaking itself. The more it is used the more it will be infused. Its very much about evolution both technically and philosophically.

Become a positive and dynamic force in the printmaking world. Become a Contemporary Printmaking adventurer and, most importantly -

Dare to be Great.

www.KeithHoward.org

In this Book
I have used a simple color code to link text to photographs or illustrations.

1 ⟶ This box, with number and yellow background, indicates that there is a corresponding photograph to help illustrate this point.

The corresponding illustration is a large version of the above. ⟶ **1**

1 ⟶ This box, without color, means that there is no accompanying illustration.

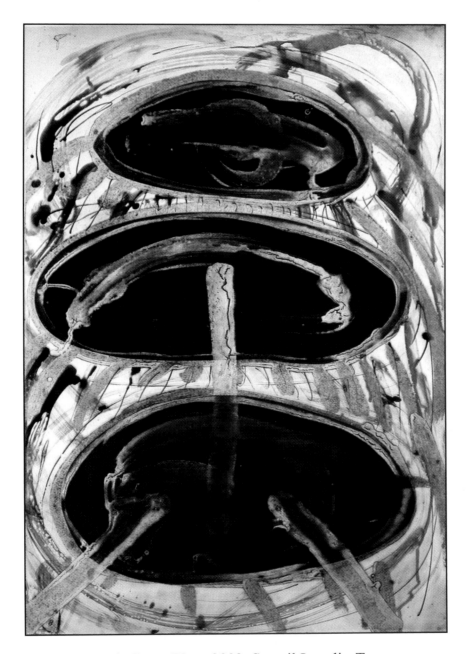

Keith Howard, **Great Plan,** 2003, Stencil Intaglio-Type,
24" x 36" demonstration print made to illustrate the chapter on
Stencil Intaglio-Type P. 97-100. See also Collectors Circle P. 243.

Bernice A. Cross, **Palm Beach,** 2003, hand worked Etched Intaglio-Type (P.129-136), 20" x 16".

Safer Intaglio Studio Setup

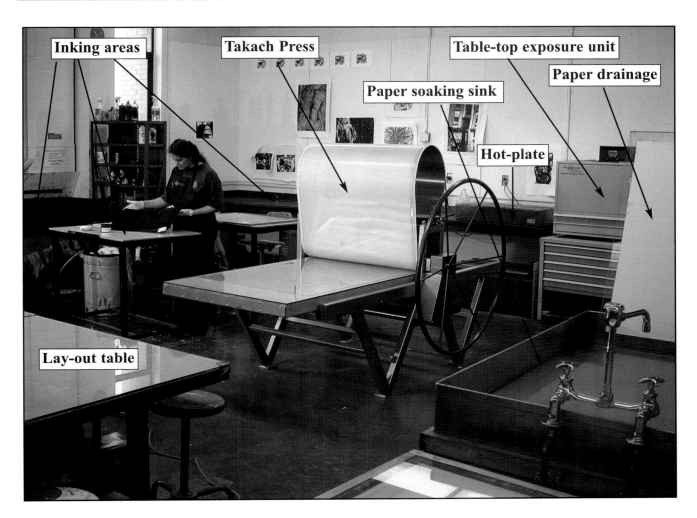

Inking areas

Takach Press

Table-top exposure unit

Paper drainage

Paper soaking sink

Hot-plate

Lay-out table

All the illustrations for this chapter were shot at the Rochester Institute of Technology Printmaking Studios. At right is our new "Extreme Etching Press", (model JZE-100) made by Polymetaal, with hydrolyic top roller adjustment, and manual or electric bed driving mechanism. This give you the choice of manually operating this press, for proofing, or switching to electric mode for edition printing. This model also has a rotational blanket system which allows hands-free operation when printing.

See more details at the:
http://www.polymetaal.nl/siteUK/ shopukwork/enter.html

Safer Intaglio Studio Setup

Introduction

Whether you have an existing toxic traditional studio, or you are building a studio, the following guidelines are the same.

As I travel around the world, giving hands-on Intaglio-Type and Acrylic Resist Etching workshops, I invariably need to re-organize existing printmaking studios to accommodate these new methods. Short term practical solutions can easily be achieved in a few hours. Some of the recommendations, I have put forth in this chapter, may require a longer term approach. Many of my suggestions are aimed at making studios *more efficient* in terms of space, practical application of techniques and movement around the studio.

In most cases converting a toxic traditional intaglio studio into a safer one is a matter or reallocation of certain tasks.

Disposal of Toxic Materials

The most important thing is to rid the studio of all solvents, acids, oil-based grounds, rosin and asphaltum powders. Disposing of chemicals safely is your responsibility. Make sure that you adhere to government disposal regulations. Do not discard these kinds of dangerous chemicals in the rubbish bin or down the sink. Most institutions have a Health and Safety Department or officials. Seek professional disposal advice. If you have a private studio look in the yellow pages or go on-line to look for health and safety equipment stores, or locate the closest university or college Health and Safety Officer and ask their advice for disposing of dangerous goods.

I have noticed that many printmakers who do commit themselves to safer practices still hang on to some of their dangerous chemicals in a belief that they may need them 'some day'. Generally, and hopefully, these chemicals stay locked away never to be seen again. While there are dangerous chemicals in your studio there is always an element of risk. My best advice is to completely safely remove all of these acids and solvents. This

will symbolize a kind of purging from the old and a heralding in of the new, safer, cleaner era in your printmaking life. *There will never be a point where any of these toxic materials will ever be needed.* This speaks also to total commitment to a cleaner, healthier studio environment.

Etching Press

Your etching press will be the central and most important piece of equipment. Place the press in the studio where it is easily accessible to your printing station. Shortening the walking distance between the etching press, paper preparation and drying station will conserve your energy and save time.

Designing Work Stations

Many work stations need a access to water and sinks. If you do not have adequate sinks in your studio you may consider putting them in.

In re-designing your studio you will need to allocate space for the following:

1 ImagOn Storage Area

Look for a small darkened room or a room where there is only incandescent light. If no room exists then a storage shelf or cupboard may substitute provided that it is away from any UV light source such as a window. Allocate any area in your studio, for ImagOn storage, as long as it is away from UV light sources. (In a hot climate the ImagOn should be stored in a dry cool place.) This area can also be used to store the soda ash powder necessary for making the ImagOn developer.

2 ImagOn Laminating Area

This consists of glass topped tables. This should be away from strong daylight or any other source of UV light. ImagOn has an open working time of about 20 minutes in most studios illuminated with fluorescent or incandescent light sources.

TIP: To determine the ImagOn open working time lay a small piece of unexposed ImagOn film onto

Safer Intaglio Studio Setup

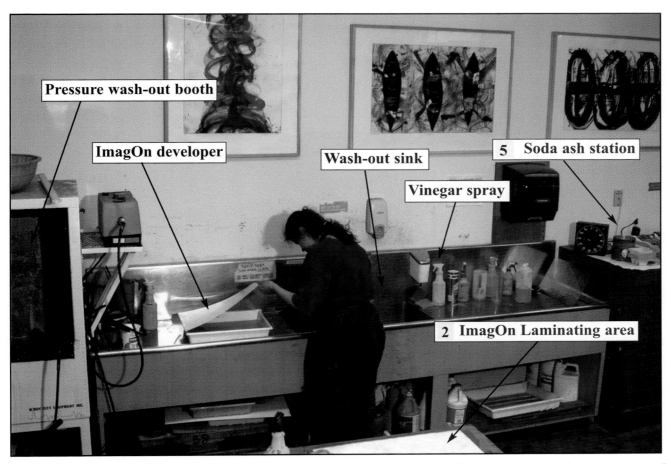

Pressure wash-out booth

ImagOn developer

Wash-out sink

Vinegar spray

5 **Soda ash station**

2 **ImagOn Laminating area**

the tabletop and cover half of it with a copper plate. Check it every 5 minutes, by lifting the copper plate, to check for a color change of the film. As soon as you notice a slight color change then subtract 5 minutes from that time and that will give you a fairly accurate working time of ImagOn in the location of your studio. Remember this test only applies for a specific local lighting condition that exists in that area of your studio. If there are other light sources, such as skylights or windows, then this will be an additional source of light that must be considered, particularly when it radiates UV light into a room.

3 ImagOn Processing Area

This area should be adjacent a sink where the developed ImagOn plate can be stabilized with the vinegar wash and rinsed with water. This area has a photo processing tray big enough to accommodate the maximum ImagOn plate size. This tray will contain the soda ash ImagOn developer.

When using the wet lamination process, for applying the ImagOn to the plate, consider using two photo trays. One for water and the other for soda ash developer. One or more developing stations may be required for a busy studio.

4 Plate Finishing Area

An area will be required for squeegeeing off the excess water from the developed and stabilized plate. This area could be on the sink top so that squeegeed water is directed into the sink. Safe working conditions in your studio should be of paramount importance. If water is present on the floor this may cause someone to slip. The best design is the one that avoids water spills.

This area can also be used for the final vinegar stabilization spray onto the freshly developed plate. The plate can be sprayed over a sink and then immediately rinsed with running tap water.

Safer Intaglio Studio Setup

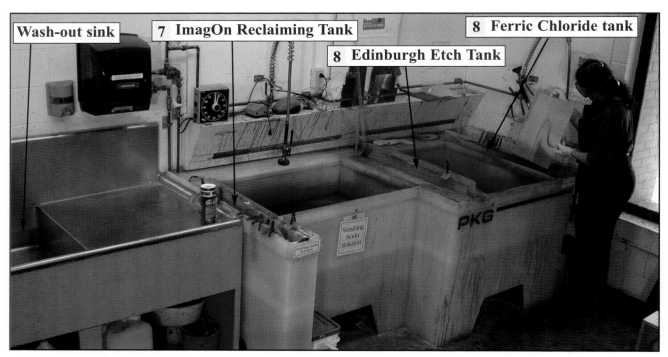

Wash-out sink | **7 ImagOn Reclaiming Tank** | **8 Ferric Chloride tank**
8 Edinburgh Etch Tank

5 Soda Ash Measuring Station

This area should be dry, but near the sink, as mixing the soda ash developer requires hot and cold water.

6 Plate Drying Station

In the R.I.T. contemporary (non-toxic) print-making studio, we installed two automatic hand-dryers, the type commonly found in public rest rooms. Heat-guns can be used for bigger plates. I do not recommend the use of hair-dryers in high usage studios as they are not designed to be kept on for long periods of time. If hair-dryers are used, for extend periods of time, they can catch on fire. A good quality heat gun, with some means of controlling the heat out-put, is well worth the investment.

TIP: The heat-gun setting should be set at a level where you can hold it about 15" from your hand without burning the skin.

7 ImagOn Plate Reclaiming Station

ImagOn can be stripped off existing metal plates by soaking the plate in a strong soda ash solution. Although this stripping solution can be placed into

a flat photo developing tray it would be far more advisable to use a vertical etching tank. The type of tank used for holding etchants such as ferric chloride is ideal for this purpose. This tank should also be positioned on the floor near a sink.

8 Ferric Chloride & Edinburgh Etch Etching Station

If you are using ferric chloride and the Edinburgh Etch, as primary copper plate etchants, I recommend using free standing vertical etching tanks or a specialized sink system, as illustrated above, where sinks and wash-out bays are combined. If both etchants are used then two free standing vertical tanks would be necessary. The vertical etching tank is extremely efficient, enabling many students to etch plates at the same time. As ferric chloride and the Edinburgh Etch are corrosive, even to stainless steel sinks, I recommend a wash-out tray, filled with water between the ferric chloride and the Edinburgh Etch tank and the sink. There should be enough space to accommodate this wash-out tray.

A larger sink/tank alternative is to have a sink designed and built from heat welded panels of polypropylene, as illustrated above. There are

Safer Intaglio Studio Setup

many plastic companies that will build such equipment. Alternatively, many printmaking supply companies sell polypropylene trays designed for holding nitric acid. These could be adapted as a wash-out sink for ferric chloride and Edinburgh Etch tanks.

I also advocate the use of professional wash-out spray systems, normally seen over stone-litho graining sinks, over the polypropylene sink. (NB When using any ferric chloride tank and wash-out system adequate eye protection should be used.)

If the Bordeaux Etch is used for etching zinc plates adequate table space should be allowed for this 'tray development' etchant . When using different etchants in your studio they all should be well labeled and separated from each other.

9 ImagOn Exposure Area

For optimum results a good plate-maker or exposure unit, as illustrated below, will be needed to fully utilize ImagOn ULTRA film. I believe that this piece of equipment is as vital to a non-toxic printmaker as a good camera is to a professional photographer. I will fully discuss exposure systems in the next chapter, but for now, it is necessary to allocate space for one in your studio.

9 ImagOn Exposure Area

There are two types of exposure systems or plate-makers. One is free standing and the other is designed to be placed onto a tabletop. There would be two considerations when deciding where it should go. The first would be to place it away from external sources of UV light such as a window or skylight. The other would be to place it in an easily accessible place in your studio.

10 Exhaust Spray Booth

Near the exposure unit should be a table space for placing the Aquatint Screen between exposures and a place where art work, stencils and plates can be readied.

Electrical outlets will also dictate where you place the exposure unit. Some exposure units require a different voltage outlet and may require special electrical outlets. This may also have a bearing on where the exposure unit is placed.

10 Acrylic Aquatint Spray Booth

The acrylic aquatint is applied to a metal plate with an airbrush. When any airbrush equipment is used, it will be necessary to exhaust any unwanted airborne spray from the studio. Professionally designed acid exhaust booths, found in traditional printmaking studios, may provide an excellent airbrush aquatint booth. The exhaust system in existing acid booths should be sufficient to exhaust any acrylic over-spray created from the application of the acrylic aquatint to the metal plate with the airbrush. It is, however, essential to have this checked by an qualified safety officer.

Safer Intaglio Studio Setup

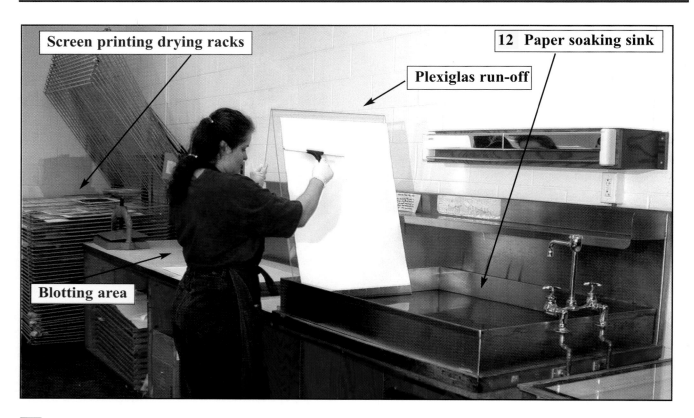

Screen printing drying racks

12 Paper soaking sink

Plexiglas run-off

Blotting area

11 Hard & Soft-Ground Area

Any free table space can be allocated to the task of applying the acrylic hard and soft-ground.

12 Paper Soaking & Preparation

Ideally there should be a paper soaking sink about 6" deep, with a cold water tap and drain. This should accommodate the largest size paper to be dampened prior to printing. A large photographic tray can substitute where a large sink is unavailable.

Alongside the paper soaking sink should be enough table space to have a plexiglas paper squeegee run-off. This run-off allows you to place the dampened paper onto the plexiglas surface and squeegee excess water so that this water runs back into the sink.

There should also be enough table space to accommodate paper blotters and paper ripping (trimming) area.

13 Hot-Plate Area

The hot-plate is a commonly found piece of

equipment used in traditional printmaking for melting rosin dust onto metal plates, for preparing grounds and also for heating intaglio ink prior to printing.

In the non-toxic intaglio studio the hot-plate is more useful for plate drying, preparing the Crackle Intaglio-Type and fusing toner onto the Polyester Litho Plate.

Most professional hot-plates require a 240V electrical outlet so placement in your studio will depend on where this outlet is located or where it can be safely installed.

14 Inking Stations

Designing inking stations will depend on the number of printmakers using the studio at any given time. In a classroom/studio environment where there is an average of 15 students inking plates there would need to be a minimum of about 3 ft. of linear table space for about one third of the class. I recommend laying a 1/4" piece of glass onto the inking tables to make clean-up easier.

Safer Intaglio Studio Setup

15   Large plate dev. & wash-out

15 **Large Plate Wash-Out Area**
Invariably there will be printmaking studios that will require facilities to handle plates that are larger than 18" x 22". To accommodate larger plates is just a matter of having everything larger. Larger developing tray, larger wash-out ·sinks, paper soaking, etching tanks and so on. I do, however, recommend a spray wash-out booth, such is used in screen printing, to wash out larger plates.

16 **Print Drying & Paper Flattening**
A good print drying rack is essential for most printmaking studios. When drying prints, without contact with any other surface, a professional screen printing drying rack is recommended. When drying and flattening prints, then flat table space is what is required. Most studios have both systems. Flattening prints will be discussed in a later chapter.

17 **Layout Tables**
If in a class room situation, or as an individual artist, working space is a necessity which generally consists of table space. Light tables and other unoccupied table space may also serve as a dual working space.

18 **Computer Room**
The use of computers is rapidly becoming an important part of contemporary printmaking and in particular to photographic and computer generated printmaking. Computers facilitate making halftones without the necessity of setting up a conventional darkroom. This presents a far better choice for halftone stencil making. It also allows printmakers greater creative freedom when it comes to integrating digital imagery with non-toxic printmaking (See P.137 - 172).

Computers have much to offer the printmakers and as such space should be made available to accommodate various pieces of computer equipment. I highly recommend Macintosh computer systems with Epson InkJet printers and HP Laser Printers. These are pieces of equipment that I have concentrated my research with. There are, however, many more choices of equipment especially in regards to printers. The information supplied on pages 137 - 172 could be equally applied to other combinations and brands of computer equipment. The most important thing to gain from these chapters is the principle of making high quality halftones.

Keen knowledge is easily transferrable!

Intaglio-Type Exposure Systems

Introduction

The Intaglio-Type techniques described in this book have evolved over a period of several years through thousands of hours of research. This technical evolution resulted from my increased understanding of the working properties of the ImagOn film. As my knowledge of the technical capabilities of ImagOn increased, so did my need for more sophisticated exposure equipment. In the beginning, the homemade exposure units worked well because my technical understanding and demands were unsophisticated.

In the late 1980's when I first started with 'non-toxic' printmaking research, my approach was directed as much by the cost of materials as by non-toxic considerations. I went out of my way to find inexpensive alternatives for everything from equipment to consumables. I started out with a simple and inexpensive exposure unit which consisted of four daylight balance 500W photo flood lamps positioned under a table. These lamps faced a portable vacuum frame (purchased used) that sat on the floor. Although this system produced good results for the gelatin-based photo intaglio process, it was not without its complications. One problem was the excessive heat created by these lamps, plus the ongoing expense of replacing these bulbs which had an active life of about 6 hours. With exposure times averaging 10 - 15 minutes, I was replacing these lamps ($25 for a set of four) every week.

I began looking for a commercial UV light source which did not burn out every few hours. I had heard that mercury vapor, metal halide, and pulse xenon were desirable lamps that gave out large amounts of UV light. Two 400W mercury vapor lamps were given to me, and, with the help of a licensed electrician, I constructed an exposure unit that had a trap-door-type shutter system. This served my needs for several years.

Once I began the photopolymer film, I realized that I would need a more sophisticated light source since the ImagOn film works best with short exposure times. Again, with the aid of an electrician, I constructed an exposure unit with a 1000W metal halide lamp, the type commonly used for highway and street lights. The exposure times were considerably shortened, sometimes to the point where they were too brief. A continuing problem was getting even even illumination over the surface of the vacuum frame. Since these industrial lamps were designed for flood lighting, even illumination was not an important consideration to the manufacturers.

I began to recognize that this low-tech approach to exposure limited the potential of the ImagOn film. What I needed was a more controllable light source. During my workshops, I had worked with many different exposure systems around the world and was becoming familiar with the technical features that made some exposure systems superior to others.

One of the greatest assets of any exposure unit is a light integrator. This light integrator measures the exact quantity of UV light emitted from the light source, meaning that exposures could be finely tuned and easily repeated. The other technical consideration is the vacuum system. Perfect contact between the ImagOn plate and the image is vital for good results.

Having worked all around the world with a wide range of exposure systems, I have concluded that the exposure unit/plate-maker is one vital piece of equipment for every Contemporary Printmaking studio. For the Intaglio-Type techniques, a good exposure unit is as important as an etching press, and I urge printmakers to budget for this equipment.

Intaglio-Type Exposure Systems

The OLEC DEC 22-28, shown above, is a tabletop exposure unit which is highly recommended for Intaglio-Type plate-making.

The greatest problems printmakers experience with the Intaglio-Type techniques result from working with inferior exposure systems. I have tested fluorescent-type exposure systems designed for screen printing emulsions, and this kind of 'soft' light does not work. No matter how much UV light it gives off, it will always yield poor results. **Under no circumstances can fluorescent-type light exposure systems be used successfully with the Intaglio-Type processes.**

The first question on everyone's mind is expense. With the help of the Olec Corporation, I have developed several exposure systems with a range of prices, and all perform well. The Olec Corporation sells their equipment in independent components or as complete units. It is possible to purchase the light integrator, light sensor, and light source separately, so a great system can be built depending upon your budget. Furthermore, the craftsmanship, design, and durability of their equipment is excellent.

We have worked together to test two light exposure systems for ImagOn film with a basic starting cost of a few hundred dollars up to the most elaborate system at a few thousand dollars. Some Olec equipment is available as reconditioned units, and these are substantially less expensive.

Intaglio-Type Exposure Systems

The Least Expensive Exposure System

|O|ne of the most affordable lamps priced at under $300 that yield a consistent and even illumination, is the *Olec Olite® 1KT-Q 1000W Quartz* 120 volt 9 amp lamp. This lamp is compact and lightweight and gives excellent results. Although there are many different varieties of Quartz Halogen lamps on the market, this one is designed with a lamp reflector specifically for imaging purposes. It offers an intense 1000W light. Even lamp illumination is a most important considerations, because it relates directly to the quality of the Intaglio-Type print.

It is possible to start with just this lamp if you have a restricted budget. An inline on/off power switch would need to be installed (available at most hardware stores). To use this simple system, just watch a clock and turn the light on and off for each exposure. The next necessity is a vacuum frame. An inferior substitute would be to place a thick piece of glass, with weights at each end, over the image in contact with the ImagOn-coated plate. This is the least expensive way to begin. However, you cannot expect ultra high-quality prints with this arrangement. One example where it would be adequate is the following: if you were laminating the halftone positive into the surface of the ImagOn, as described in the chapter on Direct Intaglio-Type, the need for a good vacuum frame is reduced. This would provide good results at a minimal cost. However, it would also be very limiting as to what stencils you could use.

The Vacuum Frame

The next most important consideration is a vacuum frame. Some printmakers may already have a vacuum frame and others may be able to purchase a used one. Some adventurous printmakers may wish to make their own vacuum frames. For construction, the two most important items are the vacuum blanket and the vacuum pump. A contact number and the Internet site for the Olec Corporation are listed in the Sources of Supply to allow follow-up inquiries.

Timing the Light Exposure

The next consideration is a means of accurately timing the light exposure. Two ways of timing are with a photographic darkroom-type timer or a light integrator. A darkroom timer is the cheapest alternative especially when using the AL 1KT lamp. A light integrator is a better investment for mercury vapor and metal halide lamp systems.

What is a Light Integrator?

A photocell measures light and a light integrator is attached to a photocell. It can be compared to a camera's light meter. Once a good light integrator and photocell are installed, it is possible to time each exposure precisely. This absolute control with exposure is an important consideration when controlled Intaglio-Type results are desirable.

A photographic timer has the ability to measure time, but it does not consider the age of the bulb and its UV light output. With metal halide lamps, the actual time that the lamp stays on increases with the age of the bulb to compensate for a lower UV output. A light integrator compensates for these changes and always gives consistent results. Each high UV light bulb has a working life of about 1000 hours. Accurate exposures can only be expected within the light bulb's recommended working life.

Intaglio-Type Exposure Systems

Olec makes five different light integrators. The least expensive is the Olix AL 111 unit. The one we tested is the Olix Ⓐl 131, as shown below. Both units work well; the one advantage the AL 131 has over the AL 111 is its programmability. The AL 131 allows you to program the integrator with different exposure modes. However, this programmability is a convenience rather than a necessity.

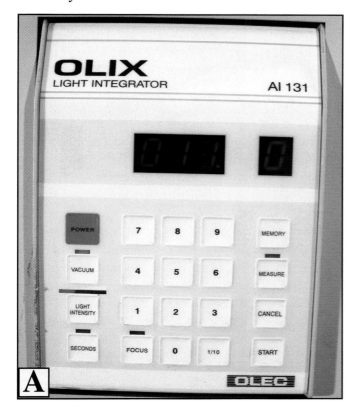

The Photocell
The photocell is a special light sensor which quantifies the amount of light emitted by the exposure lamp. There are several types of photocells available. It is important to choose the one specifically designed for ImagOn photopolymer film. The Olec photocell model PA92, which measures narrow band UV light ranging from 350-390 nanometers, is perfect for the Intaglio-Type as ImagOn peaks at 365 nanometers.

In the OLEC DEC 22 x 28 exposure unit, the photocell is positioned on the inside of the unit just above the vacuum frame, as shown in Illustration ①, on the next page. This photocell is connected via a special cable to the light integrator.

Calibrating the Photocell
When you purchase the DEC 22 x 28 Desktop Exposure Unit, the photocell must be adjusted according to the Olec owners manual that comes with the unit. The opposite illustration ① shows where this unit is located on the DEC 22 x 28 unit.

Connecting the Photocell to the Integrator
If you are assembling a custom exposure unit, the AL 1KT-Q lamp needs a QXD Box Connection to make it work in coordination with the photocell and the AL 111 or Al 131 light integrators. The QXD also allows for the connection of a vacuum frame that automates the on/off switch for the vacuum.

Upgrading to a Better Lamp
One advantage of the Olec equipment is interchangeability, allowing relatively easy upgrades from one or more components of the exposure system, to another.

The highest quality lamp I tested was the Olite AL 13®, illustration ②, which has a 1000W specially designed L 902 metal halide bulb. The metal halide lamp has a direct connection between the lamp housing shutter mechanism and the light integrator. The metal halide AL 13 is shutter-driven. The lamp is constantly running during the operation of this unit. The specific light exposure is controlled by the shutter opening and closing within the lamp housing. The Olite AL 13 does not necessarily need the QXD Box Connection unless you want the vacuum synchronized with the exposure operation.

Intaglio-Type Exposure Systems

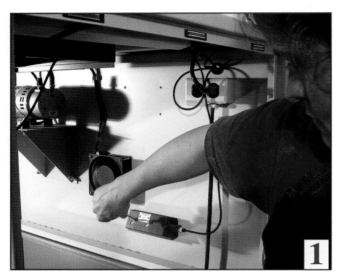

Olec DEC 22 x 28 Exposure Unit

One of the finest and most compact exposure systems I have ever used is the Olec DEC 22 x 28. This is a complete table-top exposure system. The vacuum frame has an imaging area of 22" x 28" which should accommodate most printmakers' needs. This system uses the AL 131 light integrator and the AL 13 metal halide lamp system seen in illustration 2, on the previous page.

The DEC 22 x 28 is shown on page 14.

Setting up the DEC 22 x 28

After purchasing the DEC 22 x 28 exposure unit, there are three things you must do.

1 Make sure that the photocell screw is open 3/4 of a turn. Take off the right side panel of the unit, and use a Phillips head screwdriver to turn the photocell screw.

2 While the unit is open, also disconnect the vacuum frame from its fully automated operating mode. Pull out the plug marked "frame" which is located inside the unit just behind the light integrator. Close the unit.

3 The light integrator needs to be removed from the front of the unit, and balanced to the three light settings by turning the small screws at the top end of the sensor. This balancing operation is easy and is just a matter of following the instruction manual. There are three light intensities on the AL 13 lamp: low, medium and high light output. Each of these three different intensities needs to be balanced with the photocell to read 100 on the light integrator. Balancing all three light intensities is necessary to produce the same quantity of light units on all settings. For example, if you wish to speed up the

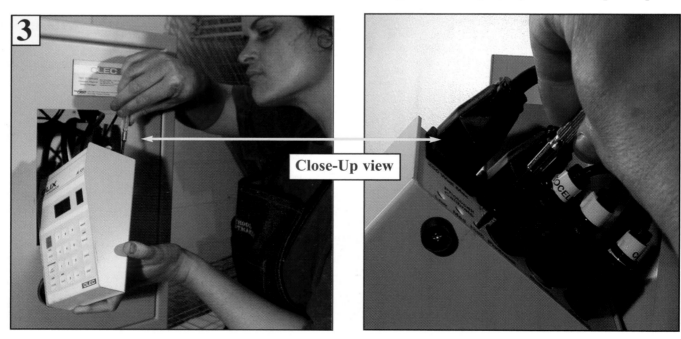

Close-Up view

Intaglio-Type Exposure Systems

exposure time by changing from the low intensity to the high intensity, the integrator will be regulating exactly the same quantity of light. The only difference between the low and the high intensity is the time the exposure takes, with the high setting reducing the time considerably compared to the low setting.

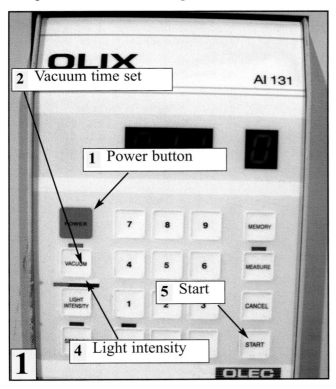

Operating the DEC 22 x 28

Most of the operations are controlled from the light integrator panel shown above.

1 Press the Power button to activate digital read-out.

2 Program the vacuum time. Press the vacuum button and dial in 14. This should give you an adequate delay before exposure for the vacuum to reach full suction. (This time may vary at a higher altitude). There is a vacuum pressure gauge on the outside of this unit that indicates when the vacuum has reached full suction. If the exposure lamp starts before the vacuum reaches full suction, then increase the vacuum time.

3a,b Open the vacuum frame by pulling the frame out of the unit, then lifting the lid. After the art work is placed in the vacuum frame, the lid is shut and the frame is pushed back into the unit.

4 Choose 'high' of the three choices of light intensities. Punch in an exposure number according to the exposure guide three pages ahead.

5 Activate the "Start" button. If you have not disconnected the fully automated vacuum feature, the vacuum will automatically start. This automation can be a very annoying feature, especially when making step tests.

Intaglio-Type Exposure Systems

When making step tests, you will need to know how to maintain the vacuum. As this procedure is not listed in the Olec operating manual, it is described as follows:

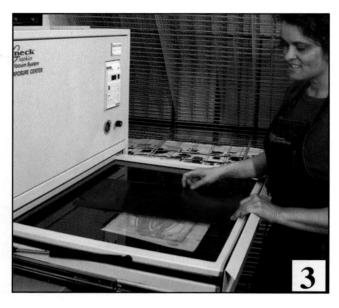

Making Step Tests with the DEC

You must fine-tune an exposure frequently, especially for the Wash-Drawing Intaglio-Type. The best method is to make an exposure step test while maintaining the vacuum pressure.

1 Expose the ImagOn plate to the Aquatint Screen

2 Place the wash drawing on top of this plate.

3 Use an opaque sheet of cardboard or piece of Rubylith to block the light during the step test. This sits on top of the vacuum frame glass. The aim is to maintain the vacuum pressure while incrementally moving the Rubylith film in exposure steps by covering a portion of the plate inside the vacuum frame.

For example, the first exposure time is 5 light units (L. U.); and you may then want to do a step test at 10 L.U., 15 L.U., 20 L.U., and 25 L.U. Since the steps will be made in multiples of 5 L.U., program the integrator to read 5 L.U.

For all exposures, I recommend placing the light intensity on the highest level to speed up the entire testing process.

Stay by the control panel and manually operate the DEC for the entire step test procedure. In this example, the image is first given five exposures of 5 L.U. Stand by the control panel; and, as soon as the lamp goes out after the first 5 L.U., press the start button again.

4 Now, to conduct the step test, push the start button to begin the 5 L.U., cycle again; and, after the 5 L.U. *immediately* pull the vacuum frame out of the unit. Although pressing the 'start' button will reactivate the vacuum, pulling the vacuum frame out from the unit ensures that the lamp will not turn on. *(This is a safety feature. It is impossible to activate the lamp unless the vacuum frame is pushed into the unit.)*

5 While the pump is engaged and the vacuum frame is out of the unit, place the piece of Rubylith film on top of the glass of the vacuum frame to block out a portion of the plate. Push the vacuum frame all the way back into the unit. When it is all the way in, the lamp will activate for another 5 L.U.

6 Stand by the control panel; and, as soon as the lamp goes out, press the start button and immediately pull the vacuum frame out again. Reposition the Rubylith film and repeat this process.

7 Complete the last step test for 25 L.U. in the same way.

This may seem at first like a lengthy and complicated procedure, but it is really quite simple and requires just a little co-ordination.

The plate is taken from the exposure unit and developed as usual.

Intaglio-Type Exposure Systems

Portable Exposure Unit

Following is a series of photographs illustrating the Portable 18" x 24" exposure unit, which was designed by the author, as it unfolds. This unit is hand-made with a stainless steel casing. It has all Olec parts with the Olec 1KT Quartz lamp. There are several price configurations depending on the components purchased. The least expensive is the basic unit with manual on-off switch, lamp, vacuum frame and pump. Adding the light integrator with sensor adds considerably to the cost. See additional information at:
<www.golsm.com>

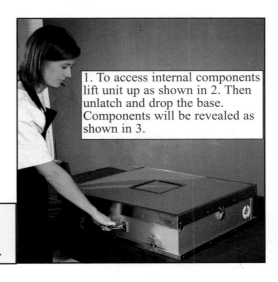

1. To access internal components lift unit up as shown in 2. Then unlatch and drop the base. Components will be revealed as shown in 3.

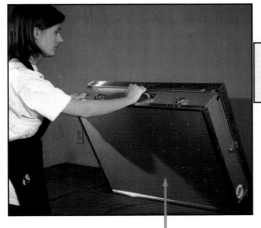

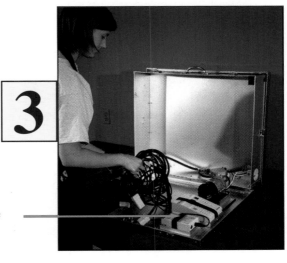

Drop this base and internal components are accessible

The unit opens up to provide a sturdy support for the exposure lamp

Intaglio-Type Exposure Systems

Place Olite 1KT Lamp on top.

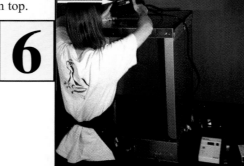

6

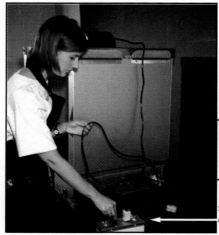

7

Plug in manual switch. The least expensive set-up.

A more expensive lamp can replace the 1KT Quartz lamp

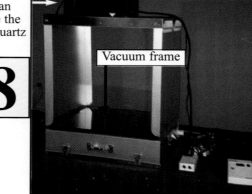

Vacuum frame

8

Exposure Guide

On the next page is an exposure guide for both the Olec DEC 22 x 28 exposure unit which uses the AL 13 metal halide lamp and the 1KT quartz lamp. There are 9 different exposures that need to be determined for various Intaglio-Type techniques. Some terminology may need clarification.

Aquatint Screen

This is a lith film screen with a 60% random 'aquatint like' opaque dot which evenly covers the entire surface of the film. Once the Aquatint Screen exposure has been calculated, it will remain constant.More information at: **<www.elizabethdove.com>**

Flash

This refers to a naked 'flash' of light onto the ImagOn film after the Aquatint Screen and image have both been exposed.

Mylar®

Refers to the Mylar drafting film. Using the word Mylar can be confusing since it is also used to describe the top layer of ImagOn film. Mylar is a general term which describes a range of plastic films. The drafting film and the top Mylar are both plastic, and both fall under the definition of Mylar.

Gouache

This is a kind of opaque watercolor paint sometimes referred to as Designer's Gouache.

Toner

This is a toner acrylic wash.

Oiled Photocopies

Any paper photocopy can be made into a kind of transparency by rubbing the surface of the photocopy with vegetable oil, as shown in Illustration 11. After the oil has saturated the paper, any oily residue can be removed by rubbing with a clean cloth. This oily residue often smears onto the inside of the vacuum frame during exposures and should be cleaned off immediately with glass cleaner and a clean rag.

Digital Halftone

This refers to digital inkjet or photographic lith film halftones. Light halftones are defined by the open dot in their darkest areas. The dense halftone refers to a 70% density of dot coverage in the blackest areas of the image.

Intaglio-Type Exposure Systems

Intaglio-Type exposure guide for the Olec DEC 22 x 28 exposure unit that uses the AL 13 metal halide lamp and the Olec Quartz 1KT lamp.

Permission is granted to photocopy this page and post it on your Olec exposure unit.

Exposure figures are in light units(L.U.) from the Olix light integrator AL 131, as described in this chapter. If a light integrator is not available, substitute light units for seconds. (Seconds are not as accurate as light units).

Type of Exposure	AL 13 → Metal Halide Light Units or sec.	1KT Quartz Light Units or sec.
Aquatint Screen	16 - 20	200
Flash	.5	5-10
Gouache on Mylar	5 - 18	100 +
Toner Wash on Mylar	5 - 28	100 - 130
Halftones---Light	15	175
Halftones-- Medium	35	200-300
Halftones---Dense	45	up to 600
Oiled Photocopy	20 -30	225

Intaglio-Type - Introduction

Intaglio-Type Terminology

Since 1994, I have been researching and developing what I have termed Intaglio-Type techniques using photopolymer film. In the beginning I took an individual research approach by developing the non-etch techniques that used unique qualities of the photopolymer film for plate making. Understanding and utilizing these qualities comprise a large body of my original research and from the very outset, I developed terminology to describe these 'new' techniques.

Language is such an important part of education, especially when it comes to teaching and describing these new photopolymer film based intaglio techniques. Consequently, I use this **new printmaking language** when teaching these techniques. During workshops I've given in Germany, Holland, Belgium and Argentina we discussed the notion of renaming Intaglio-Type techniques with Germanic, Dutch, Flemish, or Spanish names. Almost everybody agrees that the names I've given to these techniques should remain universal and thus, understandable in any language.

Furthermore, if these techniques are to be fully known in the printmaking world, they should be identified for the uniqueness that they display. I have witnessed Intaglio-Type prints in printmaking exhibitions that were described as either "intaglio print" or "etching" in their technical description. (One way that you can easily identify an Intaglio-Type print is from the plate edge created.) With well over 100,000 sq. ft. of ImagOn sold worldwide, since its inception, it is about time that the Intaglio-Type proudly take its place among other printmaking techniques. If you have employed a photoploymer film based intaglio technique and are asked to write the technique used, simply state that it is an *Intaglio-Type*. A more lengthy description could be *Non-etch Intaglio-Type* or, more specifically, a *Construction Intaglio-Type*.

Other Photopolymer Films

There were and still exist several types of photopolymer film all designed and used for making printed circuit boards. Other printmakers and myself have tested these other brands of photopolymer film and have found that Du Pont's ImagOn to be far superior. ImagOn is more user friendly while demonstrating the greatest image resolution and tonal range. There are other photopolymer films that try to equal the quality of ImagOn, but they all have downsides compared to ImagOn ULTRA. *The greatest innovation with photopolymer film research is the ability to still-develop the plate.* If you are using a photopolymer film that relies totally on hand-development then you are using an inferior photopolymer film.

Some brands promote the fact that they are thinner thus better than ImagOn ULTRA. Film salespeople who make this claim have missed the point of the tremendous creative potential of the non-etch techniques. Thinking in the toxic traditional mind-set severely retards the creative potential that photopolymer film offers printmakers. Thinner is definitely not better for non-etch techniques as it translates to less intaglio ink on the plate.

No matter how thin other brands of photopolymer film are they can never surpass the degree at which the film can be thinned for the Etched Intaglio-Type technique. The ImagOn ULTRA film can be precisely thinned to match the kind of out-put resolution required from individual images.

With the Etched Intaglio-Type (P. 129- 136), the photopolymer film can be thinned, on the plate, to about 10 microns. This allows halftones of extraordinary high resolution to be etched into a metal plate. Furthermore, the etch and non-etch Intaglio-Type techniques can be combined for more creative image exploration. This can only be done effectively if you begin with the thicker ImagOn ULTRA. Thus, with ImagOn ULTRA, there are more creative choices as there are many more plate-making options.

Intaglio-Type - Introduction

ImagOn ULTRA

Du Pont is the acknowledged world leader in photopolymer film research. ImagOn ULTRA represents the latest scientific development in photopolymer research by Du Pont. It has taken almost 18 months of solid testing to fully come to terms with the extended possibility and uniqueness of this generation of ImagOn film. The one overwhelming conclusion was that it could not be used in the same manner as the old ImagOn. Thus, an almost entirely new body of research needed to be completed before this book could be published. In the interim, I have had hundreds of inquiries about its pending publication date. My only response was that it would be forthcoming. In the meantime, in 2001, a video entitled *Keith Howard's Non-Toxic Intaglio Instructional Video* was published which is current and available. For more information see page 240.

This was the first publication of my new research with ImagOn ULTRA. Since then, I have also developed many more Intaglio-Type techniques which are fully explained in this book.

Before completing this text, I needed to thoroughly test ImagOn ULTRA in several different countries to see how it responded under different studio conditions. Thus, I introduced this film first to printmakers in Argentina, then Scotland, Germany, the USA, Belgium, and Holland. Technical problems arose in each country that were successfully addressed. This resulted in a change in methodology and an **emphasis on the importance of preliminary testing.**

The Importance of Testing

In the past, when some printmakers experienced problems with ImagOn, they were quick to blame the product. On closer examination, it was evident that they have not fully read or comprehended the instructions. Unfortunately printmakers who are not likely to read instructions rarely completely read the text including what I am now writing. Some rely mainly on the pictures combined with past experience to visually explain what they should be doing. The pictures in this book are

there to add clarity to the written text. For a more visual explanation, there is the option of my 80 minute instructional video mentioned below.

The overriding fact is that ImagOn and the techniques described in all of my books work, but there are specialized equipment, products, materials, and studio conditions that must be met before they work well. I spoke at length about this in the section entitled *Safer Intaglio Studio Setup pages 8-14*.

One essential aspect of successful Intaglio-Type printmaking is the need to do preliminary development testing. It is necessary if you want to avert technical problems.

How to Proceed

Before preliminary testing can take place, you must first learn how to laminate ImagOn ULTRA to a plate. I will..........

1. Briefly discuss Intaglio-Type plates.

2. Show how to prepare copper plates.

3. Provide a list of materials.

4. Show how to apply ImagOn to a plate.

5. Show how to make up ImagOn developer.

6. Show how to test the developer.

Once you have the correct equipment and good stencils, you should be able to make perfect Intaglio-Type prints with ImagOn ULTRA.

Intaglio-Type Plates

Almost any clean, dry non-porous flat surface can be used for Intaglio-Type non-etch techniques, such as;

1. 16 oz or .022 roofing copper, which I recommend, available from some building and plumbing supply houses although any type of

Plates & Preparation

metal plate can be used, such as, steel, aluminum, zinc or flat galvanized steel.

2. Plastics such as, P.E.T.G., Plexiglas, Lexan, acetate, Mylar, and polyester.

3. Thin plywood, provided it is sanded and sealed with several coats of water-based polyurathene. The more layers of polyurathene that are applied the less evident will be the wood grain in the final print. **Below**: Canadian printmaker, Lynda Hattin, uses tree bark to make unique ImagOn plates.

Above left, is the 6" x 4" Birch Bark plate and at right is the print from the plate.

Most plates require some kind of preparation before use from sanding the surface with wet-and-dry sandpaper to a rubbing alcohol wipe.

Part of the creative fun when working with ImagOn film is the diversity of plate-making material that can be used. Some printmakers stick with the kind of metal plate that they are most familiar with, and others seek out plate material that will creatively impact their images. No matter what plate you are using, it will require some type of preparation.

BIG TIP: Get this tool at right.

d | **Available at: <www.takachpress.com>**

Plate Making Materials

1. Recommended .022 Roofing Copper or any flat metal plate from zinc to steel

2. Electric palm sander.

3. 320 and 600 grit wet and dry sandpaper.

4. Rubbing alcohol or isopropyl alcohol.

5. Lint-free rag or cloth.

6. Small can of polyurethane (wooden plates)

7. 2" wide paintbrush.

8. Flat file or pull-tool.

Copper Plates

For the past 15 years, I have recommended purchasing .022 thick or 16 oz. roofing copper for intaglio plate making. It is a product commonly stocked by plumbing and building suppliers and is normally sold in sheets what are 3' x 8' or 3' x 10'. If purchased in this manner, a good plate cutter or metal shears will be necessary to trim the plate to a workable size. Pre-cut plates are also available from most printmaking suppliers.

This thickness of plate is such that only sharp edges need to be removed before use. It is not necessary to bevel this plates of this thickness before use, just to round the corners with a flat file or d deburring tool. This is a small hand tool which easily remove sharp edges from metal plates.

Quick Copper Plate Preparation After all sharp edges have been removed, spritz a small quantity of rubbing alcohol onto the plate and wipe the surface with a clean lint-free rag. The plate is now ready for ImagOn lamination.

Johann Feught, **"First Act. View to Hide",** 2003, Intaglio-Type/Collograph, 30" x 46".
The view more of Johann Feught's work go to **<www.ouc.bc.ca>** then type
Johann into their search engine.

Small Plate Prep. & ImagOn Lamination

QUICK LOOK

1. Prepare copper plate by sanding or by wiping with rubbing alcohol.

 1

 2

2. Spritz plate with water.

3. Remove the peel-back layer from the ImagOn.

3

4a,b

4a, b. Lay ImagOn onto wet plate.

QUICK LOOK

5. Spritz water on top of the ImagOn.

5

6a,b

6a, b. Squeegee the ImagOn down.

7. Do a final rub on the plate to remove bubbles and water.

7

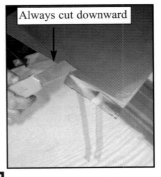

Always cut downward

8

8. Trim ImagOn edge.

9. Heat dry the plate.

9

Plates & Preparation

Copper - Longer Preparation

U se an electric palm-sander with 320 grit wet-and-dry sandpaper.

Sand using water to prevent dust. After sanding, wipe plate with a clean damp rag. Make certain that no residue remains.

If preparing a plate for the Etched Intaglio-Type technique, use 600 grit wet-and-dry sandpaper until plate surface is mirror-like. Then wipe residue from plate with a clean, damp, lint-free cloth.

Any sharp edges created by the plate cutter can also be sanded away with the de-burring tool shown at the bottom of page 27. All other corners or sharp edges can be removed with a flat file.

Plastic Plates

Do not sand plastic plates. Most plastic surfaces only require a wipe with an clean lint free rag and rubbing alcohol. It is important to use a lint-free cloth as any small cloth fibers left on the plate will cause unwanted dimples under the ImagOn as it is laminated to the plate. This will reflect in black ink specks on the finished print.

There are a variety of plastic plates that can be used. The least expensive is P.E.T.G. (Polyethylene Terephthalate) and Styrene in width thicknesses from .030 to 3/8". This type of plate, though, is extremely flexible, and the ImagOn film is reluctant to stay on. Other more expensive and stable plastics are Plexiglas or polycarbonate films such as Lexan®, Hazod® or Tuffak®. Internet searches, with all these names, reveal many distributors of the products, such as, < **www.Lairdplastics.com**>.

TIP: I recommend placing a thick sheet of polycarbonate film (Lexan) on the etching press bed to protect the bed from moisture or abrasion. Takach also have a great registration templet that can be placed under this Lexan bed protector.

Wooden Plates

Plywood, Luan, even Birch bark or, in fact, any thin wood can be used for ImagOn plate-making. Wood, however, must be sealed thoroughly with water-based polyurathene before ImagOn will adhere to it. Apply the polyurathene with a soft brush and allow it to thoroughly dry. Then, using 600 wet and dry sandpaper, lightly sand the surface until it is smooth. Repeat as necessary. Some open or large grain wood will require several coats while smaller hardwoods will require fewer coats. Each coat will diminish the wood grain effect in the final print

Zinc, Aluminum, Steel Plates

Prepare in the same manner as copper plates.

Starting Equipment

1. Fully equipped etching studio as described in the chapter on *Safer Intaglio Studio Set Up.*

2. A good exposure unit or plate-maker is essential.

3. An Aquatint Screen.

4. A Gram scale.

Starting Materials

1. ImagOn ULTRA film.

2. A piece of 1/4" thick window glass which measures about 6" larger than the largest plate to be laminated with ImagOn film.

3. Good, sharp 6" long neoprene screen printing squeegee with wooden handle. (A good, sharp medium-hard squeegee is essential). When buying this kind of squeegee, purchase the most expensive squeegee blade available. It generally cost about $1 per inch. Under no circumstances, purchase the black opaque "cheap" rubber squeegees. This WILL yield inferior results. Look instead for the type of squeegee rubber that is translucent and is, generally, an earth orange in color with a durometer or hardness of 80).

Plates & Preparation

4. Three plant misting bottles to hold water, white vinegar, and rubbing alcohol.

5 A sharp trimming knife. I recommend the Olfa Cutter with the 1" thick snap-off blades.

6. Duct tape, purchased from a hardware store. Masking tape can be substituted.

7. Copper plate. I recommend 16 oz.or .022gauge roofing copper.

8. Hand-dryer or hair-dryer.

9. Soda ash or sodium carbonate (anhydrous high-density variety) with an accurate Gram Scale.

10. Liter measuring container.

11. Two photo developing trays larger than the Intaglio-Type plates to be laminated with ImagOn ULTRA.

12 GraLab® Darkroom timer → or small electronic cooking timer.

13. 1 gal. white vinegar normally used for salad dressing. Purchase the kind that has the highest vinegar content.

14. Dish-washing gloves and eye protection.

15. 1 quart of rubbing alcohol.

Testing the Working Time, in Your Studio, for ImagOn ULTRA

ImagOn ULTRA is a light sensitive film and is particularly sensitive or reactive to UV light. If there is normal incandescent or florescent light, devoid of UV light, the working time of the film will be between 20 minutes and 2 hours.

To test the working time or the amount of time that the film can stay out in your studio without being exposed, do the following:

1. Lay a small piece of ImagOn film on the lamination table.

2. Lay a piece of copper plate or opaque card on it so that it is half covered.

3. Visually inspect the covered ImagOn film every 5 minutes by lifting the copper plate. This allows you to see if the color of the uncovered ImagOn changes. Once ImagOn ULTRA starts changing to a darker blue color it is past its light exposure tolerance point. If it takes 30 minutes to notice a color change, deduct about 20% of this exposure time to arrive at a light tolerance level for the ImagOn film.

TIP: UV light can be present in a studio either directly or indirectly through reflection from windows, doors, and skylights. The amount of UV light in these incidences will constantly vary throughout the day. Thus, the above light tolerance test may only apply for a specific time of the day. Any window can be covered with red or yellow plastic (Rubylith screen printing masking film is ideal) to prevent UV light from entering the studio.

Safe Handling

As with all photopolymers, minimize direct contact with film emulsion by wearing rubber gloves. For more details, see the Safe Handling Guide enclosed in each box of ImagOn ULTRA film.

Film Preparation Prior to Lamination

Cut ImagOn ™ ULTRA film slightly larger than the size of the plate.

When ImagOn is cut from the roll, it will naturally curl back into a small roll. Handle film carefully and avoid putting any pressure on the rolls which will leave 'dints' or impressions in the film.

Removing the Inside Peel-Back

Method for Removing Inside Peel-Back Layer

1a,b Place a piece of double-sided masking tape or Duct tape near the glass lamination slab. This creates a sticky surface which faces up. Fold the tape back on itself, so that the sticky side faces up. Then tape the ends down.

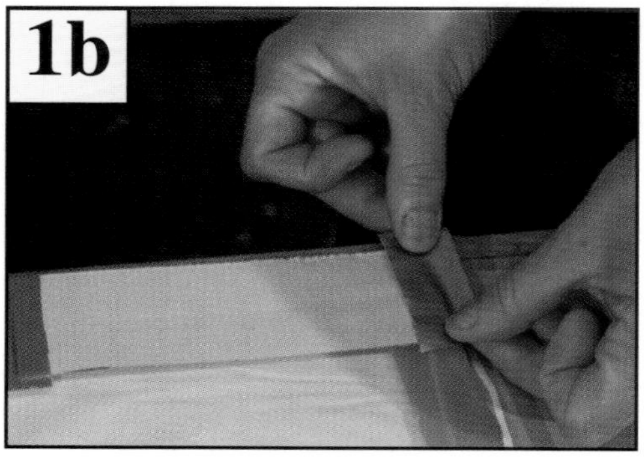

Image 1a

Image 1b

2 Press the inside of the curled ImagOn ULTRA film corner onto the sticky surface of the tape until it sticks to it.

Carefully, pull the film up and away from the tape until the inside peel-back layer separates from the film at the corner.

Image 2

3 Once the sticky tape grabs the inside peel-back layer it acts like a third hand so that you can carefully separate the peel-back layer, from the ImagOn film while using both hands.

The ImagOn film is now ready to be laminated to a plate.

Image 3

Small Plate Lamination

There are two lamination methods according to the size of the plate used. The first method is designed for plate sizes smaller than 11" x 14". If you wish to laminate larger plates, go directly to *Large Plate Lamination* on pages 37 - 40.

For best results, the ImagOn lamination procedure should be carried out as **quickly as possible**.

1. Cut film slightly larger than plate size.

2. Place degreased plate on a glass slab.

3. Liberally spritz the plate with water.

4. Remove inside peel-back layer (inside of film curl) from the ImagOn Ultra.

TIP: Peel-back layer is a soft feeling plastic and the top Mylar is crisp.

Small Plate Lamination

5 Spritz the plate liberally with water. For medium sized ImagOn plates, (between 1 and 2 sq. ft.), spritz the emulsion side of the ImagOn film as well

6a,b Place the film, emulsion side down, on top of the plate by gently lay it down from one end of the plate. If bubbles appear under the film, lift one corner of the film and lay it back down. Do this until most large bubbles under the film disappear.

7 Spritz the top of ImagOn film generously with water. This provides a frictionless surface for the squeegee lamination which happens next.

8 Gently and quickly squeegee the film from the center outward until the film is smooth. If there are any foreign particles trapped under the film, lift the closest edge of the film and remove the particle; then quickly squeegee back down.

Repeat as many times as necessary, increasing the pressure until all the water and air bubbles are no longer visible

9 With a clean rag wipe excess water off the surface by rubbing from the center outward, rubbing harder where the ImagOn is not sticking thoroughly. Pay special attention to the edges. Also, a clean rag can be used for a final wipe.

Small Plate Lamination

10 Cut the ImagOn away from the edges of the plate.

11 A final trim may be necessary to ensure ImagOn is trimmed tightly to the plate edge. Always cut in a downward direction to prevent lifting the ImagOn.

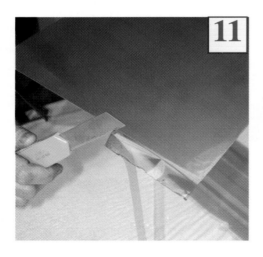

12 Using a hair dryer, set on the highest heat setting for about one minute per sq.ft. area, or hand-dryer, start drying the backside of the plate. There is normally water on the backside of the plate left after the ImagOn lamination process. After the water has been dried from the back of the plate flip it over and heat dry the front of the plate. This heat action bonds the film to the plate.

13 The laminated plate is now ready for image exposure with the UV exposure unit.

The ImagOn plate can be stored in a dark cupboard away from all light.

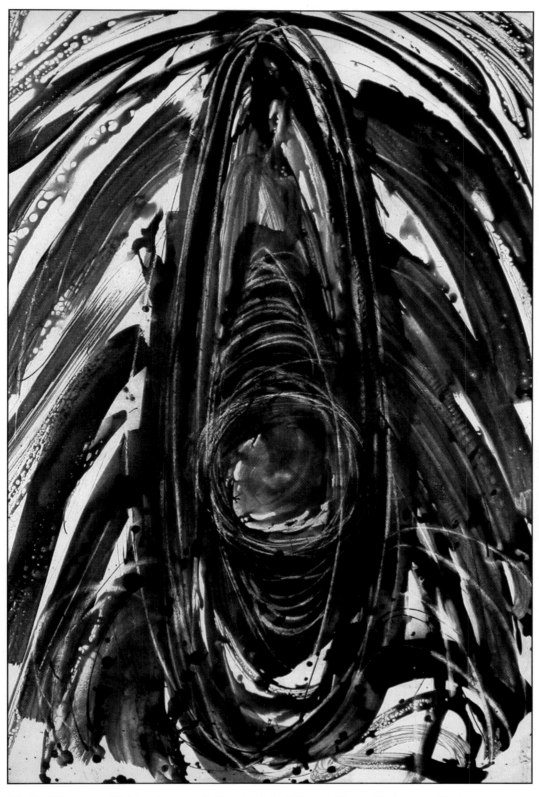

Keith Howard, 2003, **Ground Control to Major Tom, Put your Helmet on,**
2003, Spit-Bite Intaglio-Type, 24" x 36". See Collectors Circle on page 243.
More work at: **<www.KeithHoward.org>**

Large Plate Prep. & ImagOn Lamination

QUICK LOOK

1. Place the large degreased copper plate into the water tray.

2. Remove the peel-back layer from the ImagOn.

3. Float the ImagOn on top of the water, push out air bubbles and slash water on top of the film.

4. Pull the plate and the ImagOn out of the tray together. Lift under the plate and avoid pinching the film to the plate.

QUICK LOOK

5. Pull back the film, release air bubbles, and then lay it back down.

5

6

6. Squeegee the ImagOn to the plate.

6. Trim edges and heat dry the plate with a heat gun or hot-plate.

7

Plates & Preparation

Submersion Lamination for Large Plates or for more than Two Layers of ImagOn

The Submersion Lamination method should always be used for applying more than one layer of ImagOn to a plate.

1 Start this process with a clean, degreased plate or with a plate that already has one or more layers of ImagOn on it. If using a Layered Intaglio-Type plate, remove the top Mylar layer before submerging it into the water bath.

2 Place the plate in a developing tray under 1/2 inch of tap water.

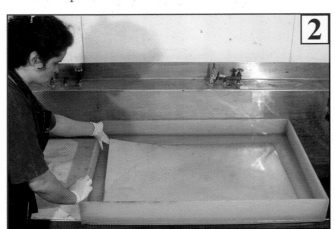

3 Remove the inside peel-back layer from ImagOn ULTRA.

4 Float the ImagOn film, emulsion side down, on top of the water and above the plate. Push out air bubbles and splash water on top of the film.

5 Remove the film and the plate together from the water, so that the film stays on top of the plate. When lifting the plate out of the water, grasp under the plate and towards the opposing edges. Avoid grasping or pinching the plate and the ImagOn film together as you remove it from the water. Wherever you do this, the ImagOn will stick prematurely, preventing you from repositioning of the film.

Plates & Preparation

6 Place the plate with the ImagOn 'floating' on it onto the glass lamination slab. There will be a thin layer of water between the film and the plate which will easily allow the film to be repositioned. There should also be water on top of the film providing a lubricant when you squeegee the ImagOn down in the next step. If there is not enough water on top of the film, liberally spritz it with water.

7a, b, c Starting in the center and working outward, quickly, gently, and carefully squeegee the film onto the plate, being careful not to wrinkle the film by pushing too hard. The film will want to stretch and wrinkle. Slowly increase the pressure and repeat. (Use a 6" squeegee with a sharp medium neoprene rubber blade).

8 If there is an air bubble under the ImagOn, lift the film at the closest edge and allow it to naturally lay down. Repeat with the squeegee as before, increasing the pressure, until all the water and air bubbles are no longer visible.

9 Trim ImagOn at the edge of the plate as you would with a standard lamination. Bond the film to the plate using a hair dryer, a heat-gun, or a hot-plate, (the drying time will be about 1 minute per square foot). Use a hot plate set hot enough not to inflict a burn. If left on a inking hot-plate, cover the ImagOn plate with aluminum foil or a disposable aluminum cookie tray to avoid exposing it to stray room light.

The laminated plate is now ready for image exposure.

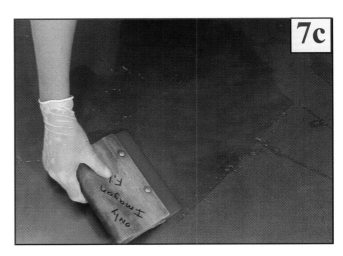

Plates & Preparation

Troubleshooting

Small Plate Lamination. Problem 1: Speckled surface under the ImagOn after lamination. **Probable cause:** Not enough lamination water from the plant mister has been applied to the plate. The final plate will reflect this. ***Solution:*** *Apply more water, with the plant mister during ImagOn lamination or use the submersion lamination method.*

Problem 2: One edge of the ImagOn film did not stick evenly. **Probable cause:** At some point, the edge of the film lifted after the initial lamination. It may have lifted when trimming the ImagOn to the edge of the plate or when removing the plate from the lamination slab. Once an edge lifts after the initial ImagOn lamination, it rarely goes back without problems unless it is addressed immediately. If an edge has lifted during the initial lamination, it can be repeated without problems provided it is done quickly. ***Solution:*** *Run the ImagOn plate through the etching press with the emulsion facing a very smooth etching bed surface. Use the same pressure you would for printing. Depending on the severity of the problem this fix-it method will work only some of the time. Some printmakers routinely run their plates through the press as a final lamination stage. If you do this make sure that the ImagOn plate faces down to a perfectly smooth, glass-like, etching press bed surface.*

Problem 3: Wrinkled ImagOn during the lamination process. **Probable cause:** You have used too much squeegee pressure when first laminating the ImagOn to the plate, or you have not laminated the plate from the center out towards the edges, in a radial manner. Also if you .have forgotten to apply water to the top Mylar surface of the ImagOn you will cause the film to grab the squeegee. The water acts as a lubricant in aiding the squeegee to lay down the ImagOn evenly. ***Solution:*** *When first squeegeeing the ImagOn on to the plate use a light pressure to adhere the film very quickly to the plate. The bigger the film, the more likely that wrinkles will occur. Applying a large amount of water onto the top surface of the film is essential to create a frictionless surface to help in the squeegeeing process. QUICK lamination is essential.*

Problem 4: The ImagOn lifts from the film during the final trimming. **Probable cause:** When cutting or trimming the ImagOn to the edge of the plate, you cut the film up and away from the plate. The up-cutting will cause the ImagOn on top of the plate to lift. The same thing can occur when using a blunt cutting blade. Some metal shears also bend or curve the plate edge during the shearing process. The ImagOn can lift from the edge of the plate depending on how the plate was cut, how sharp the sears were, and how thick the plate is. ***Solution:*** *Always use a sharp cutting knife and only cut down away from the direction that the ImagOn is stuck on the plate. Blunt metal shears bend the plate slightly at the edge. ImagOn will not stick easily to a slightly curved plate edge. This tendency is exaggerated with thicker plates. Use thin .022 roofing copper plates and sharp metal shears to avoid this problem, or have the blade on your metal shears sharpened and properly aligned to ensure optimum cutting.*

Many printmakers like the kind of edge created when ImagOn does not stick perfectly to the plate edge. I have called this the 'The ImagOn Edge'. This truly unique edge can be exaggerated by running the back of the cutting knife down the ImagOn edge at about a 45˚ angle.

Problem 5: Dimples under the ImagOn emulsion. **Probable cause:** Rough handling of the film prior to lamination creates dimples in the ImagOn emulsion that can translate into unwanted marks in the final print. Also, particles of dirt, hairs, paper, or cloth lint trapped under the ImagOn will cause dimples. The latter is, generally, the greater of the two causes. Static electricity can cause particles to be attracted to the ImagOn emulsion directly after the peel-back layer is removed. ***Solution:*** *Wet lamination is the best way to deal with dust created by static electricity. Be meticulous when inspecting the metal plate for*

Plates & Preparation

foreign particles. Use only lint-free rags, and always work on a thoroughly clean surface. Working with the submersion lamination technique will solve this problem, but only if there are no foreign particles floating in the water. To achieve maximum success you must be meticulously clean and constantly vigilant for dirt particles in every aspect of plate-making. Even though the finest speck of dirt can cause an unwanted mark, it is rarely noticed if it occurs in a ink laden area of the plate.

Problem 6: ImagOn will not stick to the plate especially with the Layered Intaglio-Type technique. **Probable cause:** There is an oily surface to the plate being laminated, or if the layered Intaglio-Type technique is being employed, the top Mylar was not removed prior to laying down the second layer of ImagOn. **Solution:***Use a different degreasing method than what was employed. Use undiluted rubbing alcohol and a clean rag to wipe the plate just prior to ImagOn lamination. With the second layer of ImagOn, make sure that the top Mylar is removed.*

TIP: Remember, also, that excessive heat on the ImagOn plate can cause the ImagOn emulsion to distort and even melt. The heat applied to the ImagOn plate should be no more than can be tolerated on your hands.

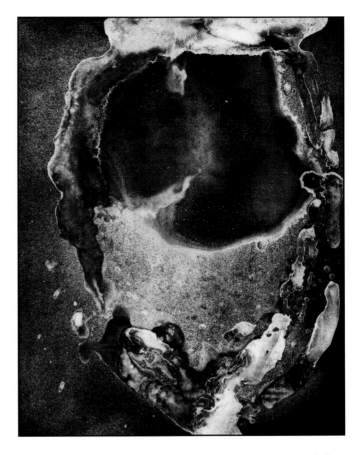

Class demonstration image by Keith Howard for the Alcohol Resist technique seen on page 224.

ImagOn Developer - Mix & Test

QUICK LOOK

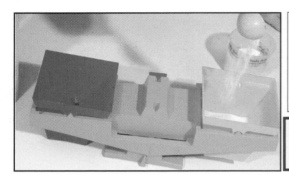

Mixing ImagOn Developer
1. Measure 10 grams of Soda Ash powder.
2. Place into 1 litre container.
3. Add 50 mls of hot water and mix until dissolved.
4. Make volume to 1 litre with room temperature water.

1

http://www.wolverinesports.com/scales.html

 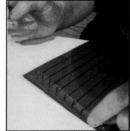

2a,b 2a,b. Divide ImagOn plate into 24 x 1/2" divisions and tape under and over one end.

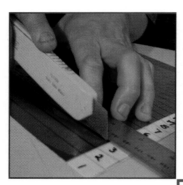

3. Cut through ImagOn to create 24 top Mylar tabs.

3

4 4. Pull off each Mylar tab every minute, while in developer, for 24 one minute segments.

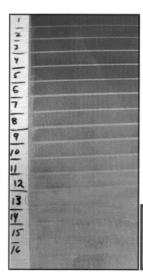

5 5. Finished test plate should show ImagOn emulsion disappearing between the 13 and 15 minute divisions. This shows that developer is the correct strength.

Mixing the developer

Materials for Mixing Developer

1. 5 lb bag of anhydrous high density soda ash.

2. Gram scale.

3. 1 litre measuring container.

4. Hot and cold water.

5. Developing tray.

6. Mixing spoon.

The ImagOn Developer

The ImagOn developer is a soft-water solution. It is made up by adding soda ash (sodium carbonate) to water. Use only anhydrous, high density, soda ash powder available from swimming pool chemical suppliers and printmaking supply companies. It is also known as 'washing soda' and is the key ingredient in Calgon Water Conditioner®. A good source is also Arm and Hammer Washing Soda®, which is commonly available in supermarkets in North America.

Mixing ImagOn Developer:

1. Measure 10 grams of Soda Ash powder.

2. Place into 1 litre container.

3. Add 50 mls of hot water and mix until dissolved.

4. Make up volume to 1 litre with room temperature water.

1 Precisely measure 10 grams of soda ash powder with a gram scale and mix it with about 1/4 cup of hot water until the powder has dissolved. ImagOn developer requires a precise amount of soda ash and, as such, a gram scale is needed.

TIP: To purchase see the web site below:

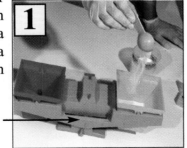

http://www.wolverinesports.com/scales.html

<www.myweigh.com>

TIP: If you do not have a gram scale use a plastic pop bottle cap from a 1 liter bottle. 10 grams equals approximately 1 level cap full plus an additional 3/4 of a cap full.

2 Room temperature water (pH+7) is then added to this dissolved soda ash solution to make a volume of 1 litre. The working temperature of the developing solution should be between 65-70°F (18-21°C). This solution is then added to a photo developing tray.

3 Pour developer into a developing tray.

It is best to use only pH=7 water or distilled water but it is far less expensive to learn how to use your studio tap water. Thus testing the developing solution, for your individual studio conditions, becomes an important part of cost saving and plate making predictability.

Testing the ImagOn Developer

Here is a very simple test which will show you the following:

1. The hardness of softness of your studio water.

2. The strength of the soda ash powder.

Testing the developer

3. How much time needed to thin the ImagOn emulsion when it comes to utilizing the Etched Intaglio-Type technique.

4. How to successfully use ImagOn ULTRA in any studio.

WHY is this test so IMPORTANT?

ImagOn ULTRA is a highly refined imaging film which has the potential to give better results than any other similar type of film. The success of this film is related to the still development method. As the developer is so essential to its success it must be tested for each locatio studio location. Once the developer has been balanced, for your studio, it will allows for a precise and perfect development each time.

If the development solution is too weak or too strong then this still-development method will not compensate for this fact, thus, producing inferior results. Weak or strong (hard or soft water) development solutions can be caused by the pH level of your local tap water or by the type of soda ash powder that is used. In Belgium and Germany, I came across a soda ash crystal that was hydrated and were about half the strength of the anhydrous variety of soda ash common in North America. Thus, if the development directions were followed using hydrated soda ash, a half strength developer would result. Plates made with this developer would not have deep enough intaglio depth to yield a good black in the final print. *Please remember this point.*

What is Involved with this Test?

Basically, ImagOn ULTRA is applied to a plate in the normal manner. **In this test the ImagOn plate is NOT exposed.** The top Mylar of the ImagOn film is cut to create 24 x 1/2" segments or strips. The plate is then dropped into the ImagOn developer. At each 1 minute interval a strip of the top Mylar is removed, while under the developer, to allow the developer to directly dissolve the ImagOn emulsion.

After the 24 x 1/2" Mylar strips have uncovered the ImagOn emulsion this step-test plate is washed and stabilized with a white vinegar wash. The test is completed by visually inspecting the plate to determine at

which point the ImagOn emulsion was completely eroded from the surface of the plate. Between the 13 and 15 minute divisions, on the plate, is the ideal point at which the ImagOn emulsion should have dissolved from the plate.

Testing Materials

1. ImagOn coated plate.

2. 1/2" masking tape.

3. Sharp snap-off blade cutter.

4. Ruler.

5. Fine water-proof felt-tip marker.

6. Mixed ImagOn developer in covered tray.

7. Darkroom timer.

8. Latex or neoprene gloves.

Testing Procedure

Test should be carried out under low ambient light.

1 Apply ImagOn ULTRA to a 9" x 12" copper plate to create the 'ImagOn plate'.

2 With a fine felt-tip marker, working directly on to the top Mylar of the ImagOn Plate, divide the 12" length of the plate into 24 segments. In other words at every 1/2" point rule a line so that the line goes across the 9" width of the plate plate, from one end of the plate to the other, in parallel strips.

Testing the developer

3 With masking tape attached to your finger carefully lift one corner of the top Mylar from the ImagOn plate. Imagine that you are facing a piano and that you are about to lift the panel that protects the piano keys. This is what you are about to do next. Lift a long flap of Mylar from the top of the plate and flap it back as you would in the piano analogy. With the top Mylar pulled back, only flip back about 1", to reveal the raw ImagOn emulsion down the entire 12" length of the plate.

4 With the Mylar flipped back attach a piece of 1" wide masking tape directly to the ImagOn emulsion.

7 Using a sharp new cutting blade and ruler cut through each pre-marked segment of the top Mylar on the ImagOn plate. Apply enough pressure to completely cut through the masking tape at the end of each Mylar segment then complete the stroke along the length of each strip.

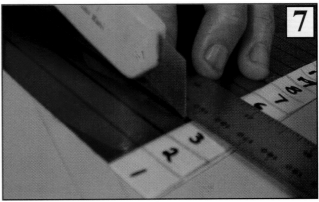

5 a , b Now stick a piece of 1" masking tape to the top of the strip of Mylar that was just flipped back. This may sound a bit confusing. We are trying to do is create finger pull-back tabs, which will easily allow the removal of the 24 x 1/2" strips of Mylar, while it is submerged in the developer.

8 Fold back each of the 24 masking tape finger-pull tabs and make sure each of the numbered segments are completely separated from each other. If not, then pulling off one tab may cause the adjacent tab also to pull off. This is not desired.

The test is now ready to commence.

6 With a waterproof marker, number each of the masking taped end tabs from 1 - 24.

9 Place the ImagOn test plate, with the 24 segments and masking tap finger-pull tabs facing up, into an ImagOn developing solution. (Wear hand protection from this point.)

Testing the developer

10a, b Set the darkroom timer onto 24 minutes. Start the timer and immediately reach into the development solution and very carefully remove the finger-pull tab marked 24. Only remove this tab. Be careful not to remove or loosen other tabs. Once the tab is completely removed discard it and wait for another 1 minute. Then pull the next adjacent tab off. Repeat this every minute until all tabs have been removed.

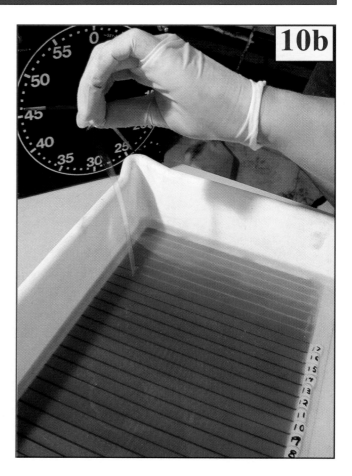

TIP: Make sure that the development tray is covered between the tab pull-back intervals. This ensures that UV light does not effect this test.

12 After removing the 24 tabs take the plate and thoroughly wash with running room temperature water. Rub the surface of the plate gently to ensure all ImagOn emulsion residue is removed.

Spritz white vinegar on to the ImagOn emulsion and rub gently with your hands.

13 Give the plate a final wash with water and wipe all water residue off the plate with paper towel. The plate can be heat dried or left to dry naturally.

Reading the Test Plate

V isually inspect the test plate, shown at right.

If your studio water has a neutral pH of 7 and if you are using the correct soda ash powder then the ImagOn emulsion should be disappearing on the 13 to 14 minute segment of the test plate. **If this is the case a 9 minute still development time would be recommended.**

Testing the developer

Test Shows Soda Ash is Too Weak

As soda ash is a water softener, you can expect to turn hard tap water into soft-water by adding soda ash to the water. If the variety of soda ash you have is hydrated, or in crystalline form, this means that it contains water. Which, in essence, dilutes its strength. Thus measuring 10 grams of this variety of soda ash will always result in a developer that is too weak. A plate test will show this immediately, as there will be virtually no deterioration of the ImagOn emulsion, at the 24 minute segment of the plate. It will mean that to use this variety of soda ash you will need to increase it weight from 10 to 20 grams and redo the test until you have a satisfactory result.

If the ImagOn emulsion is firmly entrenched on the plate at the 15, 16 minute intervals, but, is starting to disappear on around the 17 and 18 minute interval, then, this is an indication that either your studio water is hard or that your soda ash powder is too weak.

In this instance a development time of 13 minutes could be used. I do, however, recommend proportionally increasing the amount of soda ash in the developer until the ideal test plate is achieved through a development time of 9 minutes. This would mean a repeat of the previous test but with a stronger developer. If this becomes necessary then a good gram scale is invaluable.

Test Shows Soda Ash is Too Weak

If the ImagOn emulsion has disappeared before the 13 minute segment, this is evidence of soft-water. It is best to decrease the amount of soda ash, or the volume of water, in this situation rather than decreasing the development time. To do this, either re-test with 8 grams of soda ash or with 1.2 litres of water. There are two separate ImagOn adjustment methods:

1. The gram amount of soda ash is decreased until a satisfactory test plate is achieved.

2. The 1 litre recommended amount of water is proportionally increased until a satisfactory test plate is achieved.

This is a One Time Test

This generally is a one time test that you will need to do for your particular studio. If you are working in a different studio, even in the same city, you will need to redo this test. From my experience each city and country have different types of soda ash and varying degrees of hard and soft water. This simple test will ensure optimum results if your image-to-plate exposure is correct.

I cannot over stress the importance of learning how to do this ImagOn development test.

Etched Intaglio-Type Test Plate

Provided that the above plate was not exposed to UV light it could now be used as an Etched Intaglio-Type test plate. The principle by which the Etched Intaglio-Type plate works is clearly visible on this development test plate. The principle of the Etched Intaglio-Type technique is to begin by thinning the ImagOn plate. The thinner the ImagOn emulsion on the plate the higher the image resolution. The reason that a thin ImagOn emulsion yields a superior etched plate relates to image-to-plate exposure. There is less undercutting of the UV exposure light to the halftone dots of the image. The thicker the ImagOn emulsion, the greater will be the undercutting of the UV exposure light, resulting in an image with burnt-out high lights.

If, at this point you are ready for this technique, jump to the section on the Etched Intaglio-Type and follow the instructions.

Bernice A. Cross, **Dumfries**, 2003, Photo Intaglio-Type, 2" x 3".

ImagOn ULTRA Plate Development

QUICK LOOK

 1. After plate has been exposed to an image, remove the of top Mylar from the ImagOn plate.

2. Place plate into ImagOn developer for 9 minutes.

3. After development wash plate under room temperature water. 3

4. Spritz plate with white vinegar, rinse and wipe dry with paper towel.

5. Heat dry the plate with forced hot air 5

ImagOn ULTRA Plate Development

ImagOn Plate Development

Following is a standard development process recommended for most single layered Non-Etch Intaglio-Type techniques. There are variations from the standard development process for the following techniques:

1. Layered Intaglio-Type.

2. Etch Intaglio-Type.

3. Spit-Bite Intaglio-Type.

4. Construction Intaglio-Type.

The above variations will be described more fully in the chapters relevant to each technique.

Development Materials

1. Pre-mixed ImagOn developer placed in a photo development tray larger than the plate size.

2. Soft sponge.

3. Window washer squeegee.

4. Paper towel.

5. Darkroom timer or pocket electronic timer.

6. Plant mister bottle filled with white vinegar

ImagOn ULTRA Standard Development

Development is done after the ImagOn plate has been exposed to an image in the exposure unit. Wear rubber or surgical gloves and eye protection during the entire process.

1a, b Remove the top Mylar layer from the ImagOn ULTRA by running your open palm across the edge of the ImagOn plate. The hand is held at about a 45° angle to the ImagOn side of the plate. Repeat this until the Mylar comes off the plate. Once it lifts, grab it between your fingers and remove it entirely.

2 Set the timer for 9 minutes.

3 With the Mylar removed, place the plate into the developing solution so that it is completely covered.

4 Cover the developing tray with an opaque lid to keep out unwanted UV light.

5 Start the timer and allow the ImagOn plate to sit undisturbed in the developer solution for exactly 9 minutes.

TIP: For this standard development procedure the ImagOn does not require agitation or rubbing while it is in the developer.

ImagOn ULTRA Plate Development

6 After 9 minutes remove the plate from the developer solution and run it under cold water. Then use a soft sponge to lightly rub the light blue emulsion residue from the plate while under the running water. The exposed image on the plate should now be clearly visible.

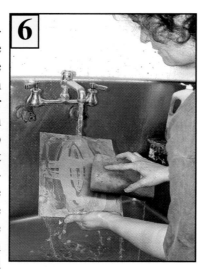

7 Stabilize the ImagOn ULTRA by spraying white vinegar on to the plate. Lightly rub the vinegar into the plate for about 30 seconds.

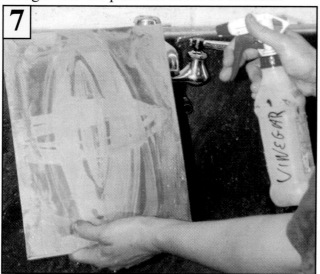

8 Do a final rinse in cold water.

9 Squeegee off the excess water and use a paper towel to blot off the remaining water.

10 The plate can be forced dry with a hand-dryer, hair-dryer or hot-plate set at about 150-200F for about 10 minutes.

TIP: One of the most convenient devices for drying the plate is a public rest room hand-dryer, especially the automatic start model shown above. This is preferable for educational purposes as these dryers are meant for high volume use.

I cannot recommend hair dryers as they are not intended for this use. A heavy-duty heat gun with temperature setting would be preferable, or a well ventilated inking hot-plate, set at a temperature that is not hot enough to cause your skin to burn.

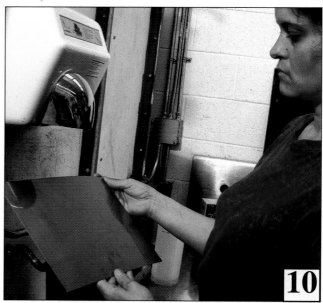

TIP: UV exposure, such as sunlight, is not an alternative for drying the plate. Some source of heat should be used, or keep the plate in a low humidity environment overnight to ensure it is dry.

Final Edge Preparation (optional)

ImagOn does create a unique edge, which I believe is part of the ImagOn aesthetic. Using this edge is inherent in preserving the integrity of this process but occasionally this edge remains unbroken. If this occurs, scrape the ImagOn edge with your cutting knife held at a 45° angle to the plate. This will cause the edge to fracture slightly thus re-creating the 'ImagOn Edge'.

ImagOn ULTRA Plate Development

If some some reason you would prefer to have a flat unbroken edge, then the edge can be sanded with the palm sander with 320 grit wet and dry sandpaper. Hold the sander at about a 45° angle to the plate and lightly sand until metal appears at the very edge of the plate.

At this point the finished plate should have a glossy blue appearance, especially in the bluest colored ImagOn areas, which will eventually register as the whiter areas of the print. The ImagOn ULTRA plate is now ready to be printed.

Trouble Shooting

Problem 1: Dimple marks on the surface of the ImagOn film. **Probable cause:** The soda ash, in the developing solution, was not thoroughly dissolved before plate development. ***Solution:*** *.Make sure to use hot water, when first mixing up the soda ash developer. Ensure that the soda ash has completely dissolved before making up the rest of the developer.*

Problem 2: Imagon film has a matt like finish in what should be the whiter areas of the plate. **Probable cause:** Either developer was too strong or the image exposure was too short. ***.Solution:*** *Remake the developer and do the Developer Test to make sure that the developer is balanced for your studio conditions. If this is OK, increase the image exposure and make another plate.*

Problem 3: Pieces of ImagOn film floats off the plate during development. **Probable cause:** There was something caught under the ImagOn during film lamination. This could be human hair, lint, dust, ImagOn edge trimmings or a host of other things. Plates that have dints in them cause ImagOn not to stick over recessed marks on the plate. It could also be improper plate preparation. If there is any grease, even finger prints, this will cause a barrier preventing the ImagOn from sticking. **Solution:** *.More often than not, slight imperfections in the plate will not be noticed in the final print. Always print the plate to determine how disruptive a potential plate imperfection will be to an image before re-doing the plate. Even if there are disruptive ink spots, these can be* removed from the plate before printing with a Q-tip. Plates can also be repaired with the liquid aquatint or even small pieces of ImagOn adhered to the plate, re-exposed and re-developed. If these measures do not work the only option is to remake the plate.

Problem 4: The top Mylar is very difficult to remove prior to development. **Probable cause:** The ImagOn plate is still warm from either the plate drying process or from too much heat given off during the exposure process. ***Solution:*** *Drop the ImagOn plate into the developer, for a couple of seconds, then take it out, and the remove the top Mylar. This action cools the plate down quickly and makes it easier to remove the Mylar.*

Guide to Problem Free Plate-Making

I cannot stress how important it is to do the preliminary Development Testing. Once this element of the process has been stabilized, if problems occur, it is a matter of looking else where to solve the problem.

Solving technical problems, with ImagOn techniques, can be a bit of a mystery to the beginner. First, you must have an understanding of how the process works. This is experienced based. Then it is a matter of listing the most probable causes of the problem and going through the process of testing to find the cause. Sometimes problem solving involves eliminating various elements that could have contributed to the problem, and, whatever is left will most likely be the cause. The soundness of this approach will depend on how familiar you are with each aspect of the technique. One way to develop a sound understanding of the ImagOn techniques is to think about how each aspect of a technique works and why it works. If you do not do this, problem solving and trouble shooting can be a frustrating hit and miss nightmare. No matter what unexpected results occur, all of theses techniques are scientifically governed. Good research and problem solving is a highly creative process that will require you to re-evaluate and re-think your methodology constantly.

Aquatint Screen & Image Exposure Test

QUICK LOOK

1. Prepare a 9" x 12" plate with ImagOn.

 2. Place Aquatint Screen, emulsion facing down, on to the ImagOn plate.

3. Use Rubylith or opaque card to block out the UV light and enable a step-test to be made. **3**

4 **4. A printed Aquatint Step-Test, the blackest area is the correct exposure.**

Aquatint Screen - Testing

Introduction

An Aquatint Screen, designed specifically for Non-Etch Intaglio-Type techniques, is a film-based screen manufactured through high-end commercial printing image-setters. The Aquatint Screen looks like a gray piece of polyester, somewhat like the old style Halftone Screen. It has a dot structure which is random and opaque. Halftone Screens will NEVER work for Intaglio-Type techniques because they are composed of translucent dots.

The opaque, random dot structure of the Aquatint Screen has been designed to closely simulate the dot structure of a conventional black intaglio aquatint. There has been intense research done in designing the optimum Aquatint Screen. The best Aquatint Screens available are sold only by ImagOn suppliers and are guaranteed for ImagOn platemaking. If these screens are not mishandled, they will last for many years.

ImagOn applied to a copper plate creates an ImagOn plate which is first exposed to the **A**quatint Screen and then exposed to a wash-drawing image. The plate is developed in soft water and stabilized with a vinegar wash. It is then heat-dried and printed.

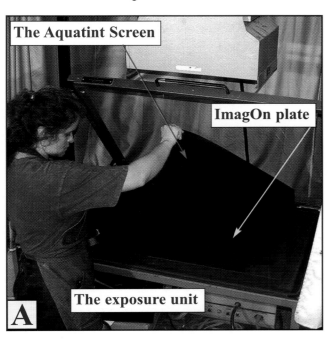

The Aquatint Screen

ImagOn plate

The exposure unit

A

Why the Aquatint Screen?

GOOD Aquatint Screens are *ABSOLUTELY NECESSARY* when employing Intaglio-Type Non-Etch painting and drawing techniques. With Non-Etch Intaglio-Type methods, the tonal range of an image is carried in the varying depth of the ImagOn film. While no etching occurs in the metal plate, there is an equal degree of intaglio etch that occurs in the ImagOn film. The depth of the etch is more than enough to yield the richest intaglio black. In this regard, the soft-water developer acts in the same manner as nitric acid in the toxic conventional etching process. Before ImagOn can yield a complete tonal range, the ImagOn plate must first be exposed to the Aquatint Screen and then, separately, to the image.

The Aquatint Screen performs the same function as a toxic traditional rosin aquatint by imparting a tooth to the ImagOn film whereby the ink can cling onto the plate. If an Aquatint Screen exposure is not used, open areas in an image will not hold ink and will open-bite. When open-biting occurs, areas of an image that should print as black will print as white. The tonality on the ImagOn plate is created by the varying degrees the wash-drawings filter the UV light, as the drawing is 'burned' into the ImagOn plate in the exposure unit. This is the Non-Etch miracle of ImagOn photopolymer film.

There are other types of screens available; some are better than others. If you wish to have excellent and consistent results, I recommend screens made specifically for ImagOn. These screens give a random dot which simulates conventional rosin aquatint structure. (See <**www.elizabethdove.com**>).

Before using an Aquatint Screen, a step exposure test should be done to determine the best Aquatint Screen exposure for your exposure unit. Once the correct Aquatint Screen exposure has been determined, this exposure should remain consistent.

Aquatint Screen - Testing

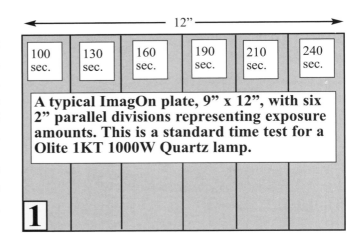

Different Exposure Units

Each type of exposure unit will require different exposure times. When ascertaining where to begin the Aquatint Screen test exposure give careful consideration to the type of exposure lamp you will be using. Exposure units with high UV light output and high Wattage (1000W to 5000W) will give exposure times in as little as 5 seconds or 5 light units (L.U.), while Quartz lamps will require exposure times as much as 5 minutes. Also the distance of the lamp from the ImagOn plate will greatly effect the exposure length.

Sophisticated exposure units rate lamp exposure both in light units (L.U.) and seconds. A L.U. is a type of light exposure meter reading that measures the exact amount of UV light emitted from the exposure lamp. Typically, as high out-put UV exposure units lamps get older, the amount of UV light emitted decreases. Thus, the L.U. is automatically adjusted to compensate for this UV fall-out.

TIP: Under NO CIRCUMSTANCES use an exposure unit that has fluorescent or black light as the main exposure lamp. This light source is too soft, resulting in grayed out images. Use only point light sources such as metal halide, mercury vapor, pulse Zeon, or Quartz halogen lights. (See chapter on Exposure systems, P. 15 - 24.)

Aquatint Screen Exposure Test

1 Start with a 9" x 12" ImagOn plate. Divide the plate into six 2" parallel segments and expose each segment for the following exposure "suggestions":

When using a 1000W Quartz lamp (placed about 20" above the ImagOn plate), make the first exposure 100 sec. and then each successive step an additional 30 sec. long. Six segments later you will have a step-test with the following exposure times; 100 sec., 130 sec., 160 sec., 190 sec., 210 sec. and 240 sec.

2 When using 1000W Metal halide or Mercury Vapor lamp (placed at about 24" above the ImagOn plate), the exposure segments should be 5 sec. Six segments later you will have the following exposure times on the step-test strip: 5 sec., 10 sec., 15 sec., 20 sec., 25., and 30 sec.

3 Next, the plate is still developed for 9 minutes, stabilized with a vinegar wash, dried, and printed, as normal. The test division that records the richest mezzotint-like black is the correct exposure for the Aquatint Screen.

In order to be more economical and efficient in the necessary testing requirements for successful Intaglio-Type printmaking, I will describe how to make two tests in one.

Aquatint Screen - Testing

Two Tests in One - Aquatint Screen Step Test & Image Exposure Test

Many of the Non-Etch Intaglio-Type techniques will require two separate exposures: the first exposure is to the Aquatint Screen and the second is to the image. The following test plate is made in a similar manner.

1 Laminate a 9" x 12" copper plate with ImagOn, and divide the plate into 6 x 2" segments along the plate length.

Above is a graphic illustration of a 9" x 12" plate, divided into 6 segments. As we are using a high output UV light source, each segment will receive only a 3 L.U. or sec. exposure.

2 Put the ImagOn plate in the exposure unit and place the Aquatint Screen, emulsion down, in contact with the ImagOn plate.

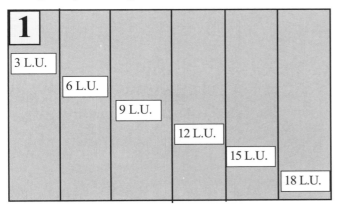

3 Engage the vacuum and expose each segment to a quantity of UV light from the exposure unit. It is EXTREMELY IMPORTANT to keep the vacuum of the exposure unit running during the Aquatint Screen step-test. When this test is completed, turn off the vacuum to enable the placement of the Mylar image on top of the plate.

4a,b Use Rubylith masking film or a piece of opaque cardboard placed on top of the vacuum frame glass to shield each segment after exposure. (Protect eyes from any potential UV light exposure.) The exposure time of each segment will be relative to the strength and type of light source used.

4a This illustration shows a high output UV light source during the exposure step procedure. With a high output UV light source such as this, segments can be as low as 3 L.U. or seconds. Thus, as illustrated in **4b**, after the plate has been exposed for 6 segments, the last segment will have received 18 L.U. or sec. exposure.

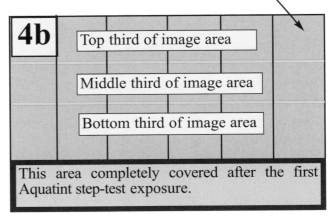

Aquatint Screen - Testing

5 After exposing the Aquatint Screen to the six segments on the ImagOn plate, open the vacuum frame and replace the Aquatint Screen with the wash-drawing stencil.

6 Re-engage the vacuum.

7 Keep about 2" of the length of the short side of the plate completely covered with the Rubylith or cardboard. This covered part will reflect ONLY the Aquatint step-test segments. The rest of the plate will be divided into thirds, where each third will be exposed to the image with increasing amounts of the UV light. See also illustration **4b** .

8 Expose the entire image area to a quantity of light equal to one third of the total 'Aquatint Screen' exposure given to the plate. In this example, that would be 6 L.U. or sec.

9 Move the Rubylith or card to cover the top third of the plate, and expose the rest of the image area for 6 additional L.U. or sec.

10 Move the Rubylith or card to cover the middle third of the plate, and expose the rest of the image area for 6 additional L.U. or sec.

By now, this plate would have been exposed in two separate exposure sessions: the first session to the Aquatint Screen and the second to the image.

11 Still develop the plate in the soda ash developer, stabilize with a vinegar wash, heat dry, and print the plate.

12 This test print shows a series of step exposures that indicate the following: firstly, its shows where the correct Aquatint Screen is. (Marked with a yellow X, in illustration 12, as the blackest square at the bottom of the illustration); secondly, it gives an image exposure to help you decide where to continue testing to obtain the best image exposure. (Also, marked with a yellow X.)

The initial observation made of the print should indicate a rich mezzotint-like black in one of the Aquatinted segments. The segment, whichever it is, will be the correct exposure for the Aquatint Screen.

The image area of the plate will show an under, a correct, or an over-exposure. The most important thing that this image exposure test reveals is how image exposure effects the printed results. It also shows how the image can be adjusted and manipulated through exposure. The longer the exposure, the lighter and more contrasted the printed image. The shorter the exposure, the lighter and less contrasted will be the resultant print.

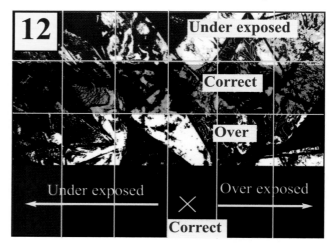

The Flash Exposure
There is an additional exposure that can be given directly to the plate after the Aquatint Screen and image exposure. This is called the 'Flash', which amounts to a small amount of UV light exposure given just to the ImagOn plate. This flash exposure was first developed by Elizabeth Dove as a way of extending the tonal range of the Intaglio-Type non-etch print. Although it is not absolutely necessary, it compensates for the high contrast nature of the Intaglio-Type print by extending the tonal range at the light end of the tonal scale.

Aquatint Screen & Image Exposure Test

Flash Exposure Set-up

Although your exposure unit can be used for flash exposures, it can be difficult to work with high out-put UV light sources because the the amount of UV light needed for the flash exposure is extremely low. **T**hus, I recommend that you purchase the low cost Olec Olite-1KT Quartz 1000W lamp and housing and suspend it above a table at a distance of exactly 30" from table to bulb. **This distance of 30" is very important.** As the Flash exposure is directly to the naked ImagOn plate, there is no need for a vacuum frame. You can attach an in-line off/on switch to the 1KT lamp, or to a timer, as you will require flash times from 5 - 15 seconds.

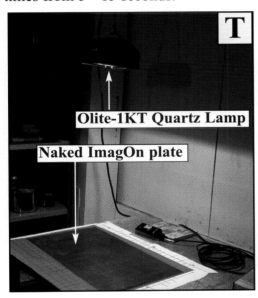

Flash Test Exposure Step-by-Step

Unfortunately, there is no way around the fact that flash exposure testing is time-consuming. For some printmakers, the amount of difference that it makes to the image does not warrant the trouble involved. I have tried my best to shorten the testing, but this method will only work for the specific Olite 1KT lamp illustrated here. Other light sources could be used but, undoubtedly, will require different exposure times. Again, no test can be successful unless you have correctly balanced your soda ash developer (as shown on pages 43-48).

After the Aquatint Screen and Image exposures have been calculated, it is time to commence the flash testing.

As the flash exposure introduces slightly more UV light onto the ImagOn plate, the image exposure already calculated will be effected. The flash exposure will be lengthening the total UV light exposure to the plate. Thus, the perfect image exposure becomes a combination between the flash and image exposure. To achieve optimum results, you must find that perfect ratio exposure. This will come with experience.

TIP: When making a test flash exposure, make a separate small plate for this purpose.

1 After the ImagOn plate has been exposed to both the Aquatint Screen and the image, take it to the Flash Exposure area directly under the 1KT lamp. Place a piece of Rubylith or opaque card across about 1/4 of the plate, and expose the plate for 5 seconds. This covered area, at first, will receive NO FLASH . This is important as it allows you to compare the results that the flash exposure has on the rest of the image.

2 Now move the Rubylith or opaque card further along the plate to cover up an additional 1/4 of the plate. At this point, half the plate will be covered. Give the plate another flash exposure of 5 seconds.

3 Move the Rubylith or card along the plate to cover 3/4 of the plate, and give it an additional 5 seconds exposure.

4 Develop the plate for 9 min. in the soda ash developer, rinse with vinegar, wash, and heat dry.

5 Print the test plate. Choose the segment that yields the greatest tonal range. In this instance, (illustration 5 on the next page) it would be the 10 second segment. Further refinement can be attained by doing 1 second step units around the best test segment, from the 5 second increment step-test.

Aquatint Screen & Image Exposure Test

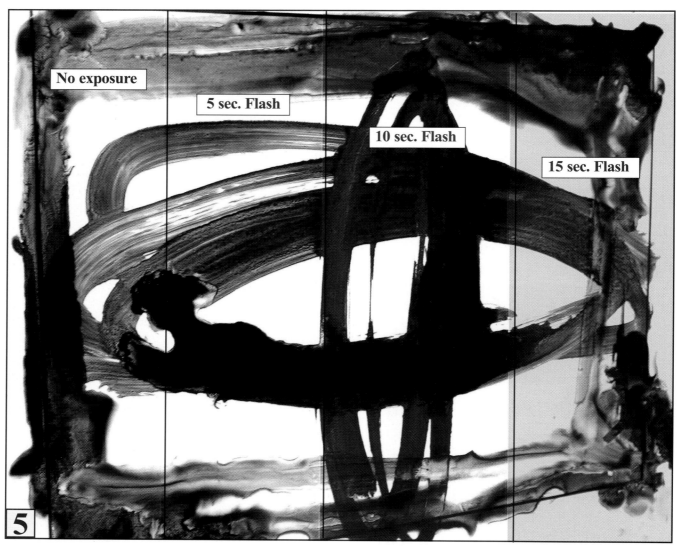

No exposure

5 sec. Flash

10 sec. Flash

15 sec. Flash

5

Troubleshooting

One of the most important ways of avoiding problems is to balance your particular variety of soda ash developer with your local water supply. It is impossible to make an accurate Aquatint Screen without dong this first. (See pages 43 - 48.)

When determining the optimum test exposure for the Aquatint Screen initially, it is good to be aware of the following points:

1. If the Aquatint Screen has not received enough exposure, the light source, from the exposure unit, will not have penetrated the Aquatint Screen structure sufficiently to harden the ImagOn emulsion on the plate. If you look at the Aquatint Screen under a magnifier, you will notice a random black dot structure with clear space between the dots. It is the clear spaces where the UV exposure light needs to penetrate the Aquatint Screen. UV light exposure hardens the ImagOn emulsion. Thus if not enough light gets through these spaces, most of the ImagOn emulsion will wash off the plate creating an UNDER-EXPOSURE or what looks like open-biting.

NB. Open-biting is a term used in traditional etching where the aquatint dot structure of the plate is completely eaten away by the nitric acid. Thus, what should have been an area that held ink will wipe clean during the printing process. The resultant print will show little to no ink in areas that should have held ink.

Aquatint Screen & Image Exposure Test

2. If too much light penetrates these clear spaces, the light burns under each black dot of the Aquatint Screen and OVER-EXPOSES the ImagOn plate. Both under and over exposed Aquatinted areas look grayed out with the major difference being the amount of ImagOn emulsion being exposed. In the first instance, not enough is being exposed; in the second, too much is being exposed. The correct exposure lies somewhere in between these two extreme exposures.

Once the Aquatint Screen exposure has been established for your particular exposure unit, it should stay stable (affected only by the fall off of light due to aging exposure system lamps). The next exposure issue is the Image Exposure. Whether the image is a wash-drawing, photocopy, inkjet halftone, or direct drawing onto the top Mylar of the ImagOn plate, an exposure test is needed to determine the best exposure for each media type.

The golden rule with Intaglio-Type IMAGE exposure is: THE SHORTER THE EXPOSURE, THE DARKER THE RESULTING IMAGE. THE LONGER THE EXPOSURE, THE LIGHTER WILL BE THE PRINTED IMAGE.

When you are exposing images made on single-sided drafting Mylar, the density of the pigment will effect the exposure times. A step exposure test is needed to find the exposure time that is right for the wash/drawing. Almost any painting or drawing media can be used, such as, graphite pencils, gouache, china markers, acrylic paint, and Sharpie markers.

Each different type of mark-making media has different light stopping power. Where the Mylar stencil is made of a combination of different types of media, it is extremely difficult to obtain a full tonal range on a print. The general rule is to stick with one type of media when making Mylar wash-drawings. Some media have approximately the same amount of light stopping power, such as, toner-wash and graphite pencil. In this instance,

good results can be made when these two media are combined.

In other instances, especially where different media have been used and there is no way of remaking the Mylar wash-drawing, there are two choices for making better stencils. The first is to scan the wash-drawing, and print out a digital stencil as explained in the chapter on digital imaging. The second is to make hand-cut Rubylith stencils to isolate different areas of the Mylar image, so that different amounts of UV exposure light can be given to compensate for the differing media used. This can be most easily accomplished with stencils that have definable areas that can be stenciled out. If media is intricately entwined, such an option is virtually impossible. In these instances, a duo-tone plate may be warranted.

Duo-Tone Intaglio-Type
This method requires making two plates of the same image: one under-exposed plate, and the other, over-exposed. Each plate is inked separately and printed, in perfect registration, one on top of the other. When making a black and white print, the under-exposed plate is inked with the black ink, and the over-exposed plate is inked with a dark gray ink. This duo-tone printing method allows for many different colors and color combinations to be used, also.

Damaged Aquatint Screens
In a student environment, it does not take long for an aquatint screen to get damaged. It is surprising how much abuse they can withstand and still perform well. The best way to clean an Aquatint Screen is with a soft cloth and rubbing alcohol.

To locate an ImagOn Aquatint Screen Contact: <www.elizabethdove.com>

Intaglio Paper & Preparation

When using Hahnemühle Copperplate paper

QUICK LOOK

1. For Akua ink printing, soak paper for 1 minute. For oil ink, 5 - 20 minutes.

 2. Damp paper needs draining, helped with window squeegee.

3. Alternatively, hang paper to allow excess water run-off. **3**

4 4. Blot paper with blotting paper and rolling pin.

Intaglio Paper & Preparation

Introduction

There are many manufacturers of fine artist quality paper around the world. Printmaking papers are made specifically for particular printmaking techniques to ensure stability and optimum ink transfer during the printing process. As there are many variables that affect the printmaking process, the last thing any printmaker wants is an inconsistency caused by the paper. Experienced printmakers look for a paper that is of high quality, stable, evenly made, and affordable.

Hahnemühle papers are of the highest quality; and, in my experience, are one of the most versatile papers on the market. These are mould-made papers, produced in Germany for over 300 years. Many art and printmaking supply stores sell this paper. (See Sources of Supply.)

Hahnemühle papers are distributed by Atlantic Papers in the USA and Canada. They carry more than 50 varieties of paper. I prefer the following Hahnemühle papers for intaglio printmaking:

1. *Hahnemühle Copperplate paper* is one of my favorites as it offers a choice of a warm or a bright white finish. It is a 300 gm. alpha cellulose fibre with a sheet size of 22" x 30" or 31" x 47". This paper surprises printmakers with its ability to print as well as 100% cotton fiber papers. As it is not a rag paper, it is less expensive but prints very well for all the techniques outlined in this book. It has the added advantage of a short soaking time. This makes it an excellent critical proofing or editioning paper.

2. *Hahnemühle Dürer Etching paper* presents the highest quality. It is a 300 gm. 100% cotton paper with a sheet size of 22" x 30" or 30.5" x 41.5". This paper is excellent for all intaglio work, especially for deep relief and embossed printing. I recommend this paper for printing editions.

3. *Hahnemühle German Etching paper* is 75% cotton and 25% alpha cellulose. It is 300 gm. with a sheet size of 22" x 30" or 30" x 42". It is also available in two colors - black and cream. This paper is famous for its ability to pick up extremely fine detail from intaglio plates and for its ease of use.

4. *Hahnemühle Monotype paper* is 19" x 25", 22" x 30", and 31" x 42", ideal for dry print intaglio printing using the Akua monoprint and intaglio ink. This paper should never be dampened at any point in the printing process as it will fall apart under the weight of the water in the paper.

5. *Hahnemühle German Etch* **Digital** available from 8.5" x 11" to 44" wide rolls, recommended for combination inkject intaglio printmaking. There are several textures available from very rough to photo-smooth. The paper should never be dampened.

Preparing Intaglio Paper

When using traditional oil-based intaglio inks, all intaglio printing papers need to be dampened prior to printing. This softens the paper fibers, thus enabling the pressure of the etching press to push the paper into the recessed intaglio areas of the plate.

Akua Intaglio is the first intaglio ink that can be dry-printed. Slightly more press pressure needs to be added; but this ability to dry-print is extremely well suited to multiplate printing, especially where acute registration is required. Also, with Akua Intaglio ink, you have the choice between dampened printing paper or dry. Each gives a slightly different result.

Dry-printing with Akua Intaglio and Hahnemühle Monotype paper results in a more contrasty print with little plate tone. Slightly dampened paper results in a softer, lower contrast tonal range while maintaining a good rich black.

Intaglio Paper & Preparation

Many traditional intaglio studios employ a system of blotters where the paper is taken from the soaking sink, prior to printing, and blotted between sheets of blotting paper. This ensures that water is not pooling or shimmering on the surface of the paper which would impede the printing process.

I recommend a stainless steel paper-soaking sink, with a plexiglas paper drainage surface used in the intermediate step between soaking and blotting the paper. A paper hanging rack above the sink is also very convenient.

1 To dampen Hahnemühle Copperplate, for use with Akua Intaglio ink, soak the paper for precisely 1 minute. This is important when using Akua intaglio ink. Gently push the paper under the water to ensure quick submersion.

2 Squeegee the paper to the Plexiglas drainage board with a window cleaning squeegee. This aids in draining excess water from the paper and speeds up the blotting process.

3 With experience, it is possible to employ a soak and hang system to the point where it is unnecessary to blot the paper. This not only saves time and the extra expense of blotting paper, but also prevents blotting paper fibers from falling onto the printing paper. Blotting paper fibers can create white specks on the finished print.

4 Use large sheets of blotting paper to ensure that excess moisture is removed from both sides of the plate.

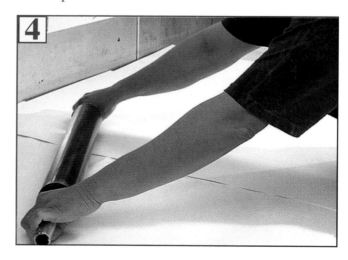

Intaglio Paper & Preparation

Hahnemühle Paper Dampening

One advantage of paper with predominantly alpha cellulose fiber content, is its ability to absorb water quickly. Hahnemühle German Etching paper is, also, extremely absorbent and is known as a 'dip' or waterleaf paper. As a waterleaf paper, it needs to be soaked only as long as it takes to submerge it in a tray of water.

Hahnemühle Copperplate paper needs to be soaked from 1 to 20 minutes depending on what intaglio ink is used. Akua intaglio requires only to be soaked for only 1 minute. When oil inks are used, the paper should be soaked for, at least, 5 minutes.

Hahnemühle Dürer paper requires a minimum soaking time of 4 minutes for Akua ink and 20 minutes for oil based ink. The length of time the paper soaks is critical only when using Akua intaglio ink. If the paper is too damp, muddy results occur when this ink is used. This point should be well remembered.

For large editions of intaglio prints, some printmakers pre-soak their paper and stack them in a plastic bag. Well dampened intaglio paper is placed between dry intaglio paper and left overnight. This is referred to as 'wet-packing'. This enables a small to large amount of intaglio paper to reach the same level of dampness to ensure greater consistency throughout the printed edition. Be aware that if the paper is left in this wet-pack for more than a couple of days, fungus and mold may start to grow on the paper.

Cutting or Ripping Paper

Hahnemühle papers have soft, irregular edges called deckle edges. This is a characteristic of fine mould-made papers. This soft deckle edge has become an important aesthetic of the print; therefore, how the paper is trimmed or resized should be considered.

O ne simple way to 'cut' the dry paper is to rip it down with the aid of a long ruler or tear-bar. Tear the paper, as illustrated, by pulling the sheet to be torn in the direction of your opposite shoulder. Often large sheets are torn in this manner to make smaller pieces of printing paper.

Final Print Preparation

There are many rituals followed by printmakers for the final preparation of the finished intaglio print. Paper that has been soaked and printed with the massive pressure of the etching press, will not dry completely flat if left to dry naturally. Depending on the type of paper, it may dry with ripples or waves. Printmakers solve this problem in a number of ways.

1 When I was giving a workshop at the Royal College of Art in Stockholm, I observed that the printmakers there had plywood panels that were hung vertically on the wall. These panels slotted onto two dowel-like pegs protruding from the wall. Immediately after the print was pulled, and while the paper was still damp, they used gummed paper tape (the same variety used to mount watercolor paper) to tape the print to a plywood

Intaglio Paper & Preparation

panel. The panel was then rehung. Several panels could be hung onto each set of dowels. As the paper dries, it shrinks slightly; but because it is taped on all four sides, it dries flat. After the print is completely dry, the paper tape is removed, and the panel is reused.

2 Other printmakers use push-pins and soft wood in place of the plywood and gum tape.

3 Wet prints can also be placed between tissue paper, blotters, and 1" thick particle board. One piece of particle board, two blotters, and one piece of tissue paper is needed for each print. These are then stacked on top of each other and left for a week or until completely dried.

4 Another print preparation option is to dry the print by leaving it on a commercial screen-printing drying rack.

After the intaglio ink is dry, the back of the paper is spritzed with water to re-dampen the fibers. It is then left to dry between blotting paper and fibrous boards. Fibrous boards are sold by hardware stores as pin-boards and are light in weight. Because this type of board is so light, it is necessary to place weights on top of the stack of boards to weight them down while the paper dries out. This procedure ensures that the prints will dry completely flat and that no wet ink will offset onto the blotting paper.

Removing Unwanted Marks

It is difficult to avoid accidental marks on the printing paper. There are a couple of solutions to this problem that can be employed either while the paper is still damp or when it is dry.

1 The first technique, shown to me by Siv Johansan, Master Printer at the Royal College of Art in Stockholm, is done to paper which is still damp. Immediately after the print is pulled, remove unwanted ink marks with a clean damp sponge by gently brushing the sponge over the ink mark. It is important to remove only a small amount of the ink with each pass of the damp sponge, as this technique also removes a small amount of the printing paper. This technique works particularly well when using Akua Intaglio ink and is best employed with ink marks well outside the printed image.

2 The second method, which is used exclusively on **dry paper**, was first shown to me by the Australian artist David Paulson. Ordinary office variety Scotch® tape is taped over the ink mark which is gradually pulled off the paper with the tape. Lightly stick the tape to the paper by gently rubbing it with your index finger while applying more pressure over the ink mark to be removed. Rip the tape back quickly to remove a

Intaglio Paper & Preparation

small portion of the dried ink. Repeat by varying the angle at which the tape is applied. For heavy deposits of ink, burnish the ink spot above the tape with your fingernail while reducing the pressure towards the outside edge of the tape. If you use the same amount of pressure over the ink mark as the surrounding area, too much paper will be removed. There is an art to this method of removing unwanted ink marks. Again, this technique works best if the unwanted ink mark is removed fractionally. It is not unusual to use 10 pieces of tape to remove one mark. After all the ink is removed, the fibrous surface of the paper has been disturbed to the point where it is necessary to burnish it down with your fingernail to blend its visual appearance with the rest of the paper surface. This technique work best with the Hahnemühle papers that have a high cotton content, such as, the Dürer and German Etching papers.

3 Another method to remove dried ink marks is to gently scrape the ink away with a sharp scalpel blade. After all the ink has been removed, the paper surface needs to be burnished with the finger nail as in the previous method.

Signing Off a Print
The most commonly accepted device for signing off prints is a 2B pencil.

Generally, there are four things that are written directly under the bottom plate mark of an image:

1st. Edition size. This is represented by a number which looks like a fraction, with the bottom number indicating the total number of prints that exist in the edition. The top number refers to the number that this print holds in the sequence of the edition. Some printmakers are organized to the point where they keep track of which print was printed first, and then number each successive print in order. From my experience, this practice is uncommon, and most printmakers feel that it does not matter which print came off the press first.

There are usually more prints made than what the edition indicates as invariably some prints are culled because of inking inconsistencies or unwanted marks. Some printmakers write on the print 'AP', which means Artist's Proof. AP's are made in addition to the edition size and usually represent approximately 10% of the edition. There are also Working Proofs (WP) and Printer's Proofs (PP).

2nd. Title of the print. This is generally written in the middle, about .25" under the print.

3rd. Artist's signature. Written to bottom right, below the right side of the plate mark. Generally, the signature does not protrude beyond the length of the plate.

4th. Date. This is generally written before or after the signature.

Some printmakers like to rearrange the order in which they sign off a print. Some will place the edition number in the middle of the page, with title to the left and signature and date to the right. How artists choose to sign off their prints is a matter of personal preference.

Bernice A. Cross, **Gent**, 2003, Photo Intaglio-Type, 3" x 2".

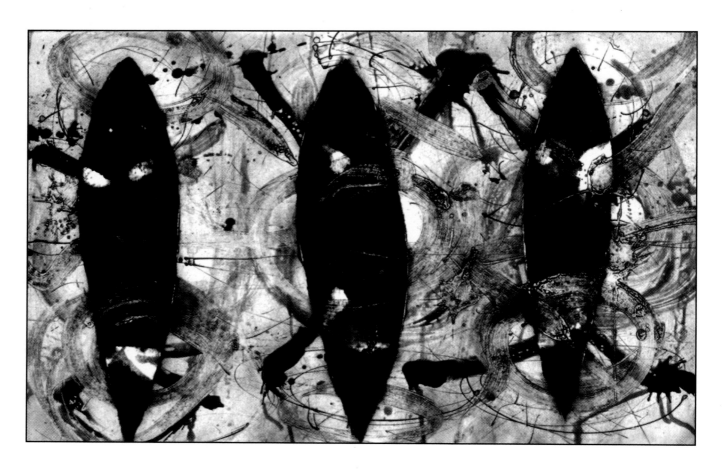

Keith Howard, **Boats float,** 2002, Stencil Intaglio-Type with Spit-Bite Intaglio-Type and Liquid Aquatint, 24" x 36". See also information on Keith Howard's Private Collectors Circle on page 243.

Close-up of Keith Howard's Layered Intaglio-Type plate inked with Akua Intaglio.

Intaglio Printing

QUICK LOOK

1. Card intaglio ink on to the plate.

2. Tarlatan wipe the plate.

3. Paper wipe the plate.

4. Print the plate.

Intaglio Printing

Introduction

Most black intaglio or etching inks are relatively hazard free provided that you avoid skin contact. Ink dryers and colored pigments increase printing ink toxicity. Intaglio inks generally do not have dryers, so a potential health health risk lies primarily in the type of pigment used. Working safely with any intaglio ink can easily be done by avoiding skin contact with the ink and by not using paint solvents for ink clean-up. This second point is the most important. Conventional oil-based intaglio inks can easily be cleaned up with vegetable oil.

All Intaglio-Type techniques are totally compatible with any oil-based or conventional intaglio ink. There are, however, some oil-based intaglio inks that are manufactured with pigments that are quite coarse. With repeated inking, they can prematurely wear out the Intaglio-Type plate. Thus, I approached Susan Rostow, President of Akua Kolor Water-based Inks in New York, and asked her to develop a new 'soft' intaglio ink that was more suitable for Intaglio-Type printing. After extensive testing, Akua Intaglio was introduced to the printmaking world in 2002 as the first 'soft' permanent water-based intaglio ink.

Although plates inked with Akua Intaglio ink can be totally wiped with phone-book paper, I prefer a preliminary tarlatan wipe which is finished with the paper wipe. Inking and printing techniques vary from printmaker to printmaker. David Jay Reed, a contributing author for this book, prefers only to use a paper wipe for the entire printing procedure. Peter Jones, from the Dublin Institute of Technology in Ireland, highly recommends to finish plate wiping with a rolled up pad of 'coat lining' fabric. This, he says, speeds up the end-wiping of a plate considerably. Some printmakers will dab ink onto a plate other prefer to use squeegee rubber to apply the ink. The inking technique presented here is how I prefer to ink plates, whether oil-based or water based inks are used.

I recommend that you try everything and determine which method suites you.

Materials for Inking

1. Old telephone books for wiping the plate.

2. Tarlatan or, as it is known in the UK, scrim.

3. Coat-lining material; alternative for final plate wiping.

4. Inking gloves.

5. Inking spatula.

6. Hand dish washing detergent.

7. Dish washing sponge.

8. Canola cooking oil.

9. Spray cooking oil.

10. Matte-board or squeegee rubber for inking the plate.

11. Newspaper for clean wiping practices.

12. Paper towel.

13. Setswell® oil based intaglio ink modifier similar to Easywipe®.

14. Intaglio ink.

15. *"NEW" Akua Oil Converter Medium Converts Akua Intaglio into an oil ink that still cleans up with soap and water. Akua Oil is highly refined archival water-soluble oil. Use it to stiffen Akua Intaglio ink and extend the range for viscosity work.*

Before Proceeding

If you do not know what kind of printing paper to use and how it is dampened for intaglio printing, go to the chapter on Paper Preparation pages 61-66.

Intaglio Printing

Intaglio Printing

The following technique is used for inking plates with Akua Intaglio water-based ink or conventional oil-based ink such as Graphic Chemical, Gamblin and Daniel Smith ink. The entire inking procedure is carried out with protective gloves.

1a, b For Akua Intaglio Ink place a knife into the ink container and stir. All other oil-based intaglio inks will most likely need mixing and modification. With oil-based inks, I recommend adding about 10% Setswell ink modifier. This softens the oil based ink and allows easy wiping. With a 2" x 2" piece of matte-board, take a small quantity of ink and apply it to the Intaglio-Type plate.

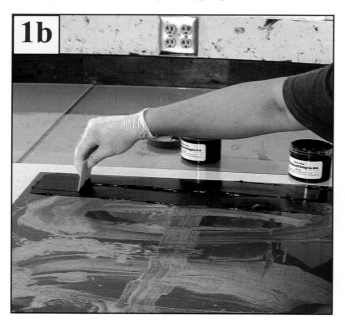

2 For high relief or deeply bitten plates, use an inking stump to push down the ink with a circular motion into the deep recesses of the plate.

TIP: Make an inking stump by rolling a small piece of etching blanket/felt, to a diameter of about 1" and then tape it around the center.

Akua Intaglio is a soft ink which feels very different from conventional oil-based inks that are tacky. It is not just a matter of squeegeeing the ink 'into' the plate with the small piece of card. Lay the ink down so that there is a thick layer of ink on the plate; then push it into the plate. If there are deeply raised or embossed areas, you may need to push the ink into these areas with an inking stump or dabber.

3 After the plate is completely covered and the ink has been pushed into the plate, use a clean, sharp piece of matte-board to squeegee the excess ink from the plate. Do this until the image on the plate is visible.

4a, b Ball up some tarlatan or scrim. I recommend the washed tarlatan, or use the tarlatan with the least amount of starch.

Balled up tarlatan is wiped across the inked plate. Exaggerated wrinkles in the tarlatan, or loose tarlatan, can uncontrollably remove the ink from the recessed intaglio areas of the plate. This is not desired. Keep the ball of tarlatan as tight as possible, wiping only the ink off the top surface of the plate.

Intaglio Printing

TIP: Tarlatan with some ink residue will initially remove the ink from the plate more than clean, unused tarlatan.

With Akua intaglio ink, the tarlatan can be recycled by washing it frequently. With oil-based inks, the tarlatan is normally not washed and kept in three different groupings according to how much ink is embedded in it. Always start the wiping process with the most ink-laden tarlatan, and exchange it for the cleaner wads of tarlatan as more ink is gradually removed from the plate.

5a, b The actual wiping motion is a long, sweeping action with one hand holding the tarlatan and the other hand, open, and preventing the plate from falling off the inking table. This hand acts as a stopper while the other hand, holding the tarlatan, sweeps towards it to remove small layers of the surface ink while, also, rotating the plate to ensure that the ink removal remains uniform. (The instructional video, listed on page 240, Sources of Supply section of the book, demonstrates this wiping motion very clearly.)

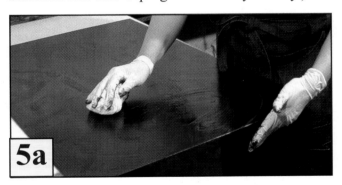

6a, b After most of the ink has been removed from the surface of the plate, lay down two pieces of phone book paper onto the plate. Rub the back of the paper to rotate-wipe the ink from the plate. Flip the paper over and endeavor to remove the ink from the plate in circular movements *using the flat part of your palms.* If the ink puts up a lot of resistance, go back and tarlatan wipe it further until there is virtually no resistance. Gradually, removed the ink from the plate, periodically replacing the phone book paper, until there is only slight resistance on the plate.

Use rotational wiping, both hands working sychronically, one hand wiping in a clockwise direction and the other anti-clockwise. This sounds complicated, but it is a very natural way to wipe a plate and easy to master. This wiping technique causes the Intaglio-Type plate to rotate on the inking table, thus making it easy to control and to wipe evenly.

TIP: Use both sides on the inking paper. You will find that the ink on one side of the printing paper allows your inking gloves to stick to the inking paper offering more control during the wiping procedure.

The plate can be wiped through to its final stage by using more phone book paper until there is no resistance from the ink on the plate.

Intaglio Printing

7 For smaller plates it may be easier to do a final wipe by supporting the plate in one hand and wiping it with the other.

8 Although not entirely necessary, a final wiping could be done with a wiping block. This is a rectangular block of wood with a Jiffy cloth (synthetic cloth used for washing dishes), stapled onto the edge. This cloth pads the block while maintaining its flatness. Make sure that several layers of Jiffy cloth are wrapped around the block to ensure that the block will not damage the ImagOn plate during wiping. A final wipe of the plate is done with phone book paper wrapped around the wiping block.

Wiping Highlights on the Plate
To obtain good highlights on the plate, you may need to use small pieces of tissue paper to finger wipe certain areas. This is more necessary with etched plates as the ImagOn plate has a glass-like surface in the white areas making highlight plate wiping easy.

Final Plate Edge Wipe
Invariably, after the plate has been completely wiped, there will be ink caught under the plate. If left, this could squish out onto the printing paper during printing. To remove this ink, pinch a clean rag onto the edge of the plate and drag it around the parameter of the plate.

The Plate is Now Ready to Print.
I encourage my students to lay either a piece of acetate or newsprint onto the press bed before printing. Acetate can make a convenient register sheet for positioning the plate and paper, ensuring that the image is printed in the center of the paper for the entire edition. To do this, use a thin-line waterproof marker to outline the shape of the plate on a .020 thick sheet of P.E.T.G. or Styrene (available at www.lairdplastis.com). Centrally align a sheet of printing paper, and mark the outside dimensions on this registration sheet. With this system, students can have their own register sheet for their particular printing requirements. This method is also recommended in a printing studio where more than one person is using the press as it prevents unwanted ink marks from being transferred to the etching blanket.

Cleaning the Plate
Intaglio-Type plates are easily damaged through conventional cleaning. If you want to keep your plate for only about 10 days, dry printing them is the best way to clean the plates as Intaglio-Type plates. This is also the best short term way to clean them. Therefore, run the plate through the press with the dry newsprint on the surface of the plate. Use this method for both Akua and oil-based etching inks.

If you wish to keep both Akua and oil-inked plates for longer periods of time, do the following:

Intaglio Printing

Left; Proofing one of Keith Howard's images with Akua Intaglio ink.

1 When cleaning Akua Intaglio inked plates, place a few drops of hand dish-washing detergent onto the plate; and wash it with room temperature water and a soft sponge. Always spritz white vinegar onto the ImagOn side of the plate after washing, squeegee it clean and wipe water residue off with a soft paper towel.

2 When cleaning oil-based inks (if you intend to reprint the plate the next day), you do not need to clean the plates, especially as aggressive cleaning can damage Intaglio-Type plates. If you wish to keep the plates for more than a week, clean the plate with Canola cooking oil and a clean soft rag. I recommend the cheapest supermarket variety

Canola oil. Pour it onto the plate and wipe/blot with a clean rag to remove all ink residue. Wipe smoother areas of the plate and blot the coarse areas. Finish by spraying with spray cooking oil, such as Pam®, in those areas where the ink remains.

Keeping the Ink off Your Fingers
Traditionalists have developed a skill of clasping bent pieces of clean matte-board and picking up clean printing paper with these pieces of matte-board to avoid transferring ink from their fingers to the printing paper. In non-toxic intaglio printing, these pieces of matte-board or paper are used to pick up the inked plate, thus keeping the

Intaglio Printing

ink from transferring to your skin. Clean fingers are then available to pick up the printing paper. Working clean is extremely important.

Clean hands, in a safer printmaking studio, mean that wherever your hands go, including your mouth, ink will not follow. This pays off with cleaner working surfaces, clothes, press handles, and cleaner press felts.

Troubleshooting

Problem 1. The Akua Intaglio ink is not printing a rich black. **Probable cause:** the printing paper is too damp. *Solution: Only use waterleaf paper, such as Hahnemühle Copperplate, and only soak the paper for 1 minute. Immediately* S *queegee off excess water from the paper and blot it until it feels slightly damp. It is also possible to print with dry intaglio paper if the press pressure is increased.*

Akua Intaglio can be adversely affected by heat in which case it gets very loose, making it easy to over wipe the plate. If this happens, add Akua ink

S

thickener to stiffen it. Akua intaglio ink differs from other inks as it stiffens when it gets cold and loosens when it gets hot. It requires a different inking sensibility.

Problem 2. There are scratches on the Intaglio-Type plate after it is inked. **Probable cause**: There is grit in the ink applicator, or a small piece of ImagOn dislodged away from the edge of the plate and mixed with the ink during the inking process. *Solution: Use a clean piece of inking matte-board between each inking. Occasionally ImagOn breaks free a fraction of an inch from the crisp edge of a metal plate. There is a natural ImagOn Edge created when this happens. This is a unique characteristic of the Intaglio-Type technique. I think it is part of its unique aesthetic; and, as such, I would encourage you to emphasize this ImagOn Edge with each of your plates. You can do this by running your cutting knife along the ImagOn Edge and forcing it to have an irregular edge. This is akin to the practice of tearing printing paper instead of cutting it to create a false deckle edge. After the false Imagon Edge has been created, brush the small ImagOn particles from the plate with a soft brush.*

Bernice A. Cross, **Loch Lamond**, 2003, Photo Intaglio-Type, 3" x 2".

Intaglio Printing

Akua Intaglio Ink Troubleshooting Guide Directly from the Manufacturer.

Mix Akua Intaglio ink before using. Separation may occur at room temperatures depending upon individual pigments. Place the ink knife directly in the ink container and stir. Mix well from the bottom of the container to the top. Akua Intaglio will never harden or form a skin in the container or when left uncovered.

Ink Consistency
The ink consistency varies from stiff to loose depending upon the pigment and temperature conditions. The primary colors tend to be looser while the heavy earth pigments are stiffer. Ink will become stiff when cold and loose when warm.

To Stiffen Ink
Use Akua Oil Converter Medium to stiffen Akua Intaglio inks. Akua Oil is very stiff, highly refined archival water-mixable oil. It converts Akua Intaglio ink into oil ink that still cleans up with soap and water. Before adding the Akua Oil, work it with the ink knife till it is smooth. Then slowly work Akua Intaglio Ink into the Akua Oil.

To Loosen Ink
Work ink with an ink knife under a warm lamp, hair dryer or a hot plate set a low temperature.

Wiping the plate
Akua Intaglio is very soft ink; the process for wiping it is slightly different from wiping traditional oil-based etching inks. It applies and wipes off the plate much easier; therefore, at first you may have a tendency to remove too much ink. You will find that Akua Intaglio wipes from intaglio type plates in less than half the time than it would take with any other ink. For best results, use cheesecloth, or very soft tarlatan to wipe the surface of the plate. Roll the cheesecloth or soft tarlatan into a large ball shape. Be careful not to press your fingers into the inked surface of the plate. The ink is soft and will transfer fingerprint impressions easily.

Printing Paper
Akua Intaglio ink prints well on most standard printmaking papers. We suggest conducting a test by printing the same plate twice. Make one print on dry paper and another print on dampened paper. Your results may depend upon individual plate characteristics and type of paper used.

Printing on Dry Paper
Printing Akua Intaglio ink on dry paper offers higher contrast prints. It also eliminates the possibility of paper shrinkage making it ideal for printing multi-registered plates, and combining prints with digital inkjet or letterpress images. Increase the press pressure and use soft printmaking papers when printing on dry paper. If your print results are blotchy or inconsistent it may be necessary to dampen the paper.

Printing on Damp Paper
Damp paper may offer greater tonal values and more consistent print results for aquatints. Soak the paper for 30 seconds and blot thoroughly before using.

Re-Soaking Prints
Akua Intaglio ink is permanent. If necessary, prints may be placed in a tray of water immediately after printing. Do not soak prints too long and be careful not to rub the image until the print is thoroughly dry.

Print Drying Time
Akua Intaglio ink does not contain dryers. Heavy applications of ink, printed from deeply bitten plates, may take a long time to dry. Dry prints in a warm dry well ventilated area. We do not recommend using glossy or coated papers.

Cleaning Up
First, clean all inky surfaces, rollers, and plates with a dry rag. A textured rag such as cheesecloth or tarlatan is ideal. Using a 28-ounce liquid dish detergent bottle, fill 4-ounces of liquid dish detergent to 24-ounces of water. Use this solution with a rag for cleaning up any remaining ink residue.

Visit the manufacturers web site at <www.waterbasedinks.com> for further technical information.

Toner-Wash : Mix & Test

QUICK LOOK

Mixing Toner-Wash
1. Measure 1 teaspoon of Toner powder and place into container.
2. Add 1 teaspoon of Future.
3. Add 1 teaspoon of rubbing alcohol and mix.
4. Add 1 teaspoon of water.
5. Add 1 teaspoon of Windex.

1

2a

2b

2a,b. Brush Toner-Wash onto Drafting Mylar to test for a good black then add small amounts of rubbing alcohol, Windex or water to vary the Toner-Wash.

3

3.Close-up of typical Toner-Wash.

Toner Wash : Mix & Test

Introduction

The Wash-Drawing Intaglio-Type is a non-etch plate making process that produces drawn and/or painted effects in an intaglio print. It has the ability to produce images that display a complete tonal range while capturing extremely fine detail.

Any type of painting or drawing material can be used to make a wash-drawing onto drafting Mylar. Used photocopy toner, by far, gives the best results.

An ImagOn plate is exposed to the aquatint screen, then it is exposed, separately, to the wash-drawing. The plate is developed for 9 minutes in the soda ash solution, then processed and printed.

Following is instructions show how to make a toner-wash:

Toner-Wash Materials

1. Toner exhaust from a photocopy machine. Any laser printer toner, new or old, can also be used, also.

2. Future acrylic floor finish or any acrylic floor finish such as Johnson's Klear or Care Free. This is used as the binder (or glue) for the toner-wash.

3. Single-sided, which is best, or double-sided drafting Mylar, which is a high quality tracing film suitable for all wash and drawing media.

4. Rubbing alcohol.

5. Window cleaner or dish-washing soap.

6. A small quantity of water.

7. An assortment of brushes, dip pens, and **B**amboo pens.

8. ImagOn plate, normal exposing and processing materials.

Drawing and Wash Media

With the Wash-Drawing Intaglio-Type technique, the wash drawing or painting must be made onto a transparent or translucent surface. I recommend either single-sided architects' drafting Mylar or True-grain film. These do not wrinkle or buckle with wet media like tracing paper or drafting vellum. If non-permanent drawing materials are used, this drafting Mylar, frosted Lexan, and True-grain film can be reused.

The mark making potential of the Wash-Drawing Intaglio-Type is enormous as almost every mark can be translated into the intaglio print. Most drawing material will work. There are a few exceptions where the drawing on the Mylar appeared quite substantial but provided too little pigment to act as a light-stopping stencil during the exposure step. Media such as felt-tip markers and diluted India Ink do not work well.

Toner-Wash Step-by-Step

1 Start by mixing the toner-wash as follows:

TONER-WASH FORMULA

A. 2 parts of used photocopy toner.

B. 1 part of rubbing alcohol.

C. 1 part of Future as the binder.

D. 1 part of soapy water. *Add 10 drops of dishwashing detergent to 1 cup of water.*

2 Add 1 teaspoon of rubbing alcohol, 1 teaspoon of Future and 1 teaspoon of soapy water to a mixing container. Now **Slowly** add 2 teaspoons of used photocopy toner to a mixing container and mix it thoroughly.

TIP: Make sure not to create any photocopy 'dust'. It is best to wear a suitable dust mask if there is a possibility of inhaling the photocopy dust.

Toner Wash : Mix & Test

3 Brush the toner-wash solution onto the drafting Mylar.

4 While the toner-wash is wet interesting textures can be made by spraying on alcohol, or Windex. Brushing on water can also create soft blended areas. Dropping on rock salt on to the wet wash can also give great results.

Recycling Used Photocopy Toner

The advantage of this technique is that every photocopier has a surplus of discharged photocopy toner which is generally discarded. Not only will this discarded toner provide an endless supply of toner wash-drawing material, but also, by reusing it, you will also be recycling. The pigment density of the photocopy toner mixture is much higher than that of acrylic or gouache, allowing for a much wider exposure latitude. Therefore, the exposures for photocopy toner Wash-Drawing Intaglio-Types are about twice as long as the exposures for acrylic or gouache washes, and are therefore closer to the exposures of halftones.

TIP: Personally, I approach each toner-wash differently. I rarely (accurately) measure the ingredients. I enjoy the variety that this inaccurate mixing style gives. I start with about a teaspoon of toner powder, add about one teaspoon of Future, then a teaspoon of rubbing alcohol, and mix it thoroughly. I then paint this concoction onto drafting Mylar to see what kind of black is produced. My aim, at this stage, is to make a rich black toner-ink. If the 'ink' is not black enough, I add slightly more toner until it is. Then I add more quantities of alcohol and soapy water to disperse the toner to create a reticulated wash effect (shown **B***elow).*

Troubleshooting

Problem 1: Toner-wash is not black enough. *Solution: Add more photocopy toner to the toner wash solution. As each toner type can be expected to vary, it is a matter of doing several tests to find the best toner formula with your unique materials.*

Problem 2: There is very little pigment reticulation in the toner-wash. *Solution: Add either more rubbing alcohol or soapy water to the toner wash mixture. Again, it is a matter of adding small amounts, mixing the toner-wash, and re-brushing it onto the Mylar. Also, a reticulated wash can be accentuated by using True-Grain, textured Lexan, or Artex Textured film.*

Problem 3: The toner-wash easily wipes off the Mylar. *Solution: Add more Future or Klear to the toner-wash mixture. This is the glue, or the binder, that causes it to stick onto the film.*

Keith Howard, **Toner-Wash-Drawing**, 2003, onto single-sided drafting Mylar using both brush and bamboo pen techniques, 24" x 36".

Wash Drawing Intaglio-Type

QUICK LOOK

1. Mix toner-wash solution.

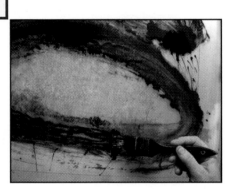

2. Paint or draw the toner-wash onto drafting Mylar.

3. Prepare ImagOn plate and expose it to Aquatint Screen.

4. Expose toner-wash-drawing to the ImagOn plate.

5. Develop the plate for 9 minutes, and stabilize with a vinegar wash; then rinse.

6. Heat dry the plate; then print it.

Wash-Drawing Intaglio-Type

Introduction

One of the key techniques in the NON-ETCH Intaglio-Type family of techniques is the Wash-Drawing Intaglio-Type. This technique takes full advantage of the Toner-Wash, described in the previous chapter. In this technique, the ImagOn plate is exposed, first, to an Aquatint Screen and, then, to a wash-drawings created on drafting Mylar. The plate is developed; then washed, stabilized with vinegar, heat dried, and printed.

The Wash-Drawing Intaglio-Type allows printmakers the greatest degree of spontaneity with both mark-making and plate making. It is a technique that any artist can access easily, provided the equipment is available. Fortunately, there are many open access studios around the country and around the world where artists can go to make prints. Generally, these artists run printmaking studios, have low monthly rentals, and provide a venue for creative exploration of all the processes described in this book. (The American Print Alliance has a book that lists such open studios, see Sources P. 242).

Materials

1. Toner-wash solution. (See previous chapter on how to make a toner-wash).

2. Single-sided drafting Mylar.

3. Assortment of brushes, drawing tools and pens.

4. Spray bottles with alcohol and water.

5. Normal ImagOn plate-making and processing equipment.

Wash-Drawing Intaglio-Type
Step-by-Step

1 Make up a toner-wash ink, as described in the previous chapter, and then the wash-drawing.

2 Prepare ImagOn test plate along with an additional image sized plate.

TIP: When working with a large plate, I recommend doing a test plate, to determine which plate exposure gives the optimum results.

3 Expose the ImagOn test plate to the Aquatint Screen. (This aquatint screen exposure should have been determined already. If not, go to the chapter on the Aquatint Screen Test, pages 53-60.)

4 Remove the Aquatint Screen, and place the wash-drawing on top of the plate. Do a series of exposure step-tests (with the Olec DEC 22 x 28) that will give you a choice of potential exposures. I recommend step tests at 5 light unit intervals from 5 -15 L.U.'s as shown below.

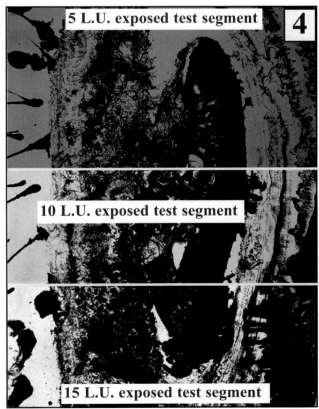

5 L.U. exposed test segment   **4**

10 L.U. exposed test segment

15 L.U. exposed test segment

Notice how the shorter 5 L.U. segment above demonstrates the darkest print with the least amount of contrast. The longer exposure gives the most degree of contrast while losing shadow

Wash-Drawing Intaglio-Type

detail. Whatever type of exposure unit is used, you will need to become familiar with test exposures to enable you, not only, to get the correct exposure for any given image but, also, to give you more image-making choices. The UV light from the exposure unit is a major image adjustment and manipulation factor.

5 With the Olec Olite 1KT Quartz lamp, at 20" above the plate, I would recommend making a test plate with the first exposure commencing at 100 seconds with step test increments of 40 seconds. Thus first expose the image at 100 seconds, then make each step after that 40 additional seconds. The plate would look very similar to illustration but with larger amounts of exposure for each step increments.

6 Once the image exposure has been determined I also advise making a step Flash exposure, to see if you can increase the tonal range of the image. See pages 57-58 for detailed description of how to make a Flash exposure.

7 Still develop the plate for 9 minutes in the soda ash developer, rinse with vinegar, wash, and heat dry.

8 Print the test plate and compare the test segments with the toner-wash drawing. Choose the best test segment exposure for the final plate.

9 Repeat the last six steps with the best exposure for the large plate.

Other Wash-Drawing Media
1. Watercolor pencil.

2. High density pigment watercolor.

3. Most black acrylic paint.

4. Designer's gouache

5. Badger Acrylic Aquatint Solution.

6. Graphic Chemical Water soluble black relief ink.

7. Graphite pencil.

Multi-Plate Wash-Drawing Intaglio-Type
Wonderful color combinations can be achieved when two or more plates are printed with various colors, one on top of the other. Although Akua process colors are one obvious color option for this particular technique, any color combination can be used. Akua make 12 different colors plus a transparent base which give the printmaker an almost infinite choice when it comes to color mixing.

The Multi-Plate technique described here for wash-drawing stencils represent one type of media. In fact this multi-plate principle can be applied to any plate making technique. This is especially so when using Mylar stencils to make the plates. As drafting Mylar is transparent

Wash-Drawing Intaglio-Type

aligning each stencil is a matter of overlaying one Mylar stencil on top of the other. This makes image registration, from plate to plate, relatively easy. It is then a matter of making identical sized ImagOn plate, exposing each drafting Mylar stencil to each plate, in total registration, and then printing them in registration. There is also a technique described for doing this in next chapter on the Pastel Intaglio-Type and also in the chapter on Process Color Intaglio-Type, pages 149 - 174.

Multi-Plate Wash-Drawing Intaglio-Type Step-by-Step

1 Start by making the first drafting Mylar stencil. Although it does not matter what media you use on this stencil, I do recommend that you limit your media to media that have similar opaque or UV light stopping properties.

2 Once the first drafting stencil is finished (and dry) place a clean piece of drafting Mylar on top and tape them together with masking tape.

3 Make additional drafting Mylar stencils as needed. If several stencils are placed, one on top of the other, it will be difficult to discern the first Mylar stencil. If this happens place the stencils on top of a light table.

4 Once the stencils have been made leave them taped together and then cut through all the stencils with a sharp snap-off cutter. This will ensure that each stencil has been cut to the identical size.

5a, b Make identical sized ImagOn plates to match these stencils and print them in any color sequence that you wish.

5a The red wash-drawing plate being printed first.

5b A three color Wash-Drawing Intaglio-Type, by Keith Howard, made with three separate Wash-Drawing Intaglio-Type plates.

5a

Printing ImagOn 1st plate

5b

Printing ImagOn 3rd plate

Keith Howard, **After the Gold Rush**, 2002, 4 plate Wash-Drawing Intaglio-Type, 9" x 12", printed with Akua Intaglio Ink.

Graham Fowler, **Sparkle Koi**, 2003, hand colored Photo-Intaglio-Type made from drawn Mylar stencil, 16" x 23". For more details see: <**www.grahamfowler.com**>

Pastel Intaglio-Type

QUICK LOOK

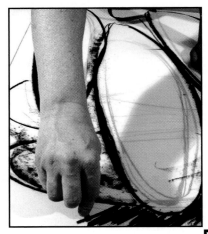

1. Use pastel or charcoal to draw onto Mylar. **1**

2 **2. Use a wet or dry rag or a bush charged with water to manipulate the pastel.** *Wet media works best.*

3 **3. Make an ImagOn step-test plate to determine the optimum exposure.**

3. Make ImagOn plates to the size of the pastel drawings and print them. Shown: a detail of the red and blue plates printed. **4**

Pastel Intaglio-Type

Introduction

Wherever a particular mark making media has the potential to offer a new visual aesthetic, I like to differentiate it by giving the technique a name. Pastel Intaglio-Type evolved largely through the work of my graduate students, Erin Holscher and Amy Williams. Wet and dry pastel offer the printmaker a unique mark-making opportunity that treads the visual aesthetic between a mezzotint and pastel-wash. (See Erin Holscher's print on page 210 and Amy William's print on 235.)

Materials

1. Colored pastels. (Prismacolor, **Nupastel**, Sanguine and red, work effectively to block out the UV light. Black pastel or charcoal work well, also.)

2. Drafting Mylar, Artex textured film, or True-Grain film.

3. Rag and smudge stick.

Pastel Intaglio-Type Step-by-Step

1 Dampen Mylar with damp rag. Using pastel or charcoal, draw directly onto drafting Mylar.

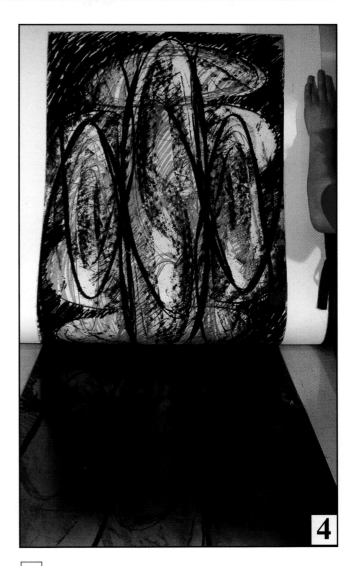

2 The wet pastel or charcoal can be manipulated on the dull surface of the Mylar with a soft rag or drawing stump.

3 A wash effect can be achieved by working into the pastel/charcoal surface with a damp rag or brush charged with water. *Wet media works best.*

4 Once the wet media has dried, make an ImagOn test plate to determine the best exposure. When working in different colored layers make the ImagOn plates to the size of the pastel drawings and print them, one on top of the other (illustrated in 4). This is a great technique to print red, blue, and yellow plates one on top of the other.

Spit-Bite Intaglio-Type

QUICK LOOK

> **START HERE**
> 1. Prepare three different concentrations of soda ash developer.
> A. 10 gms soda ash + 1 litre of water.
> B. 25 gms soda ash + 1 litre of water.
> C. 50 gms soda ash + 1 litre of water.

1. Expose a plate to Aquatint Screen and strip off the Mylar. To create negative makes, draw on the plate with a crayon.

1

2

2. Paint soda ash developer onto plate.

3. Wash the plate with water, stabilize it with vinegar, dry and print the plate.

3

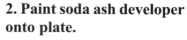

See Keith Howard's Spit-Bite Intaglio-Type on page

Spit Bite Intaglio-Type

Introduction

The Spit-Bite Intaglio-Type is a highly intuitive technique which offers the printmaker subtle watercolor type washes and a variety of drawn marks.

Three different strengths of soda ash developer are mixed and then painted directly onto an Aquatinted ImagOn plate. Stronger soda ash developer will produce a rapid degree of depth in the ImagOn plate, resulting in black areas in the final print. The weakest soda ash developers will produce the softest tones, depending on how long it sits on the plate. The key to this technique is experience and keen observation.

As the soda ash developer reacts with the ImagOn plate, it turns a blueish color. The more this blueish tinge turns light blue, the more it is eating into the ImagOn film. Thus, the deepest will be the mark produced. This is a great technique to use in combination with two layers of ImagOn film. Either, the bottom layer can be Aquatinted, independently from the top layer of ImagOn; or they can be Aquatinted simultaneously. (See the chapter on Layered Intaglio-Type, P. 107 - 110.)

Negative resist makers can be made by drawing on the ImagOn plate with a soft wax crayon. When the spit-bite developer is brushed onto the crayon marks, the crayon protects the ImagOn plate from the developing action. A white crayon-like mark results in the final print.

If you wish to make a preliminary drawing on the plate, use Crayola water-soluble markers or water-soluble pencils.

Materials

1. Soda ash and three cup sized mixing containers.

2. An assortment of brushes and water proof crayons.

3. Aquatint Screen.

Spit Bite Intaglio-Type Step-by-Step

1 Laminate the ImagOn film to the plate.

2 Mix three batches of different strength soda ash developer:

Mild - 10gms of soda ash to 1 litre

Medium - 25gms to 1 litre

Strong - 50gms to 1 litre
These can be color coded by adding watercolor.

3 Expose the ImagOn plate to the Aquatint Screen(see pages 63-72).

4 After Aquatinting the plate remove the top layer of Mylar from the ImagOn plate.

5 To make negative marks, start with crayon drawing. Crayons resist the various strength soda ash developers. Water soluble crayons dissolve with the application of the soda ash developer, which can create variable negative marks. Non-soluble crayons result in white crayon like marks in the final print.

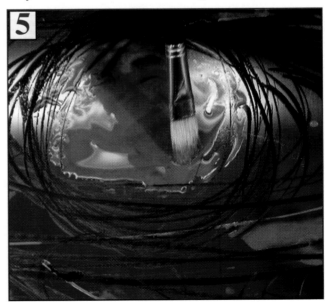

Spit Bite Intaglio-Type

TIP": Remove the crayon by heating the surface of the ImagOn plate with a hair-dryer and then rubbing the crayon off with a paper towel.

6a, b Draw or paint onto the ImagOn emulsion using one of the different strengths of soda ash developers. Illustration 6a and 6b show painting and drawing with soda ash developer. I recommend starting with the weaker strengths of developers and finishing with the strongest. Water can be added to the plate at any time to increase the subtlety of the spit-bite mark. Use paintbrushes of different sizes and bamboo pens or other types of dip pens. At any point, the plate can be washed thoroughly to stop the action of the spit-bite.

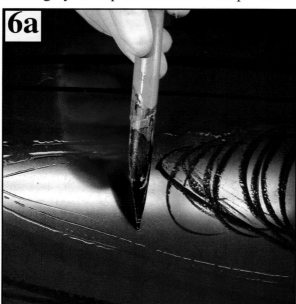

The **above** demonstration plate was printed and appears on page 36.

7 Strong developer makes darker lines; weaker developer, softer lines. The amount of time the developer sits on the plate drastically affects results. If open-bite like marks are not desired in the final print, do not let the strong developer sit on the plate for more then 4 minutes.

8 Once the spit-bite application is finished, rinse the plate as you would for still development.

9 Stabilize with vinegar; then wash, dry, and proof.

10 As long as the ImagOn plate has not been exposed to UV light, the spit-bite technique can be repeated, even after the plate has been proofed. When using Akua Intaglio water-based ink for proofing, there is no need to wash the plate before applying the soda ash spit-bite solution. However, if oil-based inks are used, the plate will need a thorough cleaning before it is reworked. Clean first with a spray cooking oil followed by a magnesium carbonate (Whiting) and water paste mixture. This degreases the plate.

11 After a final rinse, dry and heat-set the plate. The plate is ready for printing.

R.I.T. printmaking teacher, Liz Durrand, mixes potato starch with the soda ash developer to make a dry-brush, Spit-Bite, effect She also uses re-usable brush-pens made for India ink by substituting the ink for the soda ash solutions.

TIP: The Spit-Bite Intaglio-Type is a great technique for reworking the plate with paint-on Screen Filler or Liquid Aquatint.

Spit Bite Intaglio-Type

Re-work the plate with Construction Intaglio-Type
Pieces of ImagOn can be exposed to the Aquatint Screen prior to adhering them to the already worked Spit-Bite Intaglio-Type plate. In this way, more reworking of the surface can be done with the soda ash spit-bite solutions. The edges of the ImagOn film will hold ink in the final print and interact with the soft lines created by the soda ash solution.

1 Use a piece of ImagOn which is large enough to cover those areas of the plate that you wish to rework. Place this film (*which has not been laminated to the plate yet*) in the exposure unit, with the top Mylar facing the Aquatint Screen; and expose it as you would when exposing the Aquatint Screen to an ImagOn plate.

2 Remove the peel-back layer of the ImagOn film piece, and immediately stick it to the desired area of the plate. This is done by rubbing it with a dry soft cloth

ImagOn ULTRA will stick to a dry clean plate. If small pieces of Imagon do not stick to the plate, slightly dampen the plate with water. This is best done by spritzing it with water and wiping the excess water from the plate with paper towel.

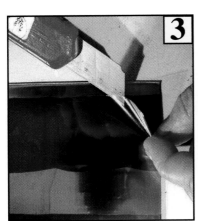

3 Remove the top Mylar from the added pieces by lifting one Mylar edge with a small cutter.

4 Rework the image with more soda ash solution. When finished, wash, stabilize with vinegar, and do a final rinse with water. Dry and proof the plate. If more reworking is warranted, add more pieces of ImagOn or paint on more soda ash. *Knowing how long to leave the spit-bite soda ash solution on the plate is a matter of experience.*

Troubleshooting
Problem 1: Blackest marks open-bite in the final print. **Probable cause:** The soda ash spit-bite solution was left on the plate too long. Open-bite occurs because the spit-bite developer is left on the ImagOn plate too long. This is most likely to happen with the strongest spit-bite developer *Solution: Decrease the amount of time the developer sits on the ImagOn plate; or decrease the strength of the soda ash developer, relative to the amount of time it is left on the plate. Knowing when the soda ash developing solution has been left on long enough is a matter of experience.*

Following is a guide to how long the soda ash developer can remain on the plate before it open bites.

Maximum Working Time for Soda Ash Developing Solutions

1. **Mild** soda ash solution
10 gms to 1 litre of water → 16 mins.

2. **Medium** soda ash solution
25 gms to 1 litre of water → 8 mins.

3. **Strong** soda ash solution
50 gms to 1 litre of water → 4 mins.

Mezzo Intaglio-Type

QUICK LOOK

1. Expose the ImagOn plate to the Aquatint Screen.

2. Develop the Aquatinted plate, wash, stabilize with vinegar, rewash, and dry.

3. Paint Speedball Screen Filler directly onto the developed aquatinted plate.

4. Interesting lines can be created if the screen filler is allowed to partially dry, and is then washed off the plate.

5. After the plate has dried, it can be printed.

Mezzo Intaglio-Type

The Plate

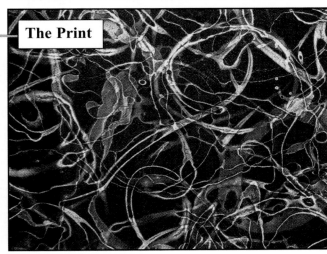

The Print

Introduction

All Mezzo-Type (abbreviated name) non-etch techniques commence by exposing the plate to the Aquatint Screen, fully developing it, stabilizing with vinegar, washing, drying, and then applying Screen filler.

There are three different approaches to the Mezzo-Type technique:

1. Additive technique onto a dry plate where the Speedball Screen filler, or some other acrylic painting medium, is added to the dry Mezzo-Type plate. The screen filler is allowed to dry and the plate printed to reveal the Mezzo-Type image.

In this technique, the developed Aquatinted ImagOn plate, which resembles the surface of fine sandpaper, is filled in with various thicknesses of Screen filler. If the plate was printed without the addition of screen filler, it would print completely black. When screen filler is added to the plate, the thicker the screen filler deposit, the lighter will be the resultant print.

To control the viscosity of the screen filler, add water to dilute it, or to thicken it, leave it in a photo developing tray in the sun to evaporate the water content.

Work directly onto the dry Aquatinted plate with the various solutions of screen filler, or use it

directly from the screen filler container. If you use it from the container, you may also work with a brush charged with water, to dilute the screen filler as you go.

2. The **Additive Wet-on-Wet** technique. One of the properties of the Speedball Screen Filler is that it is water-soluble when wet and water-proof when dry. Consequently, screen filler marks, made onto the Mezzo-Type plate, can be washed off after the edges have been dried. This creates a light colored edge around each screen filler mark or shape. The longer the screen filler is allowed to dry, the thicker will be this edge. This technique can be repeated several times to create highly complex images (see the illustration above).

3. The **Reductive** technique involves wearing down the developed aquatinted surface of the Mezzo-Type plate with the aid of a snake-slip stone or fine wet-and-dry sandpaper (using the dry method). The snake-slip stone is about the same size as a piece of classroom black-board chalk and is a light gray in color. It is used in stone lithography to remove unwanted marks from a litho stone. It has an abrasive quality that works well on the dry Aquatinted Mezzo-Type plate.

The aim of the reductive technique is to lighten areas of the plate with the snake-slip. The more the surface is abraded, the whiter it becomes. There is a danger that this abrasive action will

Mezzo Intaglio-Type

break through to the actual copper plate, hence, it makes sense to apply two layers of ImagOn to the Mezzo-Type plate. If this is done, follow the directions for Layered Intaglio-Type, especially the extended developing time required to develop down to the first layer. When using this technique, it is important to use a dust mask to avoid breathing in fine dust particles created with the snake slip.

Materials
1. Speedball Screen Filler.

2. An assortment of brushes.

Mezzo-Type Step-by-Step
1 Laminate ImagOn film to plate.

2 Expose the ImagOn plate to an Aquatint Screen.

3 Still develop the aquatinted ImagOn for 9 minutes, and hand develop with a soft sponge for 30 seconds until the rough aquatint texture of the plate can be felt.

4 Hunt Speedball Screen-Filler is then applied to the plate. For differing effects, this can be done when the plate is wet or dry. Tonal variations within an image are created by the amount of the screen filler in any particular mark on the plate. The thicker the screen filler, the whiter that area

will be in the resultant print.

Although Speedball Screen Filler is recommended, any number of acrylic mediums, such as Golden's gloss medium to their impasto medium can be used.

5 A wash effect can be achieved by painting the Screen Filler onto a wet plate. A dry plate will give more distinctive brush shapes. A wet plate gives subtle marks. The more water on the plate,

the greater the dilution of the Screen filler mark and the darker will be that mark. Sometimes, it will be necessary to apply the diluted Screen filler in several layers, allowing each layer to dry before applying the next.

6 Washing off partially dried Screen Filler can give you some interesting lines because the Screen filler dries at the edge of the mark before drying in the center.

7 If you heat Screen filler, either on a hot-plate or with a hair-dryer, it will crack which can create unique marks.

8 Once the screen filler is dry, the plate is ready to print.

Troubleshooting
Problem 1: There are no blacks, just dark grays, in the final print. This is caused when the plate is not completely developed, through an incorrect aquatint screen exposure, or if screen filler is used over the entirety of the plate surface. ***Solution:*** *Directly after the plate has been aquatinted, developed and dried, wipe a soft, clean, dry cloth across the surface of the ImagOn plate, as shown at* **r** *ight.*

Mezzo Intaglio-Type

If this is done, the rag will want to cling to the aquatinted ImagOn plate. This indicates a good level of 'tooth' on the plate which will ultimately result in a good rich black in the finished print. Once this has been established, you can proceed confidently, applying the screen filler, knowing that areas left untouched by the Screen filler will result in a rich black in the final print.

The plate may not have been completely developed. The rag test, illustrated on the previous page, is important as the plate can be returned to the developer for further development, if necessary.

NB: Once the screen filler has dried on the plate, re-developing it will cause most of the screen filler to fall off the plate.

Problem 2: Some areas of the plate have open-bite. This is caused by too much or too strong development. ***Solution:*** *Redo the plate and adjust the developer so that it is the correct strength. Open-biting can also indicate too short of an exposure to the Aquatint Screen. If this is the case, lengthen the exposure. One additional thing that can be done is to use the Layered Intaglio-Type technique and apply two layers of ImagOn to the plate. The bottom layer can be exposed to the aquatint screen independently of the top layer of ImagOn, or both layers can be exposed to the Aquatint Screen simultaneously. In both instances, this provides an "insurance layer "which can compensate for open-biting while allowing for a greater deposit of ink in the final print.*

Problem 3: The screen filler does not yield a crisp white in the finished print. Generally, crisp whites in the finished print mean, an absence of black ink on the print allowing for the white paper to shine through. Sometimes, the Screen filler holds a small amount of tone which translates to plate tone. ***Solution:*** *Coat theses ares of the plate with Future acrylic floor finish, allow it to dry, and re-proof the plate. Future can be added to any section of the Mezzo-Type plate to lighten other areas gradually.*

Illustration **below**: At the press, pulling one of Keith Howard's prints off the inked Mezzo-Type plate.

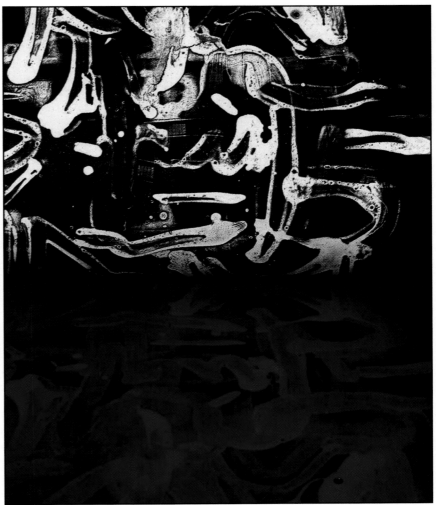

Stencil Intaglio-Type

QUICK LOOK

1. Expose the ImagOn plate to the Aquatint Screen.

2. Cut or stencil out shapes on the top ImagOn Mylar and remove them.

3. Place the plate into the ImagOn developer for 9 min. The stenciled out shapes will be the only areas to develop.

4. After the open areas have developed, remove the second part of the Mylar stencil.

5. Undeveloped areas of the plate are painted with spit-bite soda ash solutions.

6. After Spit-Bite areas are completed, the other areas of the plate are treated like Mezzo-Type. When the plate is dry, it is proofed.

See Keith Howard's Stencil Intaglio-Type print on P. 6 & 67.

Stencil Intaglio-Type

Introduction

Before commencing, you should have a working knowledge of both the Mezzo Intaglio-Type and Sprit-Bite Intaglio-Type, as the Stencil Intaglio-Type method incorporates both of these techniques.

The Stencil Intaglio-Type is a wonderful technique that uses the top Mylar of the ImagOn film as an integral part of the plate making process. After the ImagOn plate has been exposed to the Aquatint Screen, draw stencil areas onto the top ImagOn Mylar with a dry eraser marker. After the stencil shapes have been drawn, cut them out with a sharp scalpel or snap-blade cutter. Just cut through the ImagOn Mylar so that cut out shapes can be removed from the ImagOn plate. Once all the Mylar stencils have been removed, develop the plate in normal soda ash developer for 9 minutes. Only the open areas of the ImagOn plate will develop. Where the top ImagOn Mylar still exists on the plate, it will not develop.

After the plate has developed, wash and dry it. Then remove the rest of the ImagOn Mylar. Areas uncovered by this second Mylar stencil can be worked with the Spit-Bite Intaglio-Type technique. After these areas are finished, the entire plate can be worked on with the Speedball Screen Filler. Thus, a unique combination technique is possible. Once the plate is dry, it is printed. As long as the spit-bite areas are not over-exposed, they can be reworked if desired. When these spit-bite areas are completed, however, they must be fixed with a strong blast of UV light.

Materials

1. Scalpel or snap-off blade cutter.

2. Speedball Screen Filler or any Acrylic Gloss Painting Medium, such as those made by Golden Artist Color.

3. Three containers with varying strengths of soda ash solution.

4. An assortment of brushes and dip pens.

5. Dry erase markers or water soluble markers.

5. Aquatint Screen and normal plate-making materials and equipment.

Stencil Intaglio-Type Step-by-Step

1 Laminate the ImagOn film to the plate.

2 **Mix three batches of different strength soda ash developer:**

Mild - 10gms of soda ash to 1 litre water.

Medium - 25gms to 1 litre water

Strong - 50gms to 1 litre water.
These can be color coded by adding watercolor.

3 Expose the ImagOn plate to the Aquatint Screen for the normal aquatint exposure.

4 Draw areas to be stenciled with dry erase or Crayola water soluble markers.

5 Cut through the ImagOn Mylar and remove the cut out Mylar shapes. It is not necessary to cut all the way through the ImagOn emulsion to the plate.

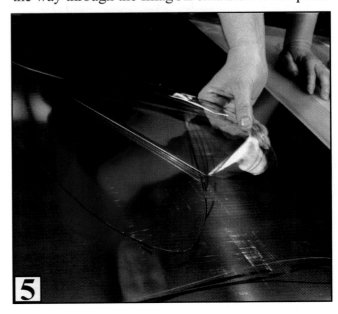

Stencil Intaglio-Type

[6] After all the ImagOn Mylar stencils have been removed from the plate, place it in the normal ImagOn developer for 9 minutes.

TIP: Cut out all of the ImagOn Mylar stencils first, and remove them from the plate at the same time. Over a period of a few minutes, ImagOn emulsion, reacting with oxygen, becomes foggy. Once all the stencils have been removed, drop the plate into the ImagOn developer as quickly as possible.

[7] After development, stabilize the 'open' areas of the ImagOn emulsion with vinegar, rinse with water and dry.

TIP: It is not necessary to dry the plate completely as the areas of the plate to be worked on next are under the Mylar that is about to be removed.

[8] Have the three previously prepared amounts of soda ash spit-bite developers ready. Remove the rest of the ImagOn Mylar.

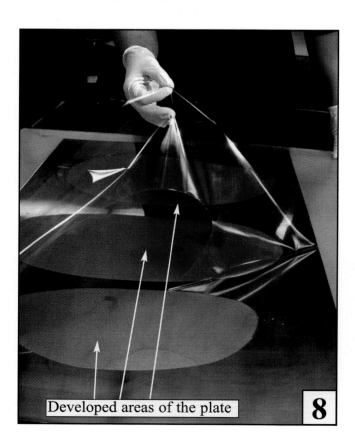

Developed areas of the plate   **8**

[9] Now, work on the dark blueish areas of the ImagOn plate with the spit-bit solutions. Try to avoid getting the spit-bite solutions on the already developed areas of the plate which will cause 'open-biting' (This may or may not be desired).

Start with the mild soda ash solution and work quickly. A working knowledge of the Spit-Bite Intaglio-Type technique is helpful (see pages 89 - 92). I would advise that you make line work with a bamboo pen and the strong soda ash solution.

TIP: If you see too much copper plate coming through the spit-bite areas of the plate, you have left the spit-bite on the plate too long. Consider using the Layered Intaglio-Type technique to prevent this.

[10] Once the spit-bite areas have been created, wash them thoroughly and stabilize with the vinegar wash.

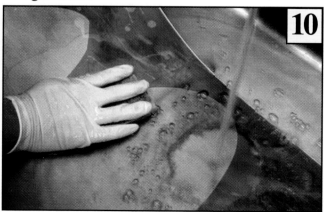

Stencil Intaglio-Type

11 Paint screen filler or acrylic gloss medium onto the plate. If you want to work with the wet-on-wet technique, described on page 94, then you do not need to dry the plate before proceeding.

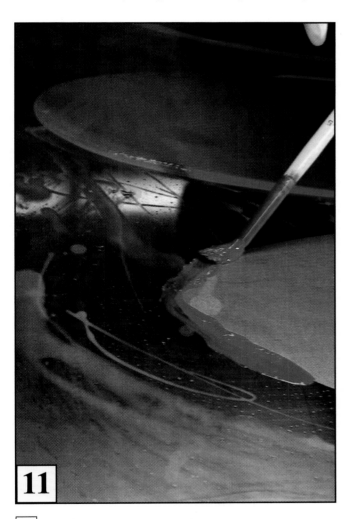

11

12 When the screen filler completely dries, the plate can be proofed.

13 Once you have proofed the plate and decided that the spit-bite areas are satisfactory, light fix the plate with a 3 minute second blast of UV exposure unit light.

Troubleshooting

Problem 1: Prin ting paper sticks to the plate. **Probable cause:** The plate was not given a final blast of UV exposure light to stabilize totally the spit-bite areas. ***Solution:*** *Take the plate to the exposure unit, place a pad of paper on top of the vacuum frame glass, and place the plate on top of it. Expose the plate for, at least the same amount of time you would for an Aquatint Screen exposure.*

Problem 2: The spit-bite areas of the plate open-bite too quickly. Probable cause: The spit-bite solution was left on the plate too long or the sequence, from mild to strong, of soda ash solutions was not employed. ***Solution:*** *Make a layered Intaglio-Type plate. Two layers of Aquatint ImagOn will allow more working time with the spit-bite solutions which, otherwise, can be weakened by the addition of more water. Normally as the spit-bite technique allows only a few minutes of working time, working fast is the best solution.*

BIG TIP*: If re-developing parts of a plate is necessary, previously developed areas of the Imagon plate can be protected from the Spit-bite developing solution by applying Vaseline. This is also a great tip to remember when reworking the Construction Intaglio-Type plate (P. 111-114).*

Problem 3. The Mezzo-Type areas of the plate did not hold a rich enough black. **Probable cause:** The ImagOn developer was too weak. ***Solution:*** *After initial development, dry the plate, and do the rag test outlined at the bottom of page 95. If necessary, the plate can be returned to the developer and sponge developed for a minute or so.*

I cannot stress how important it is to do the test outlined on pages 45-48, as balancing the developer will be one of the best ways to stave off complications with this process.

See also Keith Howard's sample prints on pages 6 & 67.

Line/Aquatint Intaglio-Type

QUICK LOOK

1. Use drafting pens, pencils, or almost any line making medium to make a drawing onto drafting Mylar or directly onto the ImagOn plate.

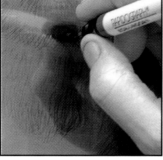

2. Prepare two ImagOn plates the same size as the drawing.

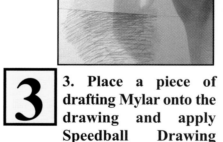

3. Place a piece of drafting Mylar onto the drawing and apply Speedball Drawing Fluid.

4. Airbrush the stencil with Badger Acrylic Aquatint Solution for Printmakers.

5. Expose and process plates as normal.

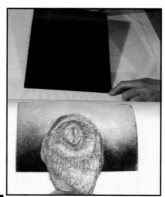

6. Print one plate after the other with the aid of a registration template.

Line/Aquatint Intaglio-Type

Introduction

Line Intaglio-Type is a NON-ETCH technique that allows for line drawing transfer to the intaglio plate. I will also demonstrate how any image can be re-worked with a second plate Aquatint Intaglio-Type. This will also involve demonstrating a simple registration technique for multi-plate registration.

Materials

1. Any drawing material, such as fine or coarse felt tip markers. (There are felt tip markers, designed for the drafting industry, that have a variety of tips which are excellent for this application. It is possible to use almost any drawing media from pencils to crayons. The main consideration is how well these drawing implements block out the UV light of the exposure unit.)

2. Single sided drafting Mylar.

3. Normal ImagOn plate-making and processing equipment.

Line Intaglio-Type Step-by-Step

1 Draw an image onto single-sided drafting Mylar. The best results occur with a line drawing that has some degree of separation between the lines. This will allow us to make a plate without the use of an Aquatint Screen exposure.

2 Prepare the ImagOn test plate along with the image sized plate.

3 Place the line drawing on top of the ImagOn plate, emulsion side down, and give it a series of step-test exposures.

4 Develop the plate for 9 minutes in the soda ash solution, stabilize it with a vinegar wash, rinse, and heat-dry.

5 Proof the plate. If the lines in your drawing are too thick or they do not have enough spacing, 'open-biting' will occur, as illustrated below in a partially inked plate.

Half inked-up Line Intaglio-Type plate with lighter 'open-bite' areas which will not hold ink.

Line/Aquatint Intaglio-Type

6 If open-biting is occurring it is possible to open up the line in the drawing by scratching it with a scalpel cutter as shown below.

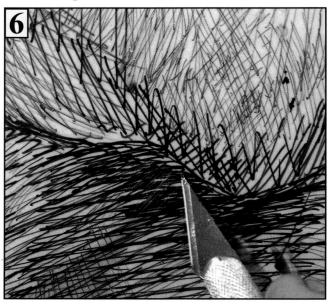

7 Once the optimum exposure has been determined from the test plate, repeat steps 1- 5 for the final plate.

Line-Etch Intaglio-Type

Go to the chapter on the Etched Intaglio-Type (pages 129-136) and follow both the plate thinning and development procedure. Expose the drawing to the thinned ImagOn plate and then process as recommended. It is also recommended that you use a small amount of talc on the plate to prevent the drawing from sticking during plate exposure. Etch the plate for 1 hour 15 minutes in fresh Ferric Chloride or 40 minutes in fresh Edinburgh Etch. Lengthen etching times for older etchants.

Combining Line Intaglio-Type with Aquatint Intaglio-Type

There are a host of printmakers who want to combine both line drawing and aquatint techniques. This method not only meets this technical challenge but also adds a new creative flexibility to the process.

Materials
1. Single drafting Mylar.

2. Speedball Drawing Fluid. (normally used for screen printing) Gum Arabic would make a satisfactory substitute.

3. Airbrush equipment. (See chapter on Acrylic Aquatint.)

4. Steel block. This is a weight used to pin printing paper to the etching press bed.

5. Photo developing tray larger than your Mylar drawing.

6. Soft dishwashing sponge.

7. Masking tape.

8. An assortment of brushes.

9. Badger Aquatint Solution for Printmakers. This is one occasion where this is used straight out of the bottle in its full-strength form. Black waterproof drafting type ink can be substituted.

10. More than one copper plate.

11. Thin plastic as a registration palette.

Line & Aquatint Intaglio-Type Step-by-Step

1 begin by cutting two copper plates exactly the same size, and laminating each plate with ImagOn.

2 Make your drawing onto drafting Mylar, and then tape a second piece of drafting Mylar directly on top of this drawing. You will be able to see the first Mylar drawing through this top drafting Mylar. This second piece of drafting Mylar will become the aquatint stencil.

3 The aim of the aquatint stencil is to create airbrush aquatint areas of tone that will

Line/Aquatint Intaglio-Type

complement the first line drawing. In the example presented in illustration 3, I have chosen to add a gradated tonal area behind the drawing of the apple and halfway up from the bottom. This creates the illusion of a table in the foreground and open darkness in the background behind the apple.

TIP: Working with two separate plates also gives me the opportunity to work with two different colored inks.

4 Use masking tape to mask out straight line areas on the aquatint stencil; then paint Speedball Drawing Fluid onto other areas to be masked out.

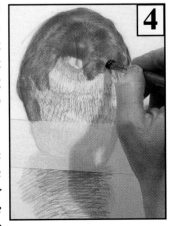

TIP: Liquid Gum Arabic by itself or with some blue water color added can be substituted for the drawing fluid.

TIP: It is not necessary to wait for the drawing fluid to dry to continue with making the airbrush stencil in the the next step.

5 Mount the aquatint stencil in the spray booth in readiness for the airbrush aquatint spray. If you have not already read the chapter on Acrylic Aquatint, it would be advisable to do so before proceeding.

6 There are two ways of approaching the airbrushing of this aquatint stencil. In the first instance, virtually any opaque airbrush paint or ink can be sprayed on this second drafting

Mylar aquatint stencil. If the airbrush spray totally blocks out the stencil, then an Aquatint Screen exposure will be required when making the second plate from this stencil.

If, however, in the second instance, you are able to apply the spray, and leave at least a 40% open area in the darkest area of the airbrush stencil, you can expose this directly to the second ImagOn plate without an Aquatint Screen exposure.

Thus, there are two distinct ways of approaching this second airbrush stencil at the plate-making stage. One will require an additional Aquatint Screen exposure step and the other will not. The second choice is preferable.

7 After the airbrush stencil has dried completely, the masking tape is removed, and the stencil is placed in a tray of water. Rub with a soft sponge until all the drawing fluid has dissolved.

Line/Aquatint Intaglio-Type

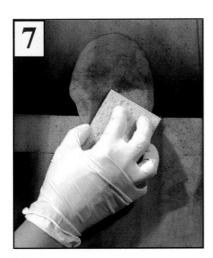

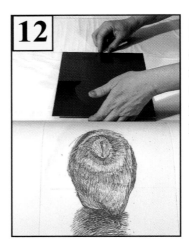

12 Using the press or block registration method, pull the first color print back and position the second plate for printing.

8 After the airbrush stencil has dried, expose it to the second ImagOn plate. Check the dot structure with a pocket microscope to see if this airbrush stencil needs to be exposed in conjunction with an Aquatint Screen. If it does, then do so. If not, expose this stencil for the same amount of time you would normally expose an Aquatint Screen.

The reason for using an Aquatint Screen or not is related to the quality of the final print. Where an Aquatint Screen is used, the image will print lighter; and where it is not, it will print darker.

9 Develop the plate in the soda ash developer, and process it as normal.

*TIP: Before you can proceed with the second plate printing, **you will need to make a registration templet**. (See the next page for this information.)*

10 It is assumed that you now have made two plates. One carries the line drawing, and the other carries the aquatint background information for this drawing. As you have two plates, you may choose to print them in two separate colors. Choose a plate to print first, and ink it up.

11 Position the first plate on the registration templet and print it.

13 Print the second Aquatint Intaglio-Type plate directly on top of the first plate.

TIP: Notice how the cutter is being used above to lift the plate off the registration templet.

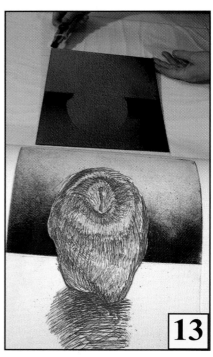

The two plate print is now finished. The concept presented here is a mere introduction in demonstrating the enormous image-making potential offered to the artist by multi-plate printmaking.

Line/Aquatint Intaglio-Type

Making a Registration Templet

1 Using a very economical type of plastic called P.E.T.G., with a thickness of .030, (See: www.lairdplastics.com) and a felt-tip permanent marker to make a registration templet. First, mark out the parameter of the paper size that you intend to use.

2 Then, position your copper Intaglio-Type plate in the center of the paper outline on the templet. Some printmakers place the plate off-center, allowing about 1" below the bottom edge of the print for signing off the print.

3 The registration templet is clamped under the top roller of the press; and the inked plate plate is positioned, ready for the printing paper. Notice the black felt-tip out line for the paper registration on the registration templet.

4 When two or more plates are printed with this registration method, it is best to leave the end of the printing paper clamped under the top press roller. This will allow you to lift the printing paper back, remove the printing plate, and replace it with the second printing plate. Printing the second plate involves lowering the clamped paper down onto this second printing plate and running it back through the press.

When a rotational blanket system is employed on an etching press, this method is cumbersome. Thus, the next method is recommended.

Blocking Registration

The next registration method uses unprinted newsprint as the registration templet and relies on the printer getting a small amount of printing ink on the back-side of the printing plate.

5 A piece of unprinted newsprint is placed onto the press bed. The inked Intaglio-Type plate is placed roughly in the center of this paper. Of course, you have the option to measure this placement before hand as demonstrated in the previous registration method.

6 The dampened etching paper is positioned on top of the plate; it is run through the press.

7a, b A block of steel is placed at the end of the printmaking paper. The paper is pulled backwards over this block of steel. The weight of the block allows the paper to remain in position, ready for the second plate printing.

Demonstration Layered Intaglio-Type plate in the developer showing the top layer of unexposed ImagOn floating off during development.

QUICK LOOK

1. Expose the first layer of ImagOn to the Aquatint Screen; or in this case, a text stencil created with a laser printer onto transparent film.

2. Apply a second layer of ImagOn with the wet-on-wet method.

3. Expose the top layer to an image; or in this case, a direct stencil using leaves.

4. Develop the plate and neutralize with white vinegar. Wash, dry, and then proof it.

Layered Intaglio-Type

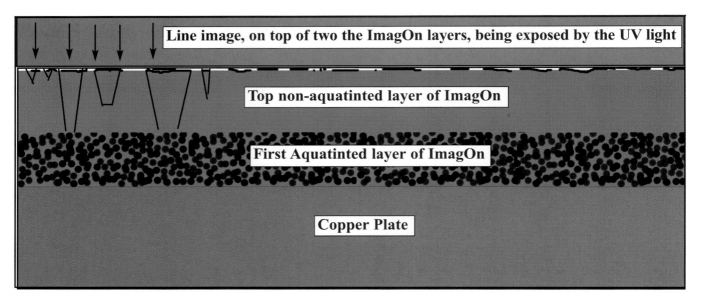

Line image, on top of two the ImagOn layers, being exposed by the UV light

Top non-aquatinted layer of ImagOn

First Aquatinted layer of ImagOn

Copper Plate

Introduction

Originally, I developed the Layered Intaglio-Type to compensate for stencils that resulted in open-bite areas in the final print. This technique involved applying a layer of ImagOn, aquatinting that layer, and then applying a second layer. An image would be exposed to this double layered ImagOn plate, and open areas of the top layer would develop down to the first layer. It was an "insurance layer" where almost any type of stencil could be successfully used without fear of open biting (unwanted open areas on a print that should print as black, but, don't) this was a simplistic application of the technique.

Ink-Emboss with Intaglio-Type

The implications of using two layers of ImagOn went beyond this "insurance layer" as greater deposits of ink were left on the plate, especially in the blackest areas. The result is ink embossing, is highly sought after by those etchers who like deeply bitten plates. There are several variations that can be employed for greater ink embossment:
1. Two layers of ImagOn are applied to the plate and aquatinted; then, a third layer is applied to which the image is exposed.

2. One layer of ImagOn is applied to the plate and aquatinted; then, two layers are applied on top and exposed to the image.

3. Three layers of ImagOn are applied to the plate, either exposed to the image or aquatinted, and then exposed to the image.

Layered Image with Intaglio-Type

Once the principle of open-biting is understood, the under-layers of the Layered Intaglio-Type plate can also be exposed to an image. This technique opens up a totally unique manner of plate-making. *In many stencils, open-biting can be created by not exposing an image which has open black areas to the aquatint screen. Once this point is understood, the creative potential of this technique can be more fully realized.*

Layered Intaglio-Type

In any traditional nitric acid-etch hard-ground technique where a line width is more than about 1/8th of an inch, open-biting will occur. In such instances, if open-biting is not desired, the plate needs to undergo a secondary "toxic" rosin aquatint and further nitric acid etch.

With the Layered Intaglio-Type technique, if the bottom layer of ImagOn is aquatinted, any thickness of line exposed to the top layer will be realized as a black area in the final print. This occurs in the plate during development where the image on the top layer develops down to the bottom second layer.

Layered Intaglio-Type

Drawing with toner-wash and various dip pens onto drafting Mylar makes a stencil which is ideal for this technique. There are also drafting pens with various thickness nibs that can be used for stencil making. These can be used when drawing directly on to the top Mylar of the ImagOn plate in the Direct Intaglio-Type technique.

There is no reason for the bottom layer of ImagOn to be always exposed to the aquatint screen. Other patterns or imagery can be substituted for the aquatint screen. In illustration on page 110, the bottom layer was exposed only to text. This variation further opens up the Layered Intaglio-Type technique to new dimensions of creative image development.

ImagOn ULTRA requires wet-lamination for successive layers (See the chapter on ImagOn lamination, pages 37 - 40). Following is a step-by-step description of the basic two layered technique. Applying a third layer is the same procedure as applying a second. I advise against using more than three layers of ImagOn at one time. By the time the developer has reached the bottom layer of film, the top layer will have over-developed. If more than three layers of ImagOn are desired, apply them after the three layer ImagOn plate has been completely developed. (See the next chapter on Construction Intaglio-Type).

Layered Intaglio-Type

1 After the first layer of ImagOn has been applied to the plate, it can be imaged, Aquatinted, or simply left unexposed.

2 Remove the top Mylar from the first layer of ImagOn before applying the second layer. Apply the second layer of ImagOn using the wet-lamination technique. We lamination is especially important with this technique as one 'dry' layer of ImagOn will instantly and prematurely stick to the another.

3 The Layered Intaglio-Type requires a prolonged development. Development is done in two stages: Stage ONE is normal still development for 9 minutes. Stage TWO requires that you sponge develop the plate for about 2 minutes. The key to successful hand development is to feel the tooth of the lower layer or layers of ImagOn with the development sponge.

4 Rinse, stabilize with a vinegar wash, rinse again, squeegee off the excess water, and dry.

5 The plate is now ready for printing.

Troubleshooting

This is by far the most difficult of the Intaglio-Type techniques to master as hand-development is required. The more layers, the more the level of difficulty. Another key to the success of this technique is to hand-develop selectively those areas of the plate that will eventually hold the most ink.

The clues to efficient development are visual, tactile, and audio. When a soft dish-washing type sponge or sponge-brush is rubbed over the plate, there is a distinctly soft, raspy sound that can be heard. Along with this sound, is a change in the tactile feel of the sponge. Keen observation along with both audio and tactile senses becomes an important indicator of successful plate-making.

Problem 1: Once a plate is proofed, the open-bite areas still print gray when they should be black **Solution:** *Clean the plate thoroughly, selectively re-develop the problem areas by hand, and re-proof.*

The greatest problem with this re-development technique is over-development. Keep a watchful eye on those areas of the plate that are most likely to over-develop. No matter what happens during re-development, I advise proofing the plate because there are always parts of the finished print where over-development is not noticeable. There is sometimes a fine line between scrapping a plate and starting over again or touching up the final print.

Applying Baby Powder to a Construction Intaglio-Type plate to prevent the ImagOn emulsion from sticking to the wash-drawing Mylar stencil.

QUICK LOOK

1. Remove the peel-back layer from the ImagOn film pieces and rub them onto the plate.

2. Rub baby powder into the surface of the ImagOn plate before image exposure.

3. Expose the ImagOn pieces to an image, or to the Aquatint Screen, or to both.

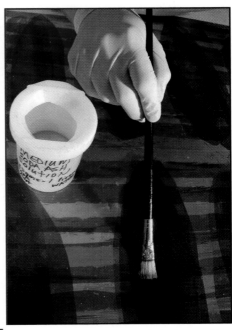

3. Brush develop with ImagOn developer. Wash, neutralize with vinegar, dry, and proof.

Construction Intaglio-Type

Introduction

The Construction Intaglio-Type is a technique where pieces of ImagOn are added to the plate and either developed and exposed together or separately. In some instances, the pieces of ImagOn are not exposed. This provides a way in which almost any plate can be creatively reworked.

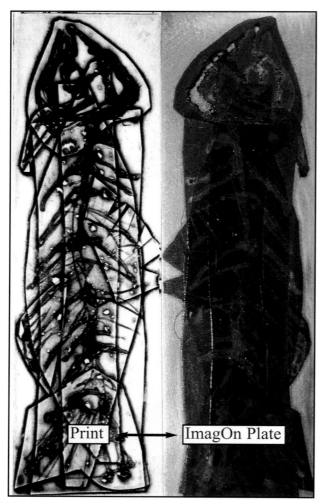

Print ⟶ ImagOn Plate

A bove: Leah Allen's "Fish", 2002, 6" x 1.5", Construction Intaglio-Type, the print is shown at left, opposite the ImagOn plate. Pieces of ImagOn were added to the plate to create the image. The pieces of ImagOn were then exposed to the Aquatint Screen followed by a spit-bite application on the plate. See also Leah's image on the outside back cover.

Materials

Same as Spit-Bite Intaglio-Type (See page 90).

Construction Intaglio-Type Step-by-Step

Any plate can be reworked with pieces of ImagOn film provided the 'carrier plate' is free of grease. The grease-free property of Akua Intaglio ink is idea if you wish to keep adding pieces of ImagOn after proofing.

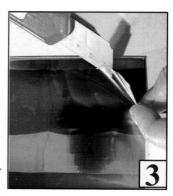

1   Cut pieces of ImagOn film to desired sizes and shapes. The circular shapes above were drawn with dry erase marker which can easily be removed before the Aquatint Screen exposure.

2   Individually remove the peel-back layer from the film, and apply the film to the plate.

3   Mylar is best removed by lifting one edge with a utility knife. Make sure not to overlap one piece of film onto another. This step can be done only after the top Mylar is removed from each piece of ImagOn film.

Construction Intaglio-Type

4 Position ImagOn pieces onto the carrier plate. Press and rub each piece of film onto the plate.

5 Once all the pieces of film have been hand-stuck to the plate, cover it with a larger piece of Mylar or ImagOn peel-back plastic and run through the etching press. This helps the smaller pieces of ImagOn to stick.

6 The ImagOn plate can be built up with a layering procedure that creates the effect of a 3D topographical map.

7 Before developing the plate, remove all the top Mylar layers from each piece of ImagOn. See point 3, which refers to removing Mylar if other layers of ImagOn are to be applied one on top of the other.

8 Development can be done in a tray with the normal soda ash developer or by brushing the developer onto the individual pieces of ImagOn film. (See the chapter on Spit-Bite Intaglio Type, pages 89-92, for more information about brush-on developing).

The Construction Intaglio-Type technique can be employed in plate-making to complement the image. One way to do this is to think of the individual strips, or set of strips, of ImagOn as different layers, as is commonly done in Photoshop. Each of the layers can be treated in a different manner.

Construction Intaglio-Type - Combination Techniques

1. If you are exposing one layer of ImagOn to leaves or other vegetation, one layer can be used with the Aquatint Screen and a second layer, on top, could be exposed without the Aquatint Screen exposure. Thus, open-bite areas from the top layer would develop down to the first layer allowing the first layer to merge through the second layer. (See the chapter on the Layered Intaglio-Type, pages 101-104).

2. This technique becomes more interesting if you use a different image or pattern between layers.

Also, the shape of the ImagOn pieces informs the design, especially if the shapes are repeated in different directions from one layer to the next. Highly intricate designs can be built up, layer upon layer. Once two or more layers have been made, it is advisable to brush-develop each piece of ImagOn individually. This allows more control of the image and prevents unwanted open-biting of the layers below.

After each development of the ImagOn, the plate should be stabilized with vinegar, washed, and heat-dried.

Troubleshooting

Problem 1: ImagOn pieces do not stick to the plate. *Solution: When reworking any ImagOn plate with the Construction Intaglio-Type technique sometimes the ImagOn pieces do not adhere to the plate. This happens especially when there are high relief areas on the plate which may have been made with the liquid aquatint or screen filler reworking techniques. ImagOn will not stick to any liquid aquatint areas. Also, ImagOn is reluctant to stick to exposed Imagon plates. If you wish to rework exposed imagOn plates, it is best to apply the ImagOn pieces by hand; then run the plate through the etching press. It is best to leave the plate until the next day to expose and re-develop it.*

Problem 2: The ImagOn plate sticks to the wash-drawing or inkjet film stencil because the top Mylar had been removed from the ImagOn plate. *Solution: Before exposing the ImagOn plate to an image rub a small amount of talcum powder into the surface of the plate with a clean dry cloth as illustrated at the beginning of this chapter.*

Problem 3: Some pieces of ImagOn did not develop. *Solution: Generally, this happens when the top Mylar of the ImagOn is not removed. It can get trapped below one or more over-layers of ImagOn. All that can be done is to remove this Mylar and re-develop. Sometimes this creates an unexpected and happy result.*

Applying a toner-wash directly to the top ImagOn Mylar layer for the Direct Intaglio-Type technique (Image by Keith Howard).

QUICK LOOK

1. Expose the ImagOn plate to the Aquatint Screen.

2. Paint Toner-Wash directly on top of the Mylar on the pre-Aquatinted ImagOn plate.

3. Re-expose the plate.

4. Remove the top Mylar from the ImagOn plate and still develop for 9 minutes. Fix with vinegar, wash, and heat-dry the plate. The plate is now ready for printing.

Direct Intaglio-Type

Introduction

The Direct Intaglio-Type is a great way to start. It is the most conservation conscious of the Intaglio-Type techniques. It uses the top Mylar covering of the ImagOn plate and also recycled toner-wash described in the Wash-Drawing Intaglio-Type chapter. It has the added advantage of the image being part of the plate ensuring optimum image-to-plate contact without the use of a vacuum frame.

If you want to work with continuous tone imagery, such is created with toner-washes, it will be necessary to Aquatint the plate before applying the toner-wash. If, however, you wish to work with line drawing, such as is created when working with drafting pens, the Aquatint exposure will not be needed. If you wish to work with lines, you can use those old fashioned dip pens, some known as Post Office or Crow Quill nibs, which can be dipped into the toner-wash solution. Bamboo pens also work well for thicker lines.

Materials

1. ImagOn coated plate.

2. Aquatint Screen.

3. Toner-Wash solution.

4. Selection of brushes and dip pen nibs.

5. ImagOn developer and normal plate processing equipment and materials.

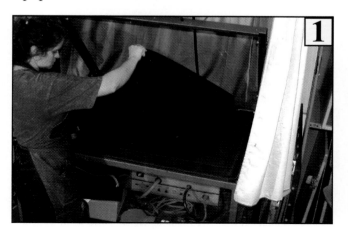

Direct Intaglio-Type Step-by-Step

1 The ImagOn plate is placed into the exposure unit and exposed to the Aquatint Screen. Illustrated is the Aquatint Screen being laid onto the Imagon plate in the exposure unit.

2 Paint toner-wash directly onto the pre-Aquatinted plate. Make sure that the wash is not more than about 1/8" thick on the surface.

3 Expose the Direct Intaglio-Type plate with toner-wash in the exposure unit. As the top Mylar of the ImagOn plate is in perfect contact with the ImagOn emulsion, the plate can be exposed without employing the vacuum.

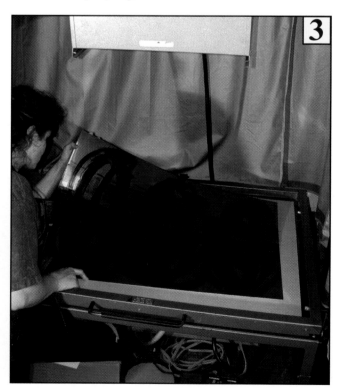

Direct Intaglio-Type

4 Pull back the top Mylar holding the toner-wash from the ImagOn plate. Notice the ghost image directly under the Mylar as you pull it off. This is an indication that the plate has received enough exposure. This Mylar toner-wash can be kept and reused to make additional plates.

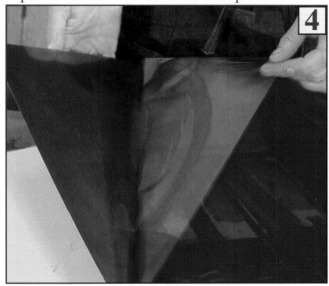

7 After the vinegar fix, wash the plate with water, squeegeeing off excess water in preparation for a final wipe with paper towel.

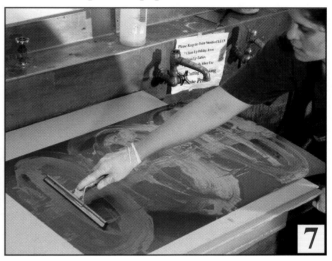

8 Heat-dry the plate with a heat gun or an industrial hand-dryer.

5 Still develop the plate for 9 minutes. During the final 20 seconds of the development period, use a soft sponge to wipe away the developed ImagOn emulsion. This presents a good chance to feel the 'tooth' of the plate indicating if the plate has fully developed.

6 After the plate has developed, wash it thoroughly. Spritz white vinegar onto the plate and rub it in.

9 The plate is ready to be inked and proofed in the normal manner.

See also Direct Stencil-making on page 108 #3. Soft-ground material, exposed directly to the plate, creates a great soft-ground substitute plate.

Crackle Intaglio-Type

QUICK LOOK

1. Remove the Mylar layer from an unexposed ImagOn plate.

2. Paint or card Gum Arabic onto the heated ImagOn plate and let the Gum dry completely.

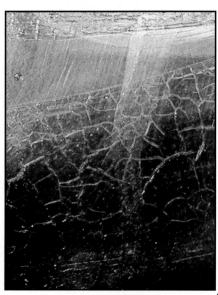

3. Still develop the plate for 8 to 9 minutes. Wash, neutralize with the vinegar wash, rinse, and dry. The plate is ready to be proofed.

Crackle Intaglio-Type

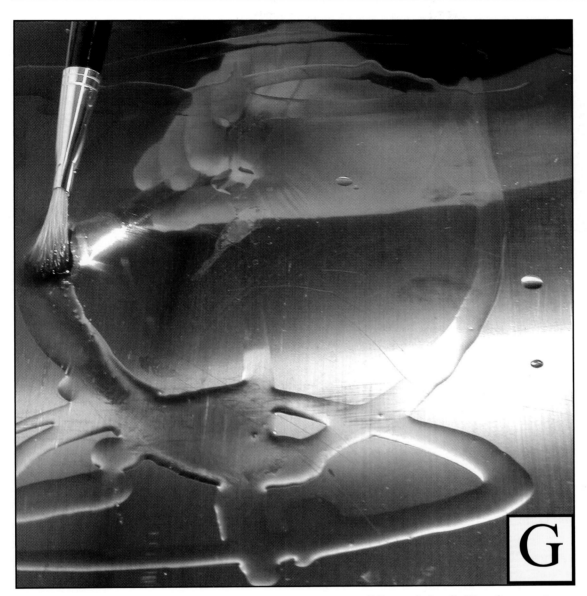

Introduction

The Crackle Intaglio-Type is a unique **non-exposure technique**. Gum Arabic is painted onto the unexposed ImagOn emulsion. It is heated until the gum cracks; the plate is developed, washed, and printed.

Materials & Equipment

1. ImagOn plate.

2. Gum Arabic.

3. Soda ash developer.

4. An inking hot-plate.

5. Brushes.

Crackle Intaglio-Type

Crackle Intaglio-Type Step-by-Step

1 Prepare an ImagOn plate in the usual manner.

2 Although a hair dryer or heat gun can be used, access to an inking hot-plate is an asset. Turn the heat setting to about 110 degrees F or just hot enough so that it will not burn your skin.

3 Remove the top Mylar. The Mylar is difficult to remove if the plate is hot.

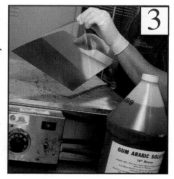

TIP: If this is the case, cool the plate under cold water before removing the Mylar.

5 Paint or card on Gum Arabic onto the ImagOn emulsion as it sits on the hot-plate. The thicker the Gum Arabic the larger the crackle will be. To selectively thin the Gum, water can be added before or after painting the Gum onto the plate resulting in finer crackles. You can first paint a design onto the plate with water, then paint Gum Arabic over the water design, following it closely as possible. Try to cover the entire plate with Gum and allow it to naturally mix with the water.

There are many interesting variations that can be applied with this technique. The ImagOn plate can be selectively brushed with *Future before applying the Gum Arabic (see illustration 5a and b).* This effects the way the plate crackles. The before and after illustrations were painted with Future, which is represented by the lighter crackled areas.

5a, b Illustrations above also show what the plate looks like with dried, crackled gum before it is developed. 5b Shows what the plate looks like after it has been developed.

Once the Gum Arabic is thoroughly dry, develop the plate in normal ImagOn soda ash developer for 8 to 9 minutes.

Thin Gum applications require shorter developing times; it may be advisable to remove it from the developer after 8 minutes.

These lighter areas of the plate were painted with Future first.

5a Plate before development.

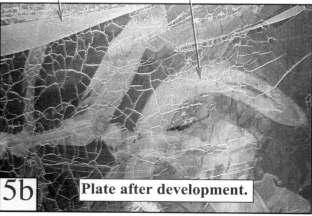

5b Plate after development.

Crackle Intaglio-Type

6 Immediately after development, thoroughly wash the plate in room temperature running water until all traces of the Gum have been removed.

7 Stabilize the plate by spritzing with a white vinegar wash.

8 Rinse the plate with water.

9 Squeegee off excess water, then wipe it with paper towel.

10 Heat dry the plate.

The Plate is now ready to proof

11 Once you have decided that the plate is finished, it should be light hardened. Put the plate, face up to the lamp, and expose it for the same time as you would an Aquatint Screen exposure.

Combination Techniques

1 One interesting combination technique is achieved by taking a plate that has been crackled, exposing it to the Aquatint Screen, and applying the **Spit-Bite Intaglio-Type** technique. Remember that the Crackle Intaglio-Type plate, in its original form, has never been exposed, thus it offers the potential to expose it to imagery.

2 Crackle Intaglio-Type works very well with the **Construction Intaglio-Type** technique as it injects a different linear element to the organic lines created by the crackle. Liquid aquatint and screen filler can also be added to the crackled plate for further plate re-working. Use unexposed pieces of ImagOn film to construct the ImagOn surface of the plate, and go through the crackle technique described in this chapter.

3 The ImagOn plate can also be Aquatinted before applying the Gum Arabic. If this is done, the developing time will need to be reduced by at least 1 minute for a total developing time of 8 minutes. If thin Gum solutions are used, the developing time should be further reduced to up to

5 minutes. If the plate is Aquatinted first, developing the plate for more than this recommended 5 minutes will result in the final print being too dark.

After the ImagOn plate has been crackled and processed and is ready to print, it is still sensitive to UV light. This allows the possibility for further image manipulation by exposing other images to the plate and re-developing it. If a portrait was to be exposed to this crackled plate, the crackle effect would disappear in the darker areas of the image, only to be visible in the lighter ones. Thus, there will be problems if this re-development is done in the normal manner; areas that had been thinned in the Crackle Intaglio-Type process will open-bite with further development. Avoid this problem by spit-bite development techniques to selectively develop any section of the plate.

Troubleshooting

Keep UV light well away from the plate during the entire procedure. If necessary, the Crackle Intaglio-Type plate can be covered with an aluminum roasting dish while it is drying on the hot-plate.

Problem 1: The first print may stick to the plate. **Probable cause:** There is some Gum Arabic left on the plate. ***Solution: Rinse the plate with water, and rub the paper off. Neutralize the plate more thoroughly with white vinegar.***

Problem 2: The Gum Arabic is too thin. **Probable cause:** It was made up with too much water. ***Solution: Either leave a jar or developing dish out in the sun and allow the water content of the Gum to evaporate, or put it in a saucepan and slowly heat it until it thickens.***

Problem 3: The crackle is too big. **Probable cause:** The Gum is too thick. ***Solution: Dilute it with water and apply it thinly.***

Applying the wrinkled ImagOn film, to the plate, prior to running it through the press.

QUICK LOOK

 1. After the exposing ImagOn film, peel back both the top mylar and the peel-back layer.

 2. Wrinkle and place the ImagOn film onto the carrier plate.

3. Cover the plate with Mylar and run it through the press.

4. Develop the plate (above) and then print the plate.

Wrinkled Intaglio-Type

Introduction

First developed by Elizabeth Dove, the Wrinkled Intaglio-Type technique enables a unique distortion of the image made possible by the 'relative' elastic properties of the ImagOn ULTRA emulsion. The ImagOn film is exposed to an image prior to laminating it to a plate. After exposure and before lamination, the peel-back and Mylar layers are removed from the ImagOn leaving just the ImagOn "elastic" emulsion. This emulsion is immediately distorted by stretching, ripping, and pulling it. Then it is adhered to the plate by running it through the etching press after which it is developed and proofed.

Beyond the Basic Concept

The concept of the Wrinkled Intaglio-Type is that simple and "interesting results" are easily obtained. Having worked with this technique for a number of years, I have found that its creative potential is governed by the various ways in which images are exposed both to the Wrinkled ImagOn film and, also, to the carrier plate film. (This technique works best if the carrier plate already has an exposed or unexposed layer of ImagOn film.) Thus, there are at least two layers of ImagOn film on the plate allowing for image overlay, manipulation, and interaction that would otherwise be impossible through any other plate-making technique.

The 'carrier layer', which has a normal layer of ImagOn film on the plate, can be left unexposed, or it can be exposed to an image or to the aquatint screen. There are a few creative combinations that are employed when working with the carrier and wrinkled layers of ImagOn.

For instance:

A. The carrier plate film layer may have a similar or totally different image than the wrinkled layer.

B. Images can be reversed from one layer to the next.

C. Images can be exposed in combination with the Aquatint Screen or without. Images exposed without the Aquatint Screen promote open-biting on one layer. This factor can be utilized if this open biting was on the top layer, thus allowing the developer to reach down through the open-bite areas to the bottom layer.

Materials

Normal ImagOn plate-making materials and equipment.

Wrinkled Intaglio-Type
Step-by-Step

The Wrinkled Layer of film is exposed to an image BEFORE it is laminated to the plate.

1 Prepare the plate as you would for an Intaglio-type.

2 Apply one normal layer of ImagOn ULTRA film to the plate. This layer could be exposed to an Aquatint Screen, an image, or to both. It could also be left unexposed.

3 Cut the ImagOn film so that it is the same size as the image or stencil (sometimes referred to as the 'film positive', 'positive', 'art-work' or Mylar drawing).

4 Place the ImagOn film into the exposure unit with the art-work on top of the film. Remember that the ImagOn film has two sides. The peel-back side is the side that is adhered to the plate. Make sure to expose through the top Mylar and not the peel-back layer side.

Tip: Some vacuum exposure frames have a highly textured mat which can impart an unwanted texture into the ImagOn film while it is being exposed. If this is the case, place a black piece of cardboard on the vacuum frame bed before exposure.

5 Expose the image to the ImagOn film.

Tip: Use the same image exposure as you would if the ImagOn was adhered to a plate.

Wrinkled Intaglio-Type

The next steps are carried out at the etching press bed

6 Remove the top Mylar from the ImagOn "carrier" plate, and place the plate on the etching press bed. Immediately spritz it with water.

7 After taking the ImagOn film (the film to be wrinkled) from the exposure unit, remove both the peel-back and Mylar layers from the ImagOn. This removal process is facilitated with masking or packing tape. One side has the stiff Mylar and the other has the soft peel-back layer. Pay attention to which side is the top and which is the bottom. The soft peel-back side of the ImagOn film is easier to remove than the stiffer Mylar side. Slightly pull back the soft peel-back layer and "dog-ear" it. Then attach a small corner of the ImagOn film to a piece of reversed (sticky side up) packing tape and pull it to uncover the Mylar layer on top (as demonstrated in illustration **7** below).

TIP: The topside is the one with the stiff Mylar.

8 Separate both the inside peel-back layer, the ImagOn emulsion, and the stiffer top Mylar layer. This makes it easier to remove quickly both layers when it comes time to wrinkle and apply it to the plate.

9 At this stage, the ImagOn carrier plate (seen in the background of illustration 10) has had the top Mylar removed and was spritzed with water while awaiting the application of the wrinkled ImagOn.

10 It is time to completely remove the top Mylar and the peel-back layer. Do this quickly while remembering that the correct side to be stuck is the side where the peel-back layer was removed. If you put this wrinkled side upside down, it will not work very well. How the film is applied is very important.

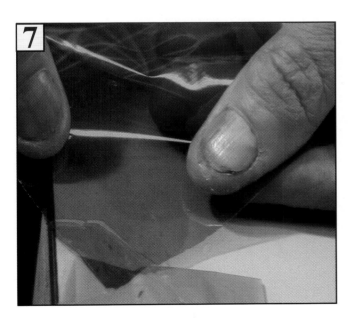

Wrinkled Intaglio-Type

TIP: Step 10 should be done quickly. If the ImagOn emulsion is left unprotected by its sandwich of plastic, it becomes brittle and hard to manipulate.

11 Stretch and wrinkle the film and position the wrinkled ImagOn onto the surface of the wet ImagOn plate. A ghost image should be present in the ImagOn film so that some control can be exercised when manipulating it.

12 Lay the discarded peel-back and Mylar pieces onto the top of the plate. This cover layer prevents the ImagOn from sticking to the etching felts.

13 Run this plate through the etching press; remove the cover layer of Mylar and peel-back pieces.

14 Still develop the plate in the normal soda ash developing solution for 9 minutes. Always cover the developing tray to avoid room light exposing the ImagOn plate.

15 While wearing rubber gloves, use a soft sponge and hand develop the wrinkled portions of the image for at least 1 minute. The tooth of the image developing should be clearly felt through the developing sponge. Concentrate this stage of the developing action to the wrinkled piece of ImagOn film.

16 Rinse with water.

17 Neutralize the plate with vinegar spray, rinse with water, heat dry and then proof.

Wrinkled Intaglio-Type

Troubleshooting

Problem 1: ImagOn top Mylar layer is difficult to remove from ImagOn film to be wrinkled *Solution: Stick masking or packing tape to the tabletop, reversing this tape so that the sticky side is up. Dog-ear the peel-back inside layer first as this is the easier layer to remove. This can be done by sticking the peel-back layer to the sticky tape and pulling. At this stage, only pull back the edge of the peel-back layer as you would to ear-mark a page in a book. There will be a small amount of ImagOn emulsion revealed. This is stuck to the sticky tape and pulled in such a manner that the the corner of the film is left behind on the sticky tape. This then reveals the top Mylar. Now, it is easy to fold it back in preparation for executing the Wrinkled Intaglio-Type technique. (Illustration 7 shows the ImagOn emulsion being stuck to the tape).*

Problem 2: The ImagOn film (to be wrinkled) becomes very brittle after both the peel-back and Mylar layers are removed. Loosing its elasticity to the point where it fractures into little pieces....*Solution.... Work as quickly as possible as the ImagOn emulsion is rapidly attacked by oxygen after the peel-back and Mylar layers have been removed. Oxidization causes the ImagOn emulsion to loose most of its elasticity. This characteristic of ImagOn film demands a rapid response when plate making using this particular technique.*

Problem 3: The image, which was exposed to the wrinkled ImagOn film, did not appear in the final print. *Solution: If the ImagOn film received the correct exposure, the most probable cause for this problem is that the Imagon film, to be wrinkled, was applied upside down. In other words, the image was exposed through the top side of the film, which is the Mylar side. If this Mylar side was stuck to the ImagOn carrier plate, it will not develop very well at all. At the very best, the blackest areas may develop. The rest of the tonal range of the image is held in the actual thickness of the ImagOn film. In this instance, it is upside down and thus hidden.*

Problem 4: The image on the carrier plate open-bites before the top wrinkled layer of ImagOn is fully developed. *Solution: When it comes to the hand development stage of the plate-making, concentrate the hand development only to the top wrinkled layer of ImagOn. Using a sponge-brush is an easy way to do this.*

Problem 5: The final print is dominated by the actual wrinkled areas and not by the actual image it was exposed to. *Solution: Not every image is suitable for the Wrinkled Intaglio-Type technique. If the image used is very abstracted, this technique will only abstract it further. It may be better to work with more discernable realistic images which would then become distorted by this unique plate-making technique.*

This plate-making technique speaks to the originality of the original print and is limited to the number of prints that the plate will print. It is impossible to accurately duplicate any plate with this technique.

Keith Howard, **Override**, 2002, Construction Intaglio-Type, 3.25" x 4.25".

Etched Intaglio-Type plate being removed from a ferric chloride etching solution. Areas that did not etch will remain a light blueish color and areas that etched will be copper in color.

QUICK LOOK

1. **Thin the ImagOn plate in a 10 gram soda ash developer for 7 to 8 mins. Wash, stabilize with vinegar wash, dry, and rub with a soft cloth and talc.**

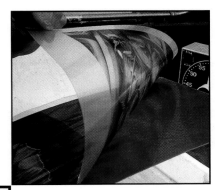

 2. **Expose an Epson halftone image onto the plate for the same length of time as an Aquatint.**

3. **Still develop the plate for 2 mins. Hand develop, as above, for about 15 sec.** **3**

4 4. **Etch the plate in ferric chloride or Edinburgh Etch solution for 1 hour, water rinse plate, dry and proof.**

Etched Intaglio-Type

UV EXPOSURE onto a thinned and unthinned ImagOn plate

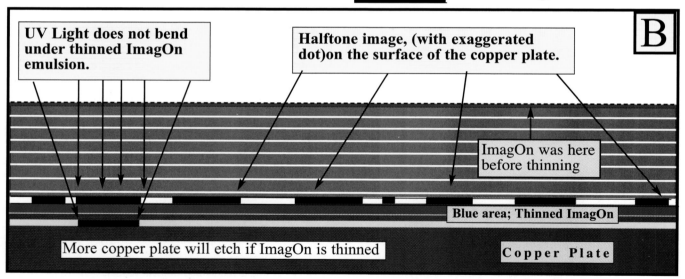

UV Light bending under ImagOn emulsion

Halftone image with exaggerated dot

A

UV light bends under halftone dots before ImagOn is thinned. White lines indicate 8 minute intervals where ImagOn will be thinned

ImagOn Ultra side view

Less copper plate will etch if ImagOn is not thinned

Copper Plate

ABOVE: ImagOn film before thinning

BELOW: After ImagOn is thinned

B

UV Light does not bend under thinned ImagOn emulsion.

Halftone image, (with exaggerated dot)on the surface of the copper plate.

ImagOn was here before thinning

Blue area; Thinned ImagOn

More copper plate will etch if ImagOn is thinned

Copper Plate

Introduction

Imagon ULTRA film is applied to the plate, and it is placed in a soda ash developing solution for 7 to 8 minutes where it is thinned. At this stage, the soda ash developer is a *Thinning Solution*. The thinned ImagOn emulsion is then exposed to a halftone image and re-developed. The plate is etched and printed.

The thickness of ImagOn ULTRA film is what enables the non-etch techniques to hold the full tonal range of an image within the thickness of the film. If you want to etch an image into a copper plate, the thickness of the ImagOn film can be a limiting factor. This is due to the UV image exposure to the plate, and way in which the UV light is diffracted by the thickness of the ImagOn film. Thinning the film on the plate reduces this diffraction proportionately. There is a simple method to thin the ImagOn emulsion while it is on the *metal plate*. Not only can the ImagOn emulsion be thinned to about a 10 micron layer, but it can be thinned to any degree depending on how long the ImagOn plate is left in the "thinning solution".

Etched Intaglio-Type

The MOST IMPORTANT Step Test

By now, you should have made a step test to determine the correct strength of the developing solution relative to the pH of the water and the type of soda ash used. This step test plate is **extremely important** in ensuring correct developer strength and, in this instance, the strength of the thinning solution. This test also shows clearly through the color change of the ImagOn, how thinning each segment affects the ImagOn emulsion on the plate.

Diagrams [A] and [B], on the previous page, demonstrate why thinned ImagOn performs so well as an etch resist.

Diagram [A] shows the ImagOn emulsion, before thinning, and the degree to which the UV exposure light bends under this thick emulsion. It also shows 8 white lines representing 1 minute intervals whereby the emulsion can be thinned.

Diagram [B] shows the emulsion, after it has been thinned for 8 minutes, and how little the UV exposure light can bend under a thin ImagOn layer.

The Etched Intaglio-Type technique is best used with halftone imagery created through inkjet laser printers, through image-setters, or in the darkroom with lith film. (See the chapter on the Digital Halftone Intaglio-Type, P. 137-148). Line drawing stencils, similar to hard-ground lines, can be made with pen and ink onto drafting Mylar.

Some textured polycarbonate films, such as, True-Grain, Artex textured film and thin textured Lexan, can also be used with pencil or crayon drawing and toner-wash techniques for hand-made stencils. The texture of these films imparts a random dot structure into the painted or drawn stencil which simulates the dot structure of the halftone image.

Tip 1: When employing the Etched Intaglio-Type method, if the image is exposed first to an Aquatint Screen and secondly, to the image, only the blackest areas of this image will etch. The use of the Aquatint Screen is meant strictly for non-etch techniques.

Tip 2: Do not expose the plate to excess light at any stage during the entire procedure. This is the one Intaglio-Type technique where it is advised to turn off room lights and work with low ambient light only.

Etched Intaglio-Type Step-by-Step

1 Prepare the copper plate by sanding with 600 grit wet-and-dry sandpaper to a mirror finish.

2 Laminate the ImagOn in the recommended manner.

3 Prepare a 10 gm soda ash developing solution. This solution is also the "thinning" and developing solution and must be precisely measured.

4 Set the timer for 7 or 8 minutes. 8 minutes is recommended for the highest resolution (400 DPI) images.

5 Remove the top Mylar from the ImagOn plate.

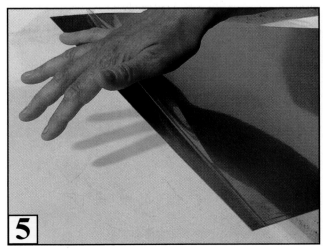

Etched Intaglio-Type

6 Place the ImagOn plate, with Mylar removed, into the thinning (developing) solution for 7 - 8 minutes. **DO NOT AGITATE SOLUTION.**

This 7 - 8 minute procedure will thin, or erode, the film sufficiently to capture the detail in a 400 line halftone. When Epson 3000 and Epson 7600 halftones are made at the highest resolution, according to the instructions in this book, the thinning time is only 7 minutes. If using an 85 line halftone, a thinning time of 5 minutes is recommended. (Go to the chapter on Digital Halftone Intaglio-Type to learn how to make Epson 3000 and Epson 7600 digital inkjet film halftones P. 137-148).

7 Put on rubber gloves. Remove the plate from the developer and rinse off the loose ImagOn emulsion in room temperature running water. Gently rub with a soft sponge until all loose residue is completely removed. At this stage, it will be difficult to detect the presence of any ImagOn on the plate as it should be very thin.

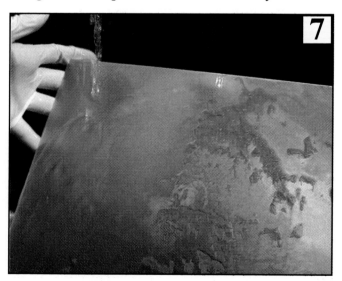

8 Remove the plate from the water and spritz with vinegar. This will stop the development. Rub the vinegar into the film very gently.

9 Pat dry with paper towel.

10 Heat dry for about 1 min. per. sq. ft. of plate.

11 With a soft cloth, rub a small amount of baby powder into the surface of the thinned ImagOn plate. This will prevent the halftone or stencil from sticking to the ImagOn emulsion during exposure.

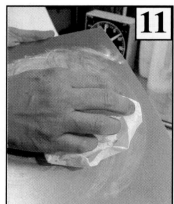

The Plate is Now Ready for Halftone Image Exposure

12 Expose the thinned ImagOn plate to a halftone positive or a line drawing in the exposure unit. Use the same exposure as you would for an Aquatint Screen exposure.

TIP: Remember that you should not be using an Aquatint Screen exposure during the Etched Intaglio-Type technique. Also, keep the vacuum on for at least 1 minute before exposure. This ensures a good plate to halftone contact.

13 After exposure, still develop the plate for 2 minutes.

14 Hand develop for 10-15 sec. using a soft sponge. This final stage of development ensures that all ImagOn emulsion residue is removed from the positive image areas on the plate. These are the areas that will eventually etch; and if a microscopic amount of ImagOn is left in these areas, it will impede the etch.

Etched Intaglio-Type

15 Take the plate from the developer and rinse it with room temperature running water.

16 Spritz with vinegar.

17 Rinse with water and heat-dry.

18 Cover the back of the plate with plastic packing tape to protect it from the corrosive action of the ferric chloride.

19 After backing the plate, make a plate hanger with the plastic packing tape.

TIP: Write your initials and the time that the plate went into the etchant on the tail end of the tape hanger (as demonstrated in illustration 19).

20 Hang the plate into the ferric chloride or Edinburgh Etch tank, and do an 'inspection etch' for about 5 minutes. Shown is the Pro-Vertical Etching Tank. (Ordering details are in the Sources and Supply chapter of this book, P. 238.).

21 Pull the plate out of the etching solution after 5 minutes, rinse with water, Inspect the surface of the plate for areas that did not etch. Areas that did not etch will remain a light blueish color. Areas that have etched will be copper in color.

22 **Brush soda ash developer into these areas of the plate that may have not etched for about 15 sec.** Wash and place the plate back into the ferric chloride for an additional 5 minutes.

Tip: Sponge brushes work best for soda ash brush developing.

23 If necessary, inspect the plate again for areas that may not be etching. You can only 'brush' develop the plate a few times before the film resist breaks down.

24 Etch the plate in the ferric chloride for 30-60 minutes or the Edinburgh Etch for 20-30 minutes; then, rinse in running water, and check the depth of the bite by proofing the plate. Because of their water-solubility, Akua Intaglio inks are ideal for both proofing and editioning the plate. If the plate has not etched sufficiently, wash the ink off the plate with soapy water and re-etch it.

Tip: Fresh ferric chloride can etch a good black in about 30 minutes. The older the ferric, the longer it will take to etch. Make a step-test plate to determine the optimum etching times.

Etched Intaglio-Type

Big Tip: *Leave the ImagOn emulsion on the plate after etching it, and complete printing the edition. The ImagOn emulsion should only be removed after the edition has been printed. If the Etched Intaglio-Type plate has not fully etched, the thin layer of ImagOn resist on the plate may hold sufficient detail to ensure a successful printing. If, however, this ImagOn layer is removed, along with some detail, conventional plate re-working will need to be employed. Ideally, the plate proofed with the ImagOn on it should have the same degree of detail as the proof pulled from the same plate, with the ImagOn removed.*

Tip : Because ImagOn has a glass-like surface, leaving the ImagOn on the plate also helps the inking and wiping of the plate.

Etched Intaglio-Type for Hand-Made Stencils
For the Etched Intaglio-Type technique to work successfully, there must be some kind of dot structure to the image. The halftone dot structure, created when images are produced through computers or even through the lith film and halftone screen process, is ideal for the Etched Intaglio-Type technique.

If you wish to have Etched Intaglio-Type images without the use of a digital halftone you can work directly onto textured Mylar. You can simulate the dot structure of a halftone, by drawing directly onto a variety of textured films, such as True-Grain film, Artex Textured Film or textured Lexan film. These films have an exaggerated tooth and when drawn on with graphite or charcoal pencils, result in a stencil with a strong random dot pattern. Toner-washes can also be applied to these textured films. The one caution, when using these textured films, is to be careful not to apply the drawing or painting medium too thickly. Thick deposits of crayon, graphite, or toner-wash can cover up the random dot structure of these Mylar type films that is necessary for the Etched Intaglio-Type plate to be completely successful.

Troubleshooting
The biggest problem, with the etched Intaglio-Type technique, is lack of accuracy, when making the soda ash developer. If the developer is too strong, the pre-thinning time of 7-8 minutes will be too long. If the developer is too hot, it may completely strip the Imagon emulsion from the plate. I was teaching a summer workshop at the College of Santa Fe where one room was unusually hot, in comparison to the rest of the printmaking studio. In the 'hot-room' the ImagOn developer acted more like a stripping solution than a developer. It would completely strip ImagOn film from a plate within the 7-8 minute recommended thinning time.

If the soda ash is too weak, a portion of the copper plate that should have etched, will not etch.

Thus, the step-test shown in the Mix and Test Chapter is extremely important in learning how to completely control the results for the Etched Intaglio-Type.

Problem 1: The ImagOn emulsion is completely gone after the pre-thinning step. **Probable cause:** The soda ash solution was either too strong, or too hot, or the length of time the plate was left in the pre-thinning solution was too long. ***Solution:*** *Go to the Mix and Test chapter of this book and redo the step-test. You will need to ascertain the correct strength of the ImagOn developer, relative to the hardness or softness of the water used, and to re-make the developer. Use a gram scale and litre measuring beaker to measure the correct amount of soda ash and water for the ImagOn developer and thinning solution. Make sure that the thinning and developing solutions are in a room which is not hotter than 70°F.*

Problem 2: The Etched Intaglio-Type plate does not completely etch. **First Probable cause:** There is still a microscopic veil of ImagOn emulsion on some areas of the plate that are not etching. ***Solution:*** *Take the Etched Intaglio-Type*

Etched Intaglio-Type

plate from the etchant about 5 minutes after it has etched. Inspect the surface to look for the tell-tail sign that the plate did not etch: blueish areas of the plate that represent slight ImagOn residue on the plate. Use a sponge brush to re-develop these areas for 15 - 30 seconds or until you can see them open up. Wash the plate, re-etch, and re-inspect. Caution: If you do this too many times, there is a chance that all the ImagOn emulsion will be removed.

Second Probable cause: Areas of ImagOn emulsion that should have developed away, remain on the plate if the halftone was exposed too long to the thinned ImagOn emulsion. *Solution: Reduce the exposure time of the halftone to the thinned ImagOn plate while it is in the exposure unit. Also, a inkJet halftone which is also comprised of thinned or inferior ink will allow the UV exposure light source to pass though it, causing some areas of ImagOn emulsion to harden. The actual halftone used should be composed of opaque dots that have good UV light stopping power. If not, a good plate cannot be expected.*

Third Probable cause: If, at some point, the ImagOn emulsion is exposed to stray UV light, it will cause the emulsion to seal the plate from the corrosive attack of the etchant. *Solution: Take every precaution to make sure the plate does not get any exposure to stray UV light. This may mean turning the room lights off and/or blocking potential light leaks from windows, doors, or skylights with masking film or black-out curtains.*

Problem 3: Some areas of the plate open-bite. **First Probable cause:** The ImagOn emulsion was developed off the plate where it was needed. *Solution: During the hand developing stage of this process, be extremely careful to avoid over-developing the most fragile areas of the plate. Generally these areas are where the plate yields the richest blacks in the final print.*

Second Probable cause: The plate was left too long in the ferric chloride or the Edinburgh Etch. *Solution: Reduce the etching time. If you notice open biting soon enough, it is possible to spray-aquatint these open-bite areas with acrylic aquatint solution or Speedball Screen Filler. First, wash the plate and de-oxidize it by putting the plate into a vinegar salt solution for a minute or so. Dry the plate and mask out areas that do not need aquatinting by painting Lanolin or Gum Arabic onto them; airbrush the acrylic or Speedball Screen Filler onto the areas that do need aquatinting. After the screen filler or acrylic has dried, wash away the Lanolin or Gum with water, and re-etch the plate.*

Problem 4: The edges of the plate over-etch. **Probable cause:** The ImagOn emulsion is extremely thin at the edge of the plate and is, generally, unprotected from the corrosive attack of the etchants. Unavoidable undercutting by the etchant occurs at the edges. *Solution: Cut the copper plate so that it is exactly 1/4" larger than the size of the halftone. Thus, when it is exposed to the ImagOn plate, there is a 1/4" edge around the plate. This border can be left on the plate for editioning or it can be removed with the plate cutter. In any case, trimming the plate is the simplest solution to this endemic problem. Knowing the outcome allows you to deal with it before it happens.*

Problem 5: There are no white areas where there should be in the final print. **Probable cause:** The copper plate was not polished enough in the initial plate preparation stage. If, for instance, the plate is sanded with 320 grit wet-and-dry sandpaper, a tooth on the copper plate is left that will eventually hold plate tone. *Solution: If necessary, polish the plate like a mirror before applying the ImagOn. Also, leaving the ImagOn emulsion on the plate for the editioning process eliminates unwanted plate tone, as correctly exposed ImagOn has a glass-like finish which does not hold any ink.*

Digital Halftone Intaglio-Type

Using an EPSON Stylus™ Pro 7600, UltraChrome ink and Apple computer with Adobe Photoshop 7

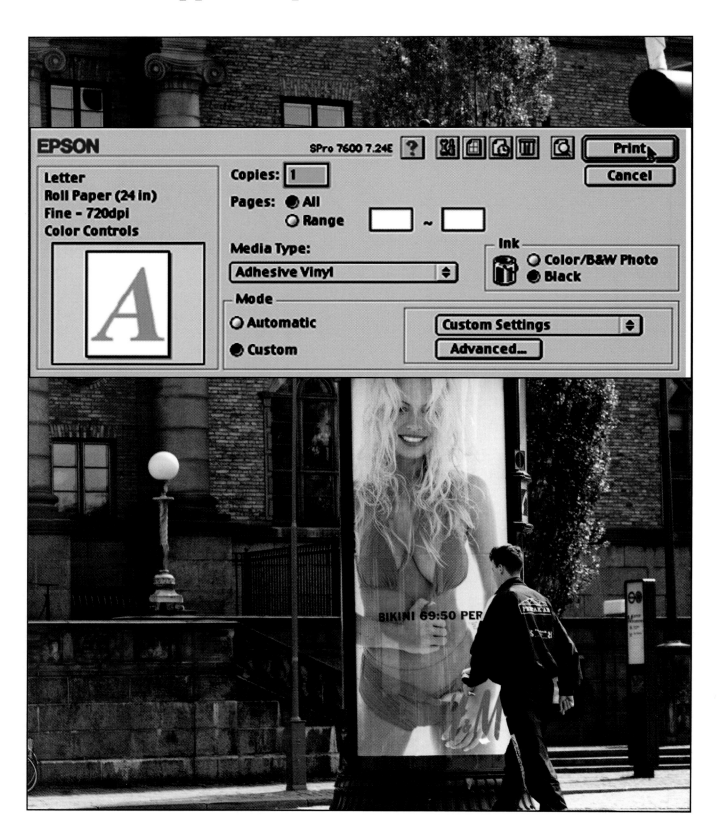

Digital Halftone Intaglio-Type

Using an EPSON Stylus™ Pro 7600,UltraChrome
ink and Apple computer with Adobe Photoshop 7

The Epson 7600 has three printer modes. The following instructions are designed for the Dual Matte Mode. Go to pages 5-13 to 5-19, of your Epson 7600 manual and change mode.

QUICK LOOK

1 Open image in Photoshop. Go to the pull down menu and highlight <Image> then <Image Size>. Resize image.

2 In the pull down menu, select <Image> <Adjustments> <Levels>. Adjust levels by aligning triangular sliders under each end of the graph. Click OK.

3 Go to the pull down menu, highlight, and select <Image> <Adjustments> <Curves>. In the Curves dialog box, click on the diagonal line; and in the <Output> box, type in **30.** Press OK.

4 Under the Apple icon, in the top left hand corner of the screen, press and drag down to <Chooser> and select the **SPro 7600**

5 Go to <Page Setup> under <File>.

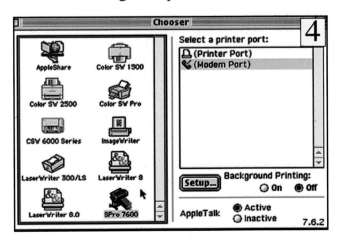

6 Select the media size under **Paper Size.** If you are using roll film, you will need to click on **Customize.**

7 Select **New** and type in the size of your image in the measurements boxes at left. Double click on Untitled and give it a name.

8 Click on **Custom** and Advanced.

9 Under **Media Type**, select Adhesive Vinyl, which then defaults to a **Print Quality** of Fine - 720dpi. Then go to **Ink,** and click on Black. Make sure that High Speed is unchecked. Press OK.

10 Visually inspect your setting on this box. Press OK.

11 Uncheck **Auto Cut.** Uncheck **Color Printing.** Press OK.

12 Make a final check of your settings. Click on OK. All dialog boxes will disappear.

13 Now go to <File> <Print> in the pull down menu. All your printer settings will be shown on this page.

14 Wait until the printer stops printing and cut the image from the roll.

Once the digital halftone is made it is exposed directly to the ImagOn plate, without an Aquatint Screen exposure, for both the Etched and Non-Etch Intaglio-Type techniques.

Digital Halftone Intaglio-Type

Using the EPSON Stylus™ 7600 with UltraChrome inks

Making a Digital Halftone on the Epson 7600 - UltraChrome™

It is assumed that the image will be printed from Adobe Photoshop. Open the image in Photoshop: go to the pull down menu and select <Image> <Mode> <Grayscale>. If this is a colored image, you may want to make a duplicate file and work on it. Also, make sure that the Epson 7600 printer driver has been chosen. This is selected in the <Chooser>.

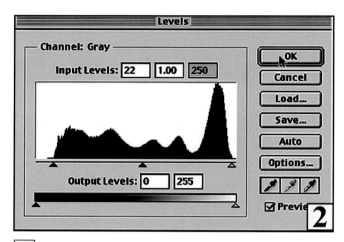

1 Go to the pull down menu and highlight <Image>; pull down to <Image Size>. The above dialog box appears. Highlight **Resolution** and make it 300 pixels/inch. Make your image the size you want within the restraints of the printer capability. The maximum printable width, for the Epson 7600, is 23.5" by whatever length desired (when roll transparent film is used in the printer). For the sample image used in this chapter, it is 23.5" x 14".

TIP: For film economy, orient your image or images to the 23.5" maximum width.

2 Go to the pull down menu; highlight and select <Image> <Adjustments> <Levels>. A dialogue box appears as follows: See illustration 2 on opposite page. Directly under the Levels graph are sliding triangular adjustments. Images vary and some will not require adjustment. Make sure the triangular adjustment points, to the left and right side of this graph, line up on the length of this graph. Click OK.

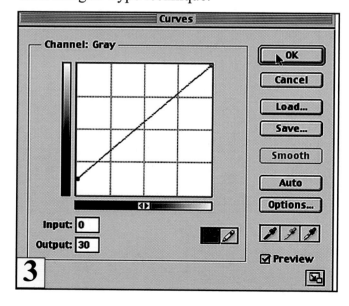

3 Go to the <Image> pull down menu; highlight and select <Adjustments> <Curves>. Dialogue box appears as follows. In the Curves dialogue box, click on the diagonal line and then in the **Output** box. Type in **30** and then press OK. Notice how the diagonal line, in the curve graph, has moved up to the left, as shown in illustration 3. The image appears as a grey and white image, not as a black and white one. Our aim is to create a halftone, which has an inherent random dot structure. In this way we will not need an Aquatint Screen exposure, just one ImagOn plate exposure to the digital halftone. While this results in the highest quality non-etch Intaglio-Type print, it also allows us to use this digital halftone for the Etch Intaglio-Type technique.

Digital Halftone Intaglio-Type

Using the EPSON Stylus™ 7600 with UltraChrome inks

4 Under the Apple icon, in the top left corner of the screen, press and drag down to <Chooser> and select the **SPro 7600**, by clicking on it, and then you will be required to select a printer port.

5 After you have chosen the correct printer port

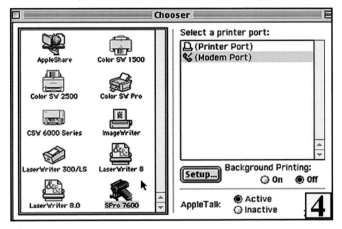

the computer looks for the connection route to the printer. If the printer is on and you have chosen the correct routing you will be prompted to go to <File> <Page Setup> in the drag down menu.

6 The below Page Setup dialog box appears. Select the media size under **Paper Size.** If you are using roll film you will need to click on **Customize**.

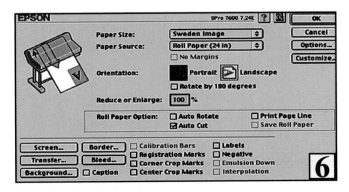

TIP: You will be using film, so do not be confused with the use of the word **Paper Size** *in this dialogue box.*

7 The above dialogue box appears. Select **New** and type in the size of your image in the measurements boxes at left. You may then wish to give this image size a name by double clicking the highlighted untitled segment of the box. Type in a name, press OK, then click **Options**:

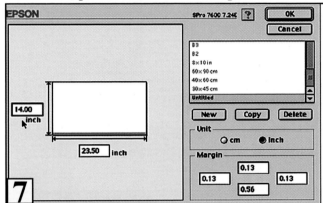

8 The above dialogue box appears. Click on **Custom,** and then Advanced.

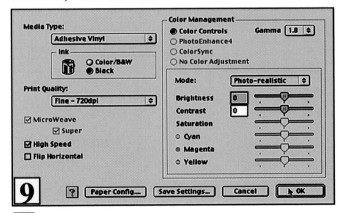

9 The above dialogue box appears. Under **Media Type**, select Adhesive Vinyl, which then defaults to a **Print Quality** of Fine - 720dpi Then go to **Ink,** and click on Black. Make sure that High Speed is unchecked. All the other settings in this box then go to a default setting. Press OK.

Digital Halftone Intaglio-Type

Using the EPSON Stylus™ 7600 with UltraChrome inks

10 The above dialogue box appears. Visually inspect your setting in this box. Press OK.

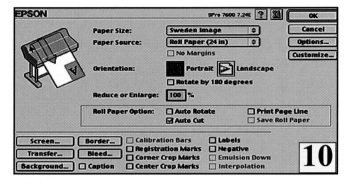

11 The above dialogue box appears. Uncheck **Auto Cut** and **Color Printing.** Press OK.

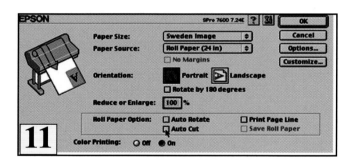

12 The final box appears above which allows you to check all the settings that the printer will use next. Click on OK. All dialogue boxes will disappear.

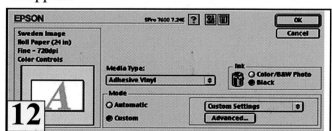

BIG TIP*: If you have not done so already you will need to change the printing mode of the Epson 7600. Go to pages 5-13 to 5-19 of your Epson 7600 owners manual and follow the steps in setting up this printer in the Dual Matte Mode.* **The instructions, given here, are designed only for Dual Matt Mode printing.** The reason for

this is that the other two choices of printing mode use a Light Black ink cartridge, which produces a translucent dot. This dot becomes over-exposed during plate-making resulting in approximately 20 to 30% of the image dropping out in the final printing.

When the Dual Matte Mode is selected the number of printer options is restricted, especially the output DPI of 720, BUT it still yields a superb digital stencil, far better in quality than the highest output resolution of the Epson 3000 printer.

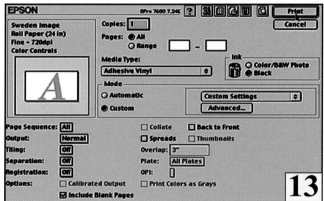

13 Now go to <File> <Print>, in the pull down menu, and the above dialog box will appear. All your printer setting will be shown on this page. *First read the TIP on this page.* Now click on Print.

A Spooling dialog box appears momentarily.

14 When the printer starts printing the above dialog box appears. Wait until it stops printing. Then follow the tip below for cutting the image from the roll.

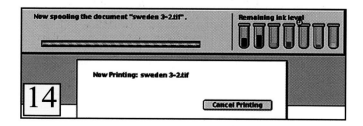

Digital Halftone Intaglio-Type

Using the EPSON Stylus™ 7600 with UltraChrome inks

*TIP: The Epson 7600 wastes a lot of film when it is automatically loaded from the roll film. You can save film by making sure that the Auto Cut has been turned off as instructed in step 11. Also if you go to page **1-27** of your Epson Stylus Pro 7600 owners manual, there is a diagram instructing you how to **Set up the Printer**. In step 8, on this page, it shows you how to use the paper release lever. It is possible to move this lever back only part way, until it actually releases the roll of film, at which point you can manually roll the film backwards on the roll. Do this until the film lines up with the "bottom edge of the paper with the row of holes, as shown" in step 7. The reason you only move this lever back part way is that the printer will think it is out of film and just keep reloading it, thus preventing you from using this film-saving tip. Once the printer has printed the film, press the film release lever all the way back and manually roll the film backwards until the top of the printed edge is visible at the top, where the arrow is pointing on page 1-27, in step 8, of this manual. Now use scissors to cut the image at the top of the image edge.*

ImagOn Plate Making with the Digital Halftone

I recommend making a small ImagOn test plate where the plate includes the darkest and lightest areas of the image. The test plate can be any size provided it includes the darkest black and white in the image. If the test plate yields a rich black and clean white then make the ImagOn plate to the size of the digital halftone. Remember that you will not need a Aquatint Screen exposure with this digital halftone as this image already has a built in random dot structure.

Troubleshooting

Problem 1. The ImagOn test plate does not produce a rich black in the final print. **Solution:** *This is probably caused by the structure of the dot in the digital halftone. Make a test digital halftone as follows:*

Digital Halftone Test

Make sure that the **Levels** have been adjusted as follows:

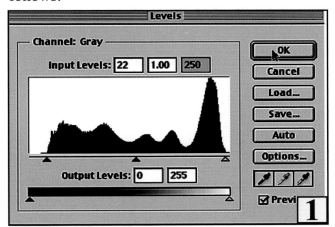

1 Open the image in Photoshop. Go to the pull down menu and highlight and select <Image> <Adjustments> <Levels>. A dialogue box appears as follows: Directly under the Levels graph are sliding triangular adjustments. Images vary and some will not require adjustment. Make sure the triangular adjustment points, to the left and right side of this "mountain like" graph, line up at the beginning and end of the graph. Press OK.

2 Click on the Rectangular Marque tool at the top left of your toolbox. Use this tool to select two or three areas of the image that cross from the blackest into the whites areas of the image.

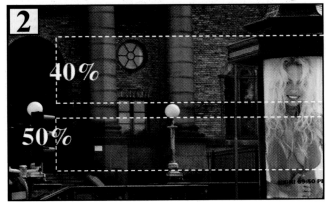

3 Go to the <Image> pull down menu, highlight and select <Adjustments> <Curves>. In the Curves dialog box, click on the diagonal line and then in the <Output> box. Type in **40** and then press OK.

Digital Halftone Intaglio-Type

Using the EPSON Stylus™ 7600 with UltraChrome inks

4 Select the Type tool from the toolbox. Click on an area just before the selected areas that were adjusted with Curves. Then change the font size to 20 and type in the corresponding output percentage Curve. Do this for each test Curve segment as shown in illustration 2.

5 Crop the image to capture the test segments; then go back to steps 5-13 to print this test image on the Epson 7600.

Then make an ImagOn ULTRA plate and expose this test digital halftone to it. Remember that the ImagOn plate only needs one exposure to this image. An Aquatint exposure is unnecessary since this digital halftone has an inherent random dot 'Aquatint' like structure included.

That test segment which yields the best tonal range, from a rich black to a crisp white, now uses the correct percentage curve to adjust the image for an optimal result.

Problem 2. The Intaglio-Type printed image drops out the highlighted tones. There are several possible reasons for this:

A. The plate was over-exposed. One reason a plate may be over-exposed is that the dot structure, in the blackest area of the digital halftone, was too congested. While an over-exposure may eventually burn through the congested dot, thus restoring the blackest tone in an Intaglio-Type print, it will also burn out the highlight (lightest gray dots) dots. .... *Solution..... Make another digital halftone test and change the <Curves> by increasing the percentage by adding 10. Thus 30% would change to 40%. You can do this in 5% degree steps also. Then make another ImagOn test print until a satisfactory tonal range is achieved.*

B. There were not enough highlight dots on the digital halftone. This generally results from scanned images with high contrast. This then relates to the nature of the original image. If it was a black and white conventional film negative,

developed in T-Max developer, it will have more contrast than a black and white film negative, developed in a C41 process. If a high contrast image is used it may be necessary to add a slight dot pattern to the whitest areas of the image. This can also be done with the expectation that these dots will drop out. ***Solution:*** Open image in Photoshop. *Go to <Image> <Adjustments> <Curves>. Illustration* **B** *appears.*

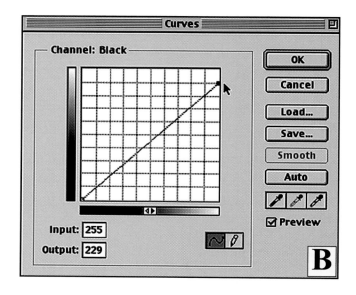

Go to the diagonal line and click it at the top and drag it down on the right side until the output number, located at the bottom left, changes from, say 255 to 229. Notice how this adds a gray dot to the digital halftone image. Reprint your digital halftone and re-do the test until a satisfactory result is achieved.

C. The mode on your Epson 7600 was not changed to Dual Matte Mode. ***Solution:*** *Change the printing mode to Dual Matte Mode.*

Using an EPSON Color Stylus™ 3000 InkJet Printer with an Apple Macintosh Computer and Adobe Photoshop 7

Digital Halftone Intaglio-Type

with EPSON Color Stylus™ 3000 InkJet Printer

The following is a description on how to use the Color Stylus Epson 3000™ Inkjet printer to make digital halftones on a Mac OS.

QUICK LOOK

1 Open the image in Adobe Photoshop 7. Go to the <Image> pull down menu and click on <Image Size>. Resize image.

2 In the <Image> pull down menu select <Adjustments> <Levels>. Adjust levels by aligning triangular sliders under each end of the "mountain like" graph. Click OK.

3 Go to the <Image> pull down menu, click on <Adjustment> <Curves>. In the Curves dialog box, click on the diagonal line and then in the <Output> box. Type in 65 and then press OK.

4 Under the Apple icon, in the top left hand corner of the screen, press and drag down to <Chooser> and select the **SC 3000.**

5 Go to <Page Setup> under <File>.

6 Select the media size under **Paper Size.** If your image size corresponds to a default size, scroll down and select it and **skip to step** **9**. If you are using a "none" default size you will need to click on **Customize.**

7 Click New.

8 Type a name in the New Paper Size box. Then type in the correct image dimensions under the Width and Height boxes. Press OK.

9 Now select Options.

10 Select **Advanced** and then More Settings.

11 On the left side of this dialog box put in the following settings:
A. **Print Quality** SuperFine 1440.
B. **Media Type** Ink Jet Back Light Film.
C. **Ink** Black.
D. **Halftoning** Error Diffusion.
E. Check Microweave.
D. Make sure that Flip Horizontal is not checked. Click on OK.

12 Click OK.

13 Click OK again.

14 Go <File> and click on Print.

15 A spooling dialog box appears with a cancel printing option button.

Once the digital halftone is made it is exposed directly to the ImagOn plate, without an Aquatint Screen exposure, for both the Etched and Non-Etch Intaglio-Type techniques.

TIP: Although these two Epson printers have been used to demonstrate the digital halftone technique, other printers will yield similar results.

Digital Halftone Intaglio-Type

Using the EPSON Color Stylus™3000, Mac OS and Adobe Photoshop version 7

Making a Digital Halftone with the Epson 3000 InkJet Printer

It is assumed that the image will be printed from Adobe Photoshop version 7. Open the image in Photoshop and go to the pull down menu and select <Image> <Mode> <Grayscale>. If this is a colored image you may want to make a duplicate file and work on it. Also, make sure that the Epson 3000 printer driver has been chosen. This is selected in the <Chooser>.

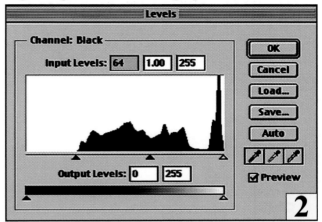

1 Go to the <Image> pull down menu and highlight <Image Size>. The above dialog box appears.

Highlight **Resolution** and make it *300 pixels/inch* and make your image the size you want within the restraints of the printer capability. The maximum printable width, for the Epson 3000, is 16.25" by whatever length desired (when roll transparent film is used in the printer.) For the sample image, used in this chapter, it is 16.25" x 9.8".

TIP:For film economy orientate your image or images into the 16.25" maximum width.

2 In the <Image> pull down menu highlight and select <Adjustments> <Levels>. A dialogue box appears as follows: In illustration 2 above, directly under the Levels "mountains" like graph, are sliding triangular adjustments. Images vary and some will not require adjustment. Click and drag these triangular adjustment points, to the left and

right side of 'mountain', so they line up at the beginning and end of this graph. Click on OK.

3 Go to the <Image> pull down menu, highlight and select <Adjustments> <Curves>. Dialogue box appears as follows.In the Curves dialogue box, click on the diagonal line and then in the **Output** box. Type in 65 and then press OK. Notice how the diagonal line, in the curve graph, has moved up to the left, as shown in illustration 3. The image appears as a grey and white image, not as a black and white one. Our aim is to create a halftone, which has an inherent random dot structure. In this way we will not need an Aquatint Screen exposure, just one ImagOn plate exposure to the digital halftone. While this results in the highest quality non-etch Intaglio-Type print, it also allows us to use this digital halftone for the Etch Intaglio-Type technique.

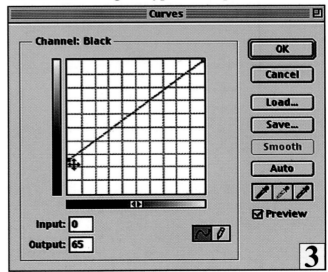

Digital Halftone Intaglio-Type

Using the EPSON Color Stylus™3000, Mac OS and Adobe Photoshop version 7

4 Under the Apple icon, in the top left hand corner of the screen, press and drag down to <Chooser>, select the **SC 3000**, by clicking on it, and then select a printer port.

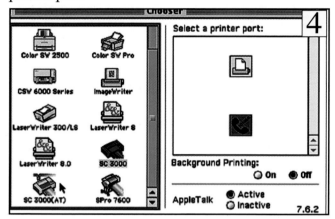

5 After you have chosen the correct printer port the computer looks for the connection route to the printer. If the printer is on and you have chosen the correct routing you will be prompted to go to <File> <Page Setup> in the drag down menu.

6 Select the media size under **Paper Size.** If your image size corresponds to a default size, shown above, scroll down and select it and **skip to step 9**. If you are using a none default size you will need to click on **Customize**.

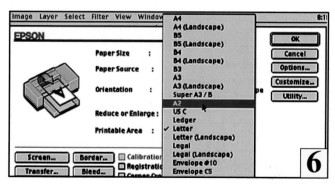

*TIP: You will be using film, so do not be confused with the use of the word **Paper Size** in this dialogue box.*

7 Click New.

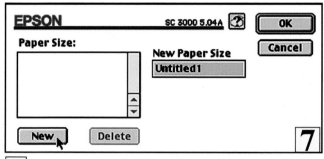

8 Type a name in the New Paper Size box. Then type in the correct image dimensions under the Width and Height boxes. Press OK.

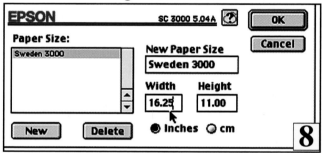

9 The above dialogue box appears. Now select Options.

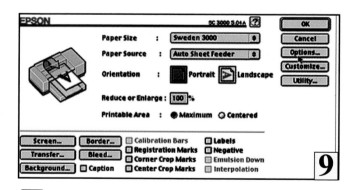

10 In the above dialogue box select **Advanced** and then More Settings.

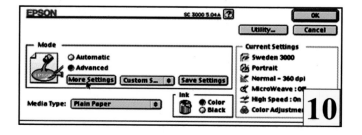

Digital Halftone Intaglio-Type

Using the EPSON Color Stylus™ 3000, Mac OS and Adobe Photoshop version 7

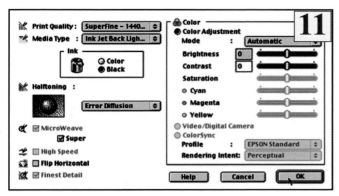

11 The following dialogue box appears.
On the left had size of this dialogue box put in the following settings:
A. **Print Quality** SuperFine 1440.
B. **Media Type** Ink Jet Back Light Film.
C. **Ink** Black.
D. **Halftoning** Error Diffusion
E. Check Microweave
D. Make sure that Flip Horizontal is not checked.

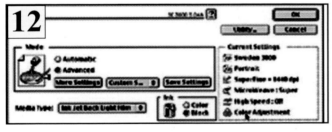

Click on OK.

12 The above dialogue box appears. Click OK.

13 The above dialogue box, with all of your setting listed, appears. Click OK.

***BIG TIP**: I always advise pre-loading your film into the printer especially if it is flat film (not from the roll). I advise supporting flat film by laying down a rigid piece of paper, into the loading tray first. Then place the film, single sheets at a time, on top of this rigid support. Press the button on top of the printer that is marked load. The loading tray lifts and the printer's rollers should engage the film and load it. There are three things that could happen:*
1.** If the printer loads the film and it catches, making all sorts of crackling noises **NEVER YANK THIS FILM OUT OF THE PRINTER,** you will break the film roll-on mechanism. **TURN THE PRINTER POWER BUTTON OFF.
At the left outside of the printer is a knob. Turning this knob towards you allows you to eject the film, caught in the printer, without damaging the roll-on mechanism.

***2.** The printer will load the film and immediately spit it out. If this happens press the **Pause** button and continue to reload it until it accepts it.*

***3.** The printer will properly load the film. In which case you can proceed to step 14 next.*

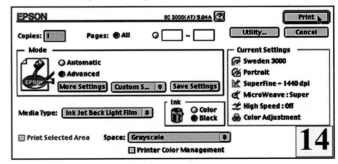

14 Go <File> and click on Print.
The above dialogue box appears.

15 A spooling dialogue box appears indicating that "Document is now Printing".

*TIP: The above dialogue may appear. You may wish to adjust your image size. Or, in many instances, if the image size is close in size to the media, I would advise clicking on **Proceed.** Generally far less clipping occurs than expected.*

Process Color Intaglio-Type (Dot Test)

By David Jay Reed

By David Jay Reed

QUICK LOOK

1. Open an Image in Adobe Photoshop.

2. Convert the image to a Grayscale.

3. In the Levels dialogue box, move the white slider to the left to eliminate all but the darkest areas.

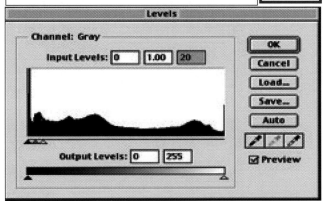

4. Create a marquee in one of the dark areas.

5. With the Color Sampler tool, sample a section of the marqueed area and make note of the percentage on the Info palette.

```
#1   K :  100%
```

6. In the Levels dialogue box, drag the black Output level to the left until the #1 K,in the Info palette, reads 100/90%.

```
#1   K : 100/ 90%
```

7. Repeat this process of sampling the dark areas but change the levels to 80%, 70%, and 60% respectively.

8. Print out the results on to a transparent medium.

9. Examine the results and select the sample that has a 80% black dot structure within it.

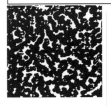

Process Color Intaglio-Type (Dot Test)

By David Jay Reed

What is a Process Color Intaglio-Type?
In the mid 1800's, new discoveries were being made in respect to color.

One of these discoveries was that minute amounts of colored pigments placed close to each other, blended into a continuous hue when seen from a distance.

In printing, it was discovered that the three pigments that worked best to achieve this blend were cyan, magenta, and yellow.

Black was added to produce contrast and a richer tone than could be achieved by just the three pigments. The four pigments became known as the process colors.

Using these pigments in pairs could produce almost any hue. For example yellow and magenta mixed together produced a red hue, yellow and cyan mixed together produced a green hue, and magenta and cyan mixed together produced a violet hue.

However, in order to create a full color continuous tone print the original image had to be converted into dots.

This was usually done with halftone screens. Four halftone screens were created and four respective plates were made from these screens and inked up with cyan, magenta, yellow and black.

Printing the plates, one on top of another, on a surface, produced the overlapping dots, which blended to create the various hues.

Traditionally this was done using lithography or serigraphy, but with the Intaglio-Type process, the image can now be placed on a number of other surfaces using **ImagOn ULTRA** film.

With the invention of Laser and Ink Jet printers came the introduction of the random dot that produced a halftone without the necessity for a screen. So now an even more natural blend can be achieved.

Below is the methodology for creating a colored image from four intaglio plates.

It is at this stage I would like to thank David LaSpina, Kenneth Ray Morton de Courville, Prof. Don Arday, and Prof. Keith Howard for so graciously contributing their knowledge to help perfect this technique.

Equipment
1. A computer with Adobe Photoshop. *These instructions are for versions **6 & 7**.*

2. An Ink jet printer.
I recommend the Epson Stylus Color 3000 or Epson Stylus Pro 7600.

3. Ink jet transparencies.
I recommend either Azon 788 4ml Clear Graphic Film, Epson Transparent film, or ImageFlow Pro Ink Jet Transparency Film by Labelon.

TIP: Whatever transparency is used, it must create a solid black dot. If the dot is not solid, some of the light source will pass through it, and the final image will not replicate the original.

4. A light source.
I recommend either the Teaneck Graphics Vacuum System Desktop Exposure Center or the Olec DEC 22 x28.

Introduction
Historically, the problem associated with the 4-colour intaglio process was the unpredictability of maintaining a uniform tonal range amongst the four plates. This tonal range was dependent upon two things: the depth of bite and the percentage of black dots associated with each tone.

With the introduction of **ImagOn ULTRA**, the uniform depth of the film has alleviated the depth of bite problem.

Process Color Intaglio-Type (Dot Test)

By David Jay Reed

However, the percentage of black dots associated with each image is still unpredictable due to the individual tonal variations inherent in each image.

So, the way I have chosen to resolve this issue is to sample the darkest tone of any image and use the Levels command in **Adobe Photoshop** to create a uniform percentage of dots across the tonal range of the image.

This procedure requires that a levels test first be conducted to establish the percentage of dots needed. Then, once this percentage has been ascertained, the four different channels are sampled, and the percentage applied to all channels.

Finally the dots are transferred, photo-mechanically, to plates coated with **ImagOn ULTRA** film. The plates are then inked, and printed.

To help you better understand the procedure, I have divided the process into three sections: the Dot test, the sampling, and the printing.

Finding the Correct Dot Density

If the final image is printed at **100%** of its tone, the dot structure will be too dense. The spaces between the dots will fill in when exposed in a platemaker and cause **ImagOn ULTRA** to burn out and fall off the ImagOn plate.

Therefore, a test should be taken to determine the correct density of the dot structure. Typically, the dot structure should be around **80%**, but this does vary from printer to printer.

The following test is for the **Epson Stylus Color 3000**.

Importing the Image

1 Scan or download a JPEG or TIFF image into your computer.

TIP: The higher the image's resolution, the higher the quality of the final print.

Line work is usually imported at around **500** dpi (dots per inch). All other images are usually brought in at **300** dpi.

I have found, however, that with this process and the Epson printers, **150** dpi also yields extremely good results.

2 Open the image in **Adobe Photoshop.**

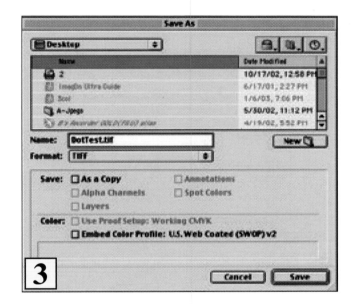

Creating a Test Image

3 Go to the <File> menu and scroll to <Save As>. In the dialogue box, make the **desktop,** or an appropriate folder, the place to save the document. Name it **Dot Test**. Make sure TIFF is selected in the *Format* box. Click **Save.**

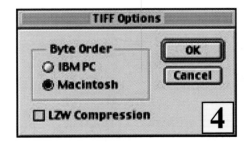

4 In the *TIFF Options* dialogue box, make sure the correct **Byte Order** is selected, ie; IBM or Macintosh. Click **OK.**

Process Color Intaglio-Type (Dot Test)

By David Jay Reed

5 **Converting the Image to Grayscale.**
Go to the <Image> menu and scroll to <Mode>. Select <Grayscale> in the submenu.

If a *Discard color information* dialogue box appears, click **OK.** The image should now be black and white.

6 **Sizing the Image.**
Go to <Image>menu and select <Image Size>. In the dialogue box, make sure the width and height size is correct and the **Resolution** is at least **150.** Click **OK**.

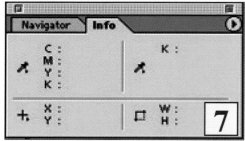

The Test

7 Displaying the Info palette. Make sure the *Info* palette is showing. If it isn't, then go to the <Window> menu and make sure < Info> is checked. A dialogue box will appear as above.

Finding the Darkest Area.

8 Go to <Image> menu and scroll to <Adjustments>. Then select <Levels> in the Submenu.

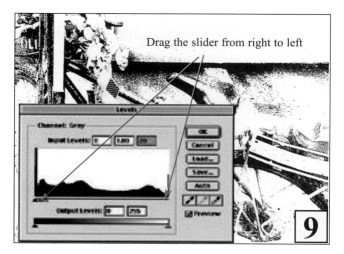
Drag the slider from right to left

9 In the *Levels* dialogue box, drag the right slider to the left until only a little amount of black remains in the image area.

This black represents the darkest area of the image. Make a mental note of the location of this black area.

Click **Cancel** in the *Levels* dialogue box. The image will return to its original tonal range.

Creating the First Test Area
Select the *Rectangular Marquee tool*, from the **Toolbox.**

Drag a marquee here

10 Press and drag a marquee approximately 1" x 1" (25mm x 25mm) in one of the dark areas that you noted earlier.

11 In the **Toolbox**, select the *Color Sampler tool* from the *Eyedropper tool* pop-out menu.

12 In the **Options** bar at the top of **Photoshop**, press on the arrow of the *Sample Size* box and select **3 by 3 Average.**

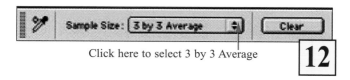
Click here to select 3 by 3 Average

Move the *Color Sampler tool* around in the marquee area until the darkest percentage is registered in the **K** section of the *Info* palette. Click.

A sample icon will appear with the number **#1** in the marquee area.

Process Color Intaglio-Type (Dot Test)

By David Jay Reed

13 In the **Info** palette, note the sample percentage for **#1 K** (Black). In this case it is **100%**.

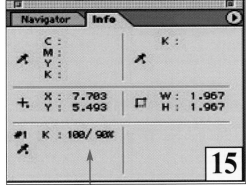

14 Go to the <Image> menu and scroll to <Adjustments>. Select <Levels> again.

Move the slider in the Levels palette until this reads 100/90%

15 In the <Levels> dialogue box, and using the *Info* palette as a guide, drag the bottom left **Output Levels** slider to the right until the **#1 K** on the *Info* palette reads **100%/90%**.

16 In this example, the number in the **Output Levels** box is **25**. Click **OK**.

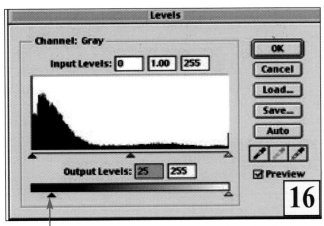

Drag this level right until 90% is reached in the *Info* palette

Now the selected area within the marquee will be a lighter shade.

Creating the Second Test Area

17 Select the *Rectangular Marquee tool*, from the **Toolbox,** and press inside the existing marquee on the image. Drag it over to the next darkest area.

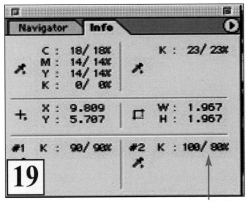

Drag the marquee here

In the **Toolbox,** select the *Color Sampler tool*

Move the *Color Sampler tool* around in the marquee area until the darkest percentage is registered in the **K** section of the *Info* palette. Click.

A sample icon will appear with the number **#2** in the marquee area. In the *Info* palette, it was **100%** again.

18 Go to the <Image> menu and scroll to <Adjustments>. Select <Levels> again.

19 In the *Levels* dialogue box, and using the *Info* palette as a guide, drag the bottom left **Output** slider to the right until the **#2 K** on the *Info* palette reads **100%/80%**.

Move the slider in the Levels palette until this reads 100/80%

Process Color Intaglio-Type (Dot Test)

By David Jay Reed

20 In this case, the number in the **Output Levels** box is **50**. Click **OK**.

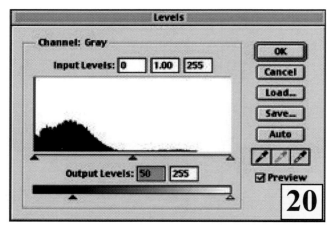

Creating the Third Test Area

21 Select the *Rectangular Marquee tool*, from the **tool box**. On the image, Press on the existing marquee and drag it over to the next darkest area.

22 In the **Toolbox,** select the *Color Sampler tool*

23 Move the *Color Sampler tool* around in the marquee area until the darkest percentage is registered in the **K** section of the *Info* palette. Click.

A sample icon will appear with the number **#3** in the marquee area.

24 Go to the <Image> menu and scroll to <Adjust>. Select <Levels> again.

25 In the dialogue box, and using the *Info* palette as a guide, drag the bottom left **Output** slider to the right until the **#3 K** on the *Info* palette reads, **100%/70%**.

26 In this case, the number in the **Output Levels** box is **76**. Click **OK**.

Creating the Fourth Test Area

27 Select the *Rectangular Marquee tool*. Press and move the existing marquee to the next darkest area.

With the *Color Sampler tool* find the darkest

point in the new marqueed area. Click. A sample icon will appear with the number **#4.**

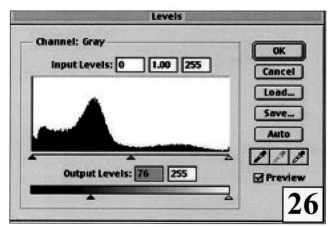

28 In the *Levels* dialogue box, <Image> <adjust> <levels>, drag the bottom left **Output** slider to the right until the **#4 K** on the *Info* palette reads **100%/60%**.

In this case, the number in the **Output Levels** box is **100**. Click **OK.**

29 Go to the *Select* menu and scroll to *Deselect* to deselect the marquee.

Printing the Transparency

You are now ready to print the test transparency.

30 The image must be flattened. To make sure it is, go to the arrow at the top right corner of the *Layers* palette and scroll to *Flatten image*. If *Flatten image* is grayed out, then the image is already flattened.

31 Place an Ink Jet transparency in the printer. In this case it is the **Azon 787n 4ml Clear Graphic Film**.

32 In **Adobe Photoshop 7**, select the <File> menu and scroll to <Page Setup>. A dialogue box will appear. Make sure the *Paper Size* and *Orientation* is appropriate for your image size. Click **OK.**

Process Color Intaglio-Type (Dot Test)

By David Jay Reed

33 In **Adobe Photoshop**, select the <File> menu and scroll to <Print>. A dialogue box will appear. Set the resolution to your desired output.

TIP: The best results have been achieved by using a high resolution in an Ink Jet printer. 1400 dpi or higher is recommended. Of course, if you want a more pixilated image, you can use a lower dpi.

Make sure the paper size is appropriate for your image size.

34 Make sure the media type is **Photo Quality Glossy Film** or equivalent.

The Ink setting must be **black.**

TIP: The printer must print a true black using black ink and not a composite of cyan, magenta, and yellow. Some printers will only only use this combination to create black. This type of transparency will not yield a good print.

35 Press the **Print** button. The printer will now print the test transparency.

Assessing the Dot Structure

On the printed transparency, use a Loupe or pocket magnifier to view the dot structure in the various test areas. The best dot structure is one that has a **80%** black dot.

TIP: Various loupes will produce different magnifications. You may have to run several tests to discover what the dot structure looks like with your particular loupe.

36 Below are three examples of how a dot structure might look if viewed in a loupe using **8x** magnification and **30x** illumination.

In this case, the best dot structure is the top left one at **80%**

From this test, it is established that for the **Epson Stylus Color 3000** printer, an **80%** level of black is required to produce a good dot structure on the **Azon 787N 4ml Clear Graphic Film**.

So, for all future images, the output should be the same. No further tests are necessary.

This is an important point to remember that this test and procedure is made for the Azon 787N film used in conjunction with the Epson 3000 printer.

However, if a different printer brand or number is used, or a different transparency film is used, then a new test will be required for that particular printer and/or transparency film.

36

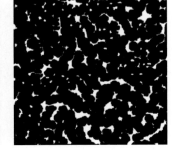

80% dot structure.
A good dot structure.

70% dot structure. The dots are too far apart.

90% dot structure. The dots are too Close together.

Process Color Intaglio-Type (Sampling)

By David Jay Reed

Process Color Intaglio-Type (Sampling)

By David Jay Reed

QUICK LOOK

1. Open an image in Photoshop and convert it to CMYK.

2. In Photoshop, select the Cyan Channel.

3. In the *Levels* dialogue box, move the white slider to the left to eliminate all but the darkest areas.

4. Use the Color Sampler tool to make a selection in the darkest area.

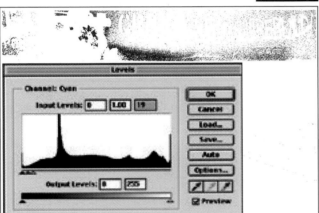

5. Select and sample the darkest areas in the Magenta, Yellow, and Black channels.

6. Reselect the Cyan channel and using the *Levels* dialogue box, move the Output Level slider until the the #1 K in the *Info palette* equals a previously established percentage. Note the Output level.

7. Adjust the Magenta, Yellow and Black channels to the same Output level as the Cyan channel.

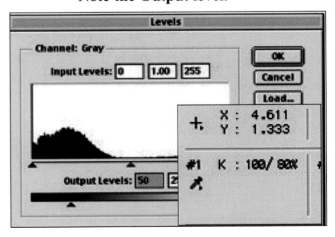

8. Add a Gaussian blur to the Cyan, Magenta, and Yellow channels.

9. Add Noise to the Cyan, Magenta, and Yellow channels.

10. Print each channel separately onto a transparent medium.

Process Color Intaglio-Type (Sampling)

By David Jay Reed

Creating the Transparencies

Once a percentage for a dot structure is established, transparencies can be made from any image using that percentage.

Importing the Image

1 Scan an image, or download a **Jpeg** or **Tiff** image into your computer.

As mentioned earlier, the higher the images resolution, the higher the quality of the final print.

Sizing the Image

2 Select the <Image> menu and scroll to <Image Size>. In the dialogue box, make sure the width and height is correct, and the *Resolution* is at least **150**. Click **OK**.

Converting the Image to CMYK

3 Go back to the <Image> menu and scroll to <Mode>. Make sure **CMYK** is selected in the submenu.

Displaying the Info Palette

4 Make sure the *Info* palette is showing. If it isn't, then go to the **<Window>** menu and scroll **to <Show Info>**. A dialogue box will appear.

In the **Toolbox,** select the *Color Sampler tool* from the *Eyedropper tool* pop-out menu.

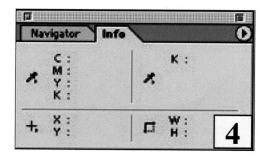

Working with Channels.

Make sure the *Channels* palette is showing. If it isn't, then go to the *Window* menu and make sure *Channels* is checked.

Sampling the Cyan Channel

5 In the *Channels* palette, click on the **Cyan**

channel to select it. All other channels should be deselected.

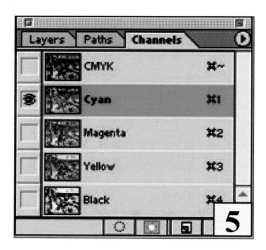

6 Go to the <Image> menu and scroll to <Adjustments>. Select <Levels> in the submenu.

7 In the *Levels* dialogue box, drag the right white slider to the left until only a little amount of black remains in the Cyan channel.

This black represents the darkest area of the image. Note in your mind the location of this black area.

Click **Cancel** in the *Levels* dialogue box.

The cyan channel will return to its original tonal range.

8 With the *Color Sampler tool* you selected earlier, and using the *Info* palette as a guide, find

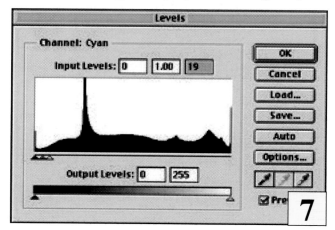

Process Color Intaglio-Type (Sampling)

By David Jay Reed

the area that you noted as being the darkest. Click on that point.

A sample icon will appear with the number **#1** in the image area.

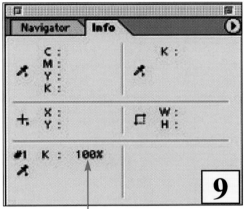

9 In this case, the percentage, according to **#1 K** (black) on the *Info* palette, is **100%**.

Percentage of black in selected area of the image.

This percentage is the maximum black that can be achieved, and will be the base by which the other channels are adjusted.

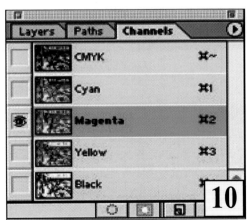

Sampling the Magenta Channel

10 In the *Channels* palette, click on the **Magenta** channel to select it. All other channels should be deselected.

11 Select the <Image> menu and scroll to

<Adjustments>. Select <Levels> in the submenu.

In the dialogue box, drag the right white slider to the left until only a little amount of black remains in the Magenta channel.

Note where the black areas are.

Click **Cancel** in the *Levels* dialogue box.

12 The magenta channel will return to its original tonal range.

With the *Color Sampler tool*, and using the *Info* palette as a guide, find the area that you noted as being the darkest. Click.

A sample icon will appear with the number **#2** in the image area.

13 In the *Info* palette, the number for **#2 K** is **100%** again.

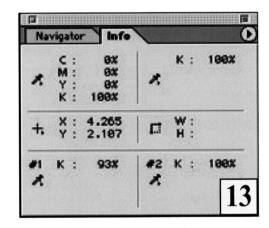

Sampling the Yellow Channel

14 In the *Channels* palette, click on the **Yellow** channel to select it. All other channels should be deselected.

Go to the <Image> menu and scroll to <Adjustments>. Select <Levels> in the submenu.

In the dialogue box, drag the white slider to the left until only a little amount of black remains in the Yellow channel.

Process Color Intaglio-Type (Sampling)

By David Jay Reed

Note where the black areas are.

Click **Cancel** in the *Levels* dialogue box.

The Yellow channel will return to its original tonal range.

15 With the *Color Sampler tool*, and using the *Info* palette as a guide, find the area that you noted as being the darkest. Click.

A sample icon will appear with the number **#3**.

In the *Info* palette, the number for **#3 K** in this case is **99%**.

Sampling the Black Channel
16 In the *Channels* palette, click on the Black channel to select it. All other channels should be deselected.

Go to the <Image> File and scroll to <Adjustments>. Select <Levels> in the submenu.

In the dialogue box, drag the white slider to the left until only a little amount of black remains in the Black channel.

Note where the black areas are.

Click **Cancel** in the *Levels* dialogue box.

The Black channel will return to its original tonal range.

17 With the *Color Sampler tool*, and using the *Info* palette as a guide, find the area that you noted as being the darkest.

Click. A sample icon will appear with the number **#4** in the image.

In the *Info* palette, the number for **#4 K** is **98%**.

NOTE: It is rare that you get so many tones of

black so close to the **100%** mark. In some images, the darkest area may be as light as **75%**.

Adjusting the channel Levels
Adjusting the Cyan Channel
18 Select **Cyan** in the *Channels* palette.

Go to the <Image> menu and scroll to <Adjustments>. Select <Levels> in the submenu.

In the dialogue box, and using the *Info* palette, drag the bottom left black **Output Levels** slider to the right until the **#1 K** on the *Info* palette reads **100%/80%**

19 In this case, the number in the **Output** box is **50**. Click **OK.**

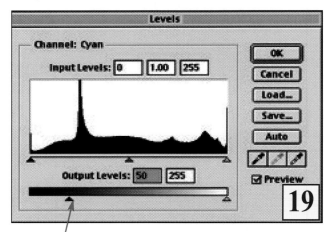

Drag slider until *Info* palette reads **100/80%**

Adjusting the other Channels
20 In order for all channels to reproduce equally, they must all have an output level of **50**. So, one at a time, select the Magenta, Yellow, and Black channels and in each *Levels* dialogue box, type **50** in the **Output Levels** box.

Preparing the Channels
Registration of the four channels is one of the difficulties in producing the final image. One of the ways to reduce this difficulty is to Blur and add Noise to the Cyan, Magenta, and Yellow channels.

Process Color Intaglio-Type (Sampling)

By David Jay Reed

This procedure will soften the image slightly, so when the final black is printed over the other three channels, any misregistration will go undetected by the human eye.

Blurring the Cyan Channel

21 Select the **Cyan** channel.

Go to the <Filter> menu and scroll to <Blur>. Select <Gaussian Blur> from the submenu.

22 In the dialogue box, make the blur between **0.5** and **1.0** pixels depending on the size of the final image.

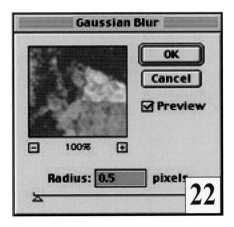

For an image that is around 12" x 16" (30.5 x 40.5cm), **0.5** is ample. Click **OK**.

Adding Noise to the Cyan Channel

23 With the Cyan channel still selected, go back to the <Filter> menu and scroll to <Noise>. Select <Add Noise> from the submenu.

In the dialogue box, make the *Noise* the same amount as the *Blur*. In this case it is **0.5%**.

24 Make sure the *Gaussian* button is selected. This will make the dot random. Click **OK**.

Do the same procedure for the **Magenta** and **Yellow** channels.

Leave the **Black** channel as it is.

Printing the Transparencies.

You are now ready to print the four transparencies.

25 As in the test, the image must be flattened. To make sure it is, select the *Layers* palette, and go to the arrow at the top right corner and scroll to *Flatten image*. If *Flatten Image* is grayed out, then it is already flattened.

Printing the Channels

The four channels will be printed one at a time. It doesn't matter in what order they are done as long as each channel is marked. This procedure can either be done manually, with a waterproof marker, or in the print dialogue box.

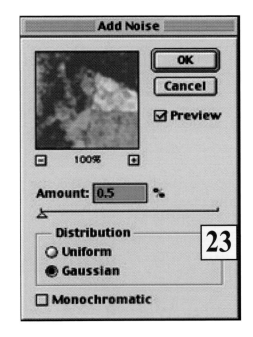

Printing the Cyan Channel

26 For this exercise, cyan will be selected to be printed first, so in the *channels* palette, select the **Cyan** channel. No other channels should be highlighted.

Place an Ink Jet transparency in the printer.

In **Adobe Photoshop**, select the <File> menu and scroll to <Page Setup>. A dialogue box will appear.

Process Color Intaglio-Type (Sampling)

By David Jay Reed

27 Make sure the *Paper Size* and *Orientation* is appropriate for your image size.

Tick the *Labels* box if the word **Cyan** is to be printed on the transparency. Click **OK.**

In **Adobe Photoshop**, select the <File> menu and scroll to <Print>.

A dialogue box will appear.

Set the resolution to your desired output. In this case it was **1400 dpi.**

Make sure the media type is **Photo Quality Glossy Film** or equivalent

28 The Ink setting must be **black.**
Press the **Print** button. The printer will now print the Cyan channel.

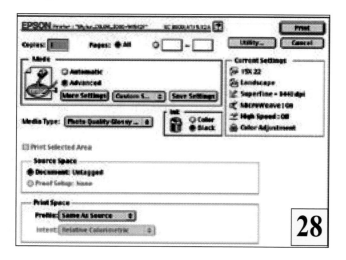

Assessing the Dot Structure

29 On the printed transparency, use a Loupe to view the dot structure.

30 The dot structure should have a **80%** black dot as established in your first test.

Printing the other channels
If the dot structure is good, then one at a time, print the Magenta, Yellow, and Black channels using the same settings as those used for Cyan.

David Jay Reed, 2002, **Ahhh... Sake!**, Process Color Intaglio-Type, 16" x 12".

David Jay Reed, 2002, **(detail) September 11th,** Process Color Intaglio-Type, 16" x 12".

Process Color Intaglio-Type (Printing)

By David Jay Reed

QUICK LOOK

1. Cut one plate and use it as a template to cut the other three plates.

2. Mark the back of each plate with directional lines that corresponds to the way it was cut.

3. Laminate the plates with ImagOn ULTRA

4. Align the previously created transparencies using the bottom left corner and side as a guide.

5. Expose and develop the plates.

6. Create a registration guide by placing the yellow plate on a substrate and drawing a line around the bottom left corner and side

7. Mix the yellow, magenta, cyan and black inks with a transparent base.

8. Ink up the separate plates with the four ink mixtures.

Process Color Intaglio-Type (Printing)

By David Jay Reed
QUICK LOOK

9. Place the yellow plate face up on the press and position it using the previously created guides.

10. Place paper on the top of the plate with an extra wide margin toward the roller.

11. Mark the press bed with tape at the point where the roller should be stopped and still hold part of the paper's margin under the roller.

12. Cover the paper with a sheet of paper and roll through the press one way and then back again to the tape mark.

13. Remove the yellow plate.

14. Place and print the magenta, cyan, and black plates using the same procedure as the yellow plate.

Process Color Intaglio-Type (Printing)

By David Jay Reed

Cutting the Plates

Now that the four transparencies have been printed, each one has to be exposed to a different plate.

Copper is the usual plate surface, but zinc or aluminum could be used.

What ever surface is decided upon, it is very important to have all four plates the same size and equal to the image size of the transparencies.

1 Using a plate cutter, cut one plate to the correct size.

2 Now place this plate on top of the second plate. Tape them together so that the two plates are securely fastened.

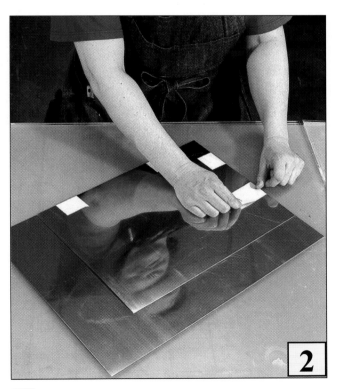

3 Use the top plate as a template to cut the bottom plate.

4 Remove the tape. Name the back of the original plate **Black** and the other **Cyan**.

5 Mark an arrow indicating the top of each plate, so that the plates always correspond to the way that they were cut.

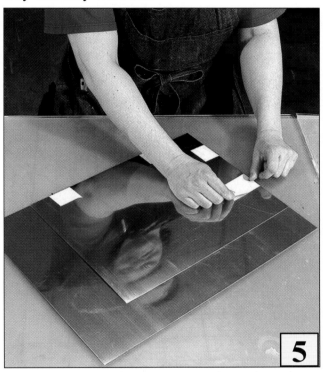

Use the Black plate as a template for the other two plates. Name these **Magenta** and **Yellow** respectively, and mark the tops with arrows.

Preparing the Plates with ImagOn ULTRA

6 Prepare the four plates and laminate with **ImagOn ULTRA** as usual.

After each plate is prepared, laminated, and heated, make sure they are placed face down, so that the emulsion side is hidden from the light.

Exposing the Images on to the plates

Typically, pin registration is used for the alignment of several plates when accuracy is important.

However, with this process it it not necessary to use pin registration, due to the **Blur** and **Noise** that has been added on the Cyan, Magenta, and Yellow plates.

Process Color Intaglio-Type (Printing)

By David Jay Reed

The technique introduced below is based on a traditional woodblock method. In this procedure, the corner and corresponding side of the plate, will be registered to the corner and corresponding side of the image on the transparency.

Aligning the Transparency to the Plate

7 Place the laminated Black plate face up on the platemaker. Make sure that the arrow on the back is pointing away from you.

8 Place the black transparency, top facing away from you, emulsion side down, on the plate so that the bottom left corner and bottom side of the transparency is aligned to the corresponding bottom left corner and bottom side of the plate.

If possible, tape the transparency to the bed of the platemaker so that it doesn't accidentally shift.

Exposing the Black Plate

Turn on the Vacuum, and expose the plate.

TIP: If using the Olec, usually 10 seconds is ample time for a good result.
However, a test should be taken.

If using the Teaneck Graphics platemaker, usually 16 seconds is ample time for a good result. Again, a test should be taken.

When the exposure is finished, remove the

transparency and plate and place the plate face down on a flat surface while you expose the other three plates.

Exposing the Cyan Plate

9 This is the exact same procedure. Place the laminated Cyan plate face up on the platemaker. Make sure that the arrow on the back is pointing away from you.

Place the Cyan transparency, top facing away from you, emulsion side down, on the plate so that the bottom left corner and bottom side of the transparency is aligned to the corresponding left corner and bottom side of the plate.

Turn on the Vacuum and expose the plate.

When the exposure is finished, remove the transparency and plate, and place the plate face down on a flat surface.

Exposing the Remaining Two Plates

Create the Magenta and Yellow plates using the same procedure that was used in the aligning and exposing of the Cyan and Black plates.

Developing the Plates

10 Mix a solution of developer made with 10g of Soda Ash per 1 litre of water

Remove the top Mylar layer from the plates just before submersion.

Place the plates in the developer and leave covered for 9 minutes. Do not agitate.
When the 9 minutes have expired, remove the plates from the developer.

Rinse with cold water, spritz with Vinegar, re-rinse, and dry.

Preparing the plates and paper registration.

There are several registration methods used in multi-plate editioning, but the one most successfully employed for this technique is using the press roller to secure the paper.

8

Process Color Intaglio-Type (Printing)

By David Jay Reed

11 Place a substrate on the press and place a sheet of etching paper on top of it. Mark around the edges to create a template for the paper.

12 Remove the paper and on the same substrate, place the yellow plate and mark the location by drawing around the same bottom left corner and side of the plate that was used to line up the original transfer.

TIP: The paper needs to be cut slightly wider than is needed, so that part of it will remain under the roller of the press after it has been rolled through.

Mixing Inks
Oil based inks. (Graphic Chemical)
Typically, the oil process colors of cyan, magenta, yellow, and black have been used to create four colour imagery.

However, in the intaglio process, the images created with these colors have often not produced an accurate color balance.

Therefore, an extra red, yellow, and black have been mixed with the existing inks, as well as the addition of a tint base extender, and tack reducer.

The mixtures are as follows:
Yellow
1 part Process Yellow + 1 part Diarylide Yellow + 2 parts extender + 3 parts tack reducer.

Magenta
1 part Process Red + 1 part Bright Red + 2 parts extender + 3 parts tack reducer.

Cyan
1 part Process Blue + 1 parts extender + 1.5 parts tack reducer.

Black
1 part Process Black + 1 part Blue Black + 2 parts extender + 3parts tack reducer.

*TIP: The amount of **tack reducer** used will vary depending on the humidity. This medium is added to break down the oil-based ink into a more*

pliable form, so it can be easily applied to and removed from the plate.

Water-based Inks (Rostow & Jung)
The new **Akua-Intaglio** water-based inks by Rostow & Jung have also proved very successful.

Process Color Intaglio-Type (Printing)

By David Jay Reed

The mixtures are as follows:

Yellow
1 part Hansa Yellow + 1 part medium transparent base.

Magenta
1 part Crimson Red + 1 part medium transparent base.

Cyan
1 part Phthalo Blue + 1 part medium transparent base.

Black
Lamp Black or Charcoal black, depending on whether a cold or warm finish is desired.

Whatever inks are used, ink up all four plates with their corresponding colors and wipe in the usual manner.

Printing
Printing is done in this order: yellow, magenta, cyan, and black.

The Yellow plate
Place the inked yellow plate face up, top facing away from you, on the press bed.
Use the ruled lines, around the bottom left corner and side, that were created earlier, as guides.

13 Precision is needed in placing the yellow plate exactly on these guides as the other three plates must be placed in the exact same location for the registration to be accurate.

Dampen the paper for about 30-60 seconds (This procedure is necessary for oil-based inks, but is optional for water-based inks).

Place the etching paper on top of the plate with the extra margin facing toward the press roller.

14 Mark the press bed with some tape where the roller will be stopped on the return pass, and still leave about 3" (7cm) of the extra wide margin under the roller.
Cover with a extra sheet of paper.

The press should be set Aquatint printing.

15 Roll the plate through one way and then back again, making sure that you stop when you reach the tape you set as a marker.

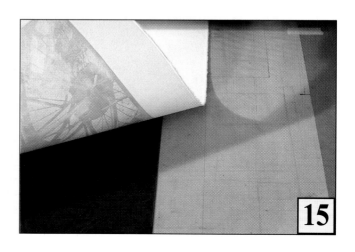

Process Color Intaglio-Type (Printing)

By David Jay Reed

16 Lift the cover paper and then the etching paper. A yellow image will be printed on the etching paper. Remove the yellow plate.

17 Using the same guide lines, place the magenta plate, face up, top facing away from you, in the same location as the yellow plate was previously placed.

Lower the etching paper and then the cover paper. Roll the plate through one way and then back again.

18 Lift the cover paper and etching paper. A combination of yellow and magenta will be printed on the etching paper.

19 Repeat the same procedure for the Cyan plate. When you view the image on the etching paper, it will be a combination of Yellow, Magenta, and Cyan.

20 Repeat the same procedure for the final Black plate. When you view the finished image, it should represent a good replica of the original image.

Remove the finished print from the press bed and place it on a rack, or under a weighted board.

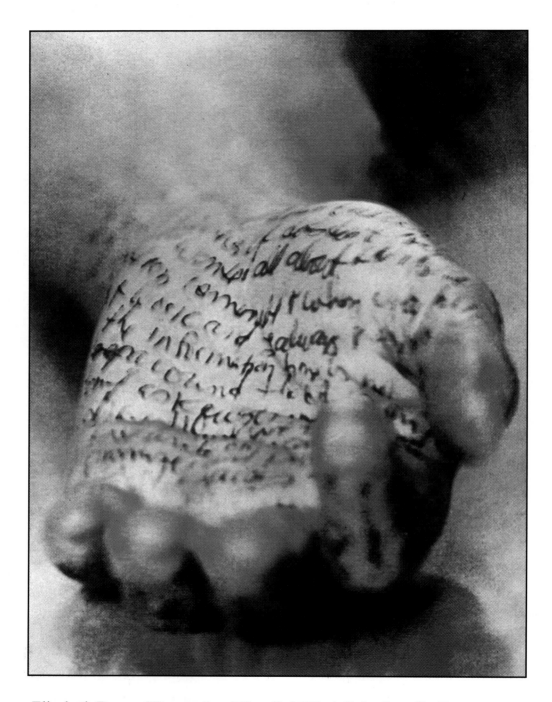

Elizabeth Dove, **"Remember When"**, 2002, 4-Color Intaglio-Type,
30" x 40" (Method for making this print is described on the next page).
See also: < **www.elizabethdove.com**>

4-Color Intaglio-Type

By Elizabeth Dove

Introduction

It is a great time to be a printmaker as there are many very talented printmakers from around the world contributing new technical knowledge to what I call "Contemporary Printmaking". The following original research was conducted by Elizabeth Dove, from the University of Montana. It presents an alternate technique for working with the process colors and computer technology.

4-color Intaglio-Type Ste-by-Step

1 Scan image into Photoshop, using a resolution of either 240ppi or 360 ppi, which is either 1/3 or 1/2 of the 720 dpi that most inkjet printers utilize. Make any desired image adjustments and color corrections.

2 Convert your file to CMYK. Working from the Channels palette split the channels into individual CMYK separations. Each channel will now be shown as a grayscale image.

3 Adjust the curves on each grayscale file from being 100% black to being 90% black; curving the blacks in this way opens up shadow detail.

4 Print to an Epson 3000, using Westar inkjet transparencies and "Ink Jet Back Light Film" as my media type.

TIP: Select a 4-head ink jet printer rather than a 6 or 7 head printer if you have a choice, the toner from the 4-heads is denser and provides better results when printing transparencies than the thinner toner than comes from 6-head inkjet printers.

5 Just prior to printing, flip each separation horizontal (using Ink Jet Back Light film as the media type will always flip them horizontal when printing to the Epson 3000, so flipping them in advance will result in a properly oriented image.

Skip this step if using another printer model that does not flip the image horizontal when printing to Ink Jet Back Light film).

5 Within the printer dialogue box, select black as the ink, Ink Jet Backlight Film as the media type, and leave it on a minimum of 1440dpi for the printout. Use the default Epson setting of Fine Dithering for the halftone dot type.

6 Prepare four identical copper plates and laminate with ImagOn Ultra in the usual manner.

7 Expose each plate to the Aquatint Screen. Expose each inkjet transparency for equal amounts of time. As an example, I expose my Aquatint Screen for 4 minutes and my ink jet transparencies for 2 1/2 minutes each. This is only an example, and it must be tested for each light source. What is important is that each of the CMYK separations be exposed for equal times. Develop as usual.

8 Prior to printing, pre-stretch your paper. I calendar my paper by running it through the etching press four times under high pressure.

9 Use Daniel Smith process inks and transparent base. Yellow is mixed 1/3 Process Yellow to 2/3 Transparent Base. Magenta is mixed 3/4 Process Magenta and 1/4 Transparent Base. Process Blue and Process Black are used straight from the cans.

10 Use a simple template registration system and a block to prevent paper shift, but many registration systems will work.

The key to getting accurate color seems to be altering the print order from what is traditional (yellow first, magenta second, cyan third and black fourth). Best results are achieved by starting printing the modified yellow first, then printing straight process blue second, straight process black third, and modified magenta fourth.

Re-working the Intaglio-Type image with a P.E.T.G. plastic plate overlaid onto the Intaglio-Type plate.

QUICK LOOK

1. You can rework an Intaglio-Type image directly onto the ImagOn plate, or additional plates can be made.

2. P.E.T.G. plastic makes a great second plate alternative which can be cut easily with a snap-off retractable cutter.

3. Place plastic plates directly on top of the ImagOn plates and either paint on screen filler or engrave directly into the plastic.

4a, b. Screen filler or liquid aquatint is applied directly to the ImagOn plate. This plate can also be engraved or reworked with a Dremel tool.

5. Once the screen filler has dried, the ImagOn plate, or successive plates, are printed.

Reworking the Intaglio-Type

Introduction

Reworking the Intaglio-Type plate is a totally difference experience from working with traditional scraping and burnishing techniques. Reworking the Intaglio-Type plate is actually fun. There are several approaches that can be employed.

Intaglio-Type plates can be reworked by doing the following:

A. You can add Speedball Screen Filler or Golden Artist Color acrylic gloss medium directly to the surface of the plate which create texture and soft tonal marks.

B. You can add carborundum grit to the screen filler and make a gritty paint-on liquid aquatint. This adds rich mezzotint-like blacks to the print (if the plate is inked with black ink).

C. The Intaglio-Type plate can be sanded or worked on with a dry-point needle or Dremel tool.

D. Additional plates can be made. I recommend a type of inexpensive plastic called P.E.T.G. which is .020 thick, the same thickness as the copper plate recommended in this text. Other copper plates can be used as well. These additional plates can be reworked with the techniques mentioned in A, B, and C.

Once the additional plates are made or the screen filler and the liquid aquatint areas have dried completely, print the plates in succession to reveal a multi-plate image-making approach to the Intaglio-Type technique.

E. You can also manipulate the artwork in favor of the plate as it takes only about 20 minutes to make a new plate. Sometimes it is better simply to rework the toner-wash drawing or other art work and make a new plate rather than rework the original plate.

E. Finally, you can combine various techniques onto one plate, such as, Wrinkled and Construction Intaglio-Type onto one plate. Of course, once new and unexposed pieces of ImagOn are added to the plate they can also be manipulated with any number of other techniques. Spit-Bite Intaglio-Type and re-exposing toner-wash or other art work to the newly added pieces of ImagOn become interesting reworking options.

The following 8 images was created over a few days by Paul Brekke, at workshop I conducted at the College of Santa Fe. They are a sampling of about 12 variations that he made. Images 4 and 8 are photographs of the ImagOn plate through various stages. Paul worked in a highly intuitive manner from image to image. The liquid aquatint and screen filler applications were extensively used. Paul also reworked the toner-wash drawing. He also employed Construction and Spit-bite Intaglio-Type methods, and he scraped back into the plates. This series illustrates the extraordinary choice of plate and image manipulation that can be creatively employed in re-working an image.

ImagOn plate

Reworking the Intaglio-Type

ImagOn plate

Most importantly, if you become familiar with the various possibilities, or the vocabulary of the Intaglio-Type, you will have endless possibilities for your own images.

Materials
1. Speedball Screen Filler or any acrylic gloss medium (Golden is recommended.)

2. Mild, medium, and coarse carborundum grit (The type used when griding litho stones flat.)

3. Dry point needles and Dremel tool.

4. P.E.T.G. plastic .020 thick or Sintra (a sign painting plastic.)

Reworking the Intaglio-Type Plate
There are three approaches that I will demonstrate: First, **Additive** techniques, second **Subtractive** techniques and third, **multi-plate** techniques. These reworking techniques can be used separately or in combination.

Screen Filler and Liquid Aquatint
Any clean Intaglio-Type plate can be added to with either Speedball Screen Filler or a mixture of screen filler and carborundum. When carborundum is added to screen filler, painted onto a plate and allowed to dry, the resulting print yields a rich mezzotint like black (if the plate was printed with black ink). The carborundum grit mixed in with the screen filler provides an ideal tooth to hold the ink.

Mixing the Liquid Aquatint
To about a dessert spoonful of Speedball Screen Filler, slowly add medium grit screen filler and mix it thoroughly with a small brush. The consistency can vary from a thin solution to one that has about the same viscosity as artist's oil paint.

In fact, any grade of carborundum grit can be mixed with the screen filler to create differing effects. The liquid aquatint technique provides a very direct and painterly approach to plate re-working, and the one great aspect of this technique is its ability to stick to both the ImagOn plate and to the P.E.T.G. plastic.

Below, notice the thickness of the brushed on liquid aquatint and also the ridge of liquid aquatint created on each side of the brush mark. This ridge not only imparts a high relief texture into the print but, also creates a tonal change within the mark in the final print. If black ink is used the tonal change goes from a deep mezzotint-like black to a dark gray. This unique feature of the liquid aquatint emphasizes the textural relief in the final print.

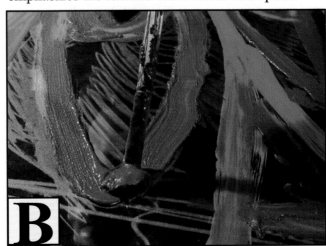

B

Reworking the Intaglio-Type

Screen filler or any variety of acrylic matte and gloss mediums can be painted directly onto the plate. The screen filler can be thinned with water, or it can be used straight out of the container. It can be applied layer upon layer to increase the relief nature of the mark. Screen filler brushed on, without the additional carborundum grit, produces low key tones in the final print. If a clean white is desired in these brushed on screen filler areas, paint Future acrylic floor finish or Golden's acrylic gloss medium directly on top of the screen filler marks.

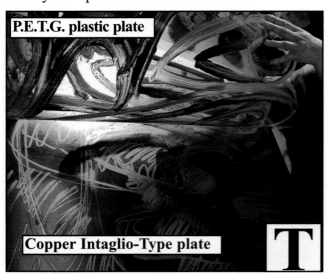

P.E.T.G. plastic plate

Copper Intaglio-Type plate

You can achieve an additional characteristics when using screen filler painted directly onto the plate. If it is applied thickly and allowed to heat dry quickly, each thick area of screen filler will dry with a unique crack, as shown in the print below.

Liquid Aquatint & the P.E.T.G. Plate

The liquid aquatint and the screen filler can be painted directly onto the P.E.T.G plastic plate.

First, place the copper Intaglio-Type plate on top of the P.E.T.G. plastic, and with a snap-off retractable blade cutter, cut the plate to the size of the metal plate. I advise cutting the P.E.T.G plastic to about 1/8" shorter on each side than the copper Intaglio-Type plate. If you want more plate tone with the P.E.T.G plastic plate, sand the surface of the plate with 320 grit sand paper.

You can also work with a dry-point needle on to the P.E.T.G. plastic plate. If editions longer than 10 prints are desired, a polycarbonate (Lexan) or plexiglass plate is substituted for the P.E.T.G. plastic plate.

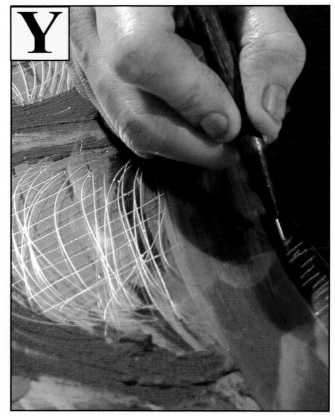

Reworking the Intaglio-Type

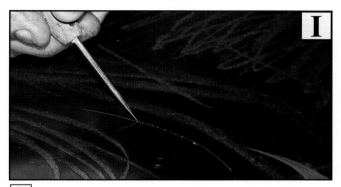

I t is also possible to use the dry-point needle to re-work the ImagOn plate. Working with a dry-point needle into the ImagOn plate, causes the line to fracture, a desired or an undesired effect, as it simulates a dry point line with a burr. If, however, you want to have a clean etched-like line, work on the plate with a dry-point needle or sharp scalpel blade directly after the plate has finished the developing cycle and has not dried.

W orking directly on to the ImagOn or the P.E.T.G. plastic plate with a Dremel tool provides a wonderful way to rework any plate. Dremel tools come with a large variety of drill-type bits that offer printmakers new mark-making facilities.

There exists an almost infinite range of possibilities when all of the previous techniques are combined with multi-plate printing techniques. The P.E.T.G. plastic plate gives you, the printmaker, the ability to make, easily and quickly, a second, or third, or as many plates as you want. These plastic plates can also be inked in relief using Akua intaglio inks and a good quality brayer.

One final plate-reworking technique is to drop the ImagOn plate into the soda ash stripping solution for about 1 minute, removing it and then washing the plate. The stripping solution will destroy the darker areas of the plate first, and in some instances will restore a plate that has been over-exposed. Leaving the plate in the stripping solution for longer periods before washing would

disintegrate of the original image even more. Using a plate reworked in this manner with a normally exposed plate, with the same image, also opens up a new visual dialogue when used with the multi-plate printing technique. At the very least this method of re-working can be done virtually on any ImagOn plate as just another way to re-see the image that you are working on. There is an unpredictablity here that is intriguing.

Printing Intaglio and Relief Together
It is a common practice for printmakers to combine intaglio and relief printing techniques on one plate. First, the plate is inked in the intaglio manner. Then, one roll of ink is applied to the surface of the plate with a brayer. The plate is then printed.

In such printing techniques, there is always an issue of requiring a certain diameter of roller to avoid lap marks. Furthermore, the brayer or roller can only be applied to the plate once and must be cleaned after each application. Otherwise the relief layer of ink becomes polluted from the intaglio layer beneath.

These technical difficulties can all be avoided by simply making a P.E.T.G. plastic plate. It can be rolled up with any relief colored ink and printed first, followed by the second intaglio plate. This first plastic plate can be reworked easily by wiping back certain areas with a clean rag, thus allowing for the original paper color to be present within the final print. Also, more than one color can be rolled onto this second plastic plate. Of course, printing can become more complex by combining additional relief rolled plastic plates. The combinations and possibilities are indeed endless.

Friedhard Kiekeben, **Tinflower**, 2002, etched copper plate using the Edinburgh Etch and then colored. 15" x 15".

New Etching Chemistry

By Friedhard Kiekeben

Corrosive Metal Salts - Etching without Acid

In Acrylic Resist Etching, metal plates are etched in metal salt solutions rather than acids. Since the first publication of the Edinburgh Etch process in 1997, I have been able to further develop, test and refine a whole range of new metal salt etching processes for all metals commonly used in intaglio printmaking and for sculptural plate-making. The system comprises specific metal salt solutions for the fast and accurate erosion of copper, brass, zinc, steel, and aluminum. All of the etching processes given below are compatible with the entire range of acrylic resist mark making methods, such as hard ground, stop out, or aquatint.

The benefits of this new etching methodology over the traditional acid etch approach are compelling, both in environmental terms and in regard to the superior quality of bitten work. Metal salt etching comprises two basic kinds of process: The Edinburgh Etch and The Saline Sulphate Etch. The Edinburgh Etch (© F.K. 1997), suitable for copper, brass and steel, consists of solutions of ferric chloride and citric acid or sodium chloride, while the new Saline Sulphate Etch (© F.K. 2002), designed for biting zinc and aluminum, comprises solutions of a copper sulphate and sodium chloride mixture. Due to their low hazard rating, the metal salt etching methods are both suitable for use in a professional printmaking environment as well in an artist's personal studio.

Cause and Effect

Traditional acid etching processes produce significant amounts of toxic fumes. In the commonly used nitric acid etch, for example, the nitrous gases produced are suspected of causing eye, nerve, lung, and kidney damage, as well as impotence and genetic defects; in contact with chlorine-based cleaning products, nitric acid can even turn into mustard gas! In industry today, regulations prohibit the use of nitric acid without fully extracted and filtrated glove units similar to those used in the nuclear industry. Regrettably, despite these compelling facts, many artists, workshops, and printmaking departments maintain that their existing measures provide adequate protection.

Safe and Simple

By contrast, the Metal Salt Etching system is free from harmful gas emissions. During etching, the chemical reaction by-products are contained within the etching solution without polluting the workshop atmosphere. The processes are not heat generating, and no vicious reactions can occur during the etching of a plate. So inert are these processes that extraction and / or containment can be seen as additional safety measures rather than essential requirements. A further benefit is that the superbly accurate etching properties of the metal salt solutions remain constant throughout their usable life, without the gradual deterioration that causes unwanted foul-biting and undercutting – a common feature with the use of conventional acid solutions.

Nevertheless, no new printmaking process, however safe or simple, would be worth its salt if the results did not equal or exceed those produced by traditional means. Perhaps, the most exciting fact about the Edinburgh Etch and the Saline Sulphate Etch is that the results are startlingly good – biting plates quickly and cleanly.

Solving the Issues of Ferric

A solution of ferric chloride salt crystals has long been valued by etchers as the most accurately biting and controllable etchant for copper plates. Ferric chloride also commends itself because it gives off no toxic vapors, neither by itself nor during etching; it is low-hazardous in occasional contact with skin and is not readily volatile if accidentally spilled in the workshop. Why, then, has ferric not always been used as the prevalent mordant in etching? The answer lies in the speed and ease of biting. The way ferric was used in the past meant that etches of a reasonable depth, as are typically required in the intaglio medium, took a very long time to accomplish, and the methods employed were often cumbersome and inefficient.

New Etching Chemistry

By Friedhard Kiekeben

A number of ground-breaking innovations have now dramatically enhanced the properties and the biting speed of this safe mordant. The problems traditionally associated with ferric chloride center around its peculiar biting chemistry: when metal plates are etched in ferric chloride, a sediment gradually builds up inside the bitten intaglio areas. If these crystalline residues are not continually removed by some means, they eventually clog up the newly formed grooves and prevent the plate from etching any further. One way of avoiding this problem is by etching the plates in vertical dip-tanks - a reliable technology from the electronics industry which was first applied to printmaking by Keith Howard. Plates are suspended in the upright position in the corrosive solution allowing sediment particles to drop out of the etched grooves and sink to the bottom of the tank. The solution needs to be agitated to accelerate the bite. A simple air pump attachment will suffice. The dip tank can also be heated for improved efficiency.

The effect of these practical measures on ferric allows its safe and effective use use in printmaking. With further chemical enhancement, (the Edinburgh Etch formula), its potential is fully realized as a mordant unsurpassed in the etching of copper, brass, and steel.

Safety Note: For safety reasons a concentrated ferric chloride based etch should not be employed for ZINC and ALUMINUM as this can cause the production of heat, flammable hydrogen gas, and acid fumes!

Chemistry of Ferric Chloride

The corrosive properties of ferric become apparent with a brief look at its chemical make up. A ferric molecule consists of one atom of iron which has three atoms of chlorine locked onto it. The bridge between iron and chlorine - which creates the chemical 'adhesion' of the molecule - is made up of two electrons (negatively charged particles) for each chlorine atom. However, since the iron atom needs eight electrons to be in a stable condition, but has only six, it tends to attract atoms it comes in contact with, such as atoms of other metals, and reacts with them to gain the missing two electrons. A substance of this kind is not, strictly speaking, regarded as acid; but due to its similar corrosive properties, is referred to as a 'Lewis acid' by chemists.

An Essential Ingredient for Etching

Ferric chloride is available from most chemical suppliers either as yellow granules or as a saturated solution, both of which are fairly inexpensive, especially if bought in larger quantities. If at all possible, the ready-made solution should be used, which for its industrial use comes in 25l or even larger containers at about 42 to 48 BE (Baume) density. The density/weight of ferric can be measured by immersing a so-called hydrometer in the solution. The Baume scale of describing the specific weight of liquids is not entirely accurate, and sometimes manufacturers give other specifications. The strength of the ferric solution can also be described as a percentage. For example 40% ferric chloride (or 40% FeCl3) denotes a ratio of 40% ferric crystals to 60% water. I find that 40% FeCl3 about equals a 42-45 BE density.

When ordering ferric, it is easiest simply to ask for a 'saturated' ferric chloride solution without referring too much to density scales that many suppliers are unsure about. Remember that liquid ferric is a heavy solution of ferric chloride salt crystals in water; the solution could not go beyond a certain strength (i.e. 48BE) unless the crystals solidify. It is easy to dilute a strong solution with water to obtain a weaker strength, but impracticable to strengthen a ferric solution which is too weak for a good etch from the outset. Even though ferric chloride is relatively safe to use, eye protection and gloves must always be worn when handling it.

The saturated ferric solution of about 42-48BE is an ideal base ingredient for making up various

New Etching Chemistry

By Friedhard Kiekeben

mordants needed in the etching workshop. Only in exceptional circumstances (i.e., very delicate etched photo-polymer work) would it be useful to obtain the much more expensive, purer but weaker, laboratory grade ferric, which actually etches less well than the impure industrial grade. Due to the variable strength of saturated ferric chloride, certain adjustments to the mordant recipes given here may have to be made. If, for example, a mix of one part ferric to three parts water does not etch as expected, simply reduce or increase the water content accordingly. This, as well as fine-tuning of the recipe, will entail some testing, but working some things out for oneself is always half the fun of printmaking!

Tip: Eye protection and gloves must always be worn when handling Ferric Chloride.

Making up ferric from granules

If ferric chloride is not available in solution, crystalline granules are available. These should be handled with caution as they are highly corrosive and require careful preparation before they can be used for etching. The granules should be kept in sealed plastic containers to prevent any absorption of moisture from the surrounding atmosphere. The etching solution is made by dissolving approximately one part of ferric crystals in two parts of warm water (about 40°C). During this process, heat and hydrochloric acid gas are generated, so adequate ventilation and full protection are essential.

For reasons of safety and quality, use a ready-made ferric chloride solution whenever possible.

TIP: Before using fresh etching solution take the 'sting' out of it to prevent uncontrolled biting. Either insert a blank piece of metal of the kind that is to be etched in the bath and allow it to completely dissolve, or add a small amount of exhausted mordant to the fresh mix.

The Discovery of the Edinburgh Etch:
The Vertical Tank Approach

My aim in developing the new Edinburgh Etching solutions was to fully harness the eroding power of ferric chloride. Artists in the past mainly resorted to mechanical devices enabling them to eliminate the sedimentation problem associated with the ferric bite. In its traditional form, this meant placing etching plates in trays face down while rocking the bath continually. This method produced reasonable results on copper plates, but a good etch could take hours. Due to its generous filling with mordant and vigorous agitation, a dip-tank represents the best facility for the mechanical removal of the crystalline sediments that ferric chloride generates as it etches metal. The Pro-Vertical Tank ia a reasonably priced etching tank, shown below, takes several 18" x 24" sized plates and

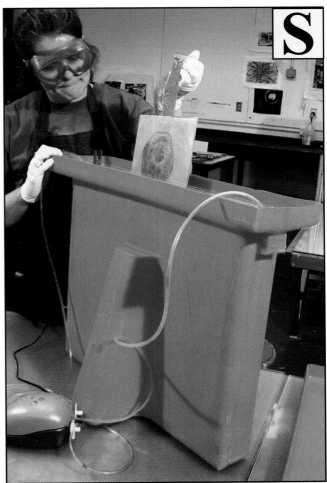

New Etching Chemistry

By Friedhard Kiekeben

many medium sized ones. Larger tanks can be custom made by most professional acid unit manufacturers, preferably from welded polypropylene. For small-scale work, even a square bucket will make a serviceable etching tank, especially if fitted with an aquarium aeration pump.

Go to <**.www.marmitplastics.com**> for more information.

Aeration

One or several tubes of fish tank 'airline' are fitted to a rod on one or two ends of the tank. The air outlets should point upwards and are connected to a powerful fish tank aeration pump. The powerful stream of bubbles rising on the side of the tank produces a circular flow within the solution which activates the etch mechanically. Aquarium shops also supply small valves which can be inserted in the airline in order to regulate the air flow and the resulting current inside the tank.

Aquarium pump

A New Catalyst: Citric Acid

In the course of my research, I approached the issue of activating the ferric etch from a new

angle, searching for additives to ferric chloride which might be able to dissolve the sediment as it is produced.

After experimenting with a variety of possible substances, I tried a new kind of non-toxic additive normally more associated with food rather than etching - citric acid. It turned out that a citric acid solution mixed at a certain ratio with a ferric chloride solution not only speeds up the bite of ferric but produces an entirely new kind of mordant with outstanding biting properties. Different kinds of metal require a different mix of this mordant I then called 'the Edinburgh Etch'. On copper, brass, and mild steel, I found the unique property of the Edinburgh Etch to be consistent throughout: the etch process takes place with the utmost precision and without the build-up of sediment typically associated with unmodified ferric chloride. In chemical terms, this is due to the fact that the individual molecules of the metal salts produced during biting are locked into the clamp-like carbon rings of citric acid atoms, thus keeping them dissolved. They are no longer allowed to solidify as crystals which would impede biting and result in a slower and coarser etch. So, the main obstacle usually encountered with ferric chloride is literally being dissolved by the new mordant.

Monona Rossol recently expressed concerns over the modified balance of acidic compounds of the Edinburgh Etch in contrast to pure ferric chloride. In practice, this is a valid issue in the now obsolete ferric / citric based etching solution for zinc which I advocated in the 1998 publication "Non-Toxic Intaglio Printmaking" by Keith Howard. Soon after publication, I noticed the possibility of a runaway chemical reaction in this heat-generating process which can trigger the release of chlorinated fumes during open biting. Consequently, this particular process has since been replaced by the new Saline Sulphate Etch which entails no such hazards. The crucial catalyst contained in the Edinburgh Etch, citric acid, is widely available from larger chemical

New Etching Chemistry

By Friedhard Kiekeben

suppliers and suppliers to the food industry. This white powder ordinarily finds its way into cakes or fizzy lemonade rather than into an etching tray. It should be obtained as 'anhydrous citric acid'. Its handling and storage is about as non-toxic as a chemical could be. Do, however, wear a dust mask and suitable goggles when dispensing the fine powder. Anhydrous citric acid powder is now available both from chemical and printmaking suppliers.

Tip Warning: It is absolutely essential that different kinds of metal are always etched in different etching facilities, such as in separate tanks or trays. A metal plate accidentally placed in the wrong tank or tray causes electrolytic processes, contaminates the solution, and, in the case of a zinc or aluminum plate inserted in a dip tank, can even lead to violent chemical reactions.

Edinburgh Etch for Copper

Copper sheets are supplied by printmaking suppliers, or, more cheaply, by an industrial sheet metal dealer. Industrial copper (and zinc sheets) tend to have a more or less pronounced rolling-texture which may become visible during open biting. In practice, this is rarely a problem; any thickness of sheets ranging from about 0.5mm to 1.2mm, or 0.2" – 0.5" is suitable for intaglio printmaking. Printmaking suppliers also sell copper sheets of the more expensive 'hammered' variety, as these do not have any rolling texture.

Intaglio marks, made with acrylic grounds on copper plates and etched in Edinburgh Etch, are of the best possible quality. Lines, textures, and open areas are cut into the metal as if with a razor blade; even the finest detail registers accurately on the bitten plate which, in turn, produces a crisp intaglio print.

For large edition sizes of, perhaps 40 to 50 prints, professional workshops often have copper intaglio plates steel-faced prior to printing; the electrolytic coating hardens the surface and renders the plate more durable. If, however, an etching project is executed from the outset using brass or steel plates, no steel-facing is needed for a large edition, as the plate itself will already have the required durability for a large edition.

In a ferric-based etching solution fortified with citric acid, copper plates can now be etched face up in a tray. The Edinburgh Etch erodes copper about twice as fast as pure ferric, and the hindrance of sedimentation does not occur.

For this very controlled etch process which neither generates heat nor gas bubbles, a fairly concentrated solution is normally used. The tray method can safely be employed even in an artist's studio lacking ventilation, given that basic precautions, such as the use of goggles and gloves, are followed.

Frequent rocking of the tray is not essential to the quality of the etch but can speed up the biting action. Working with ferric-based mordants does not necessarily require fan assisted fume extraction as long as good general ventilation, such as an open window, is ensured. During over 10 years of intensive use of ferric chloride, I have, however, encountered two cases of printmakers who were hypersensitized to the smell of ferric chloride. In rare cases such as these, fume extraction and the use of an inorganic respirator are, of course, mandatory and, preferably, an alternative process should be used.

The non-sedimenting properties of the Edinburgh etch are enhanced by the use of a dip-tank in which agitation takes place automatically. This results in very speedy biting times for copper plates. For instance, a black aquatint, a crisp line, or a well-developed open bite ridge are already deeply etched at about 20°C after a 30 - 40 minute immersion in a dip tank aerated with an aquarium pump.

The Edinburgh etch mixture, given on the following page, is a universal mordant to be used in both flat trays or upright tanks. If no citric acid

New Etching Chemistry

By Friedhard Kiekeben

is available, a saturated ferric chloride solution can also be used, but the etch will be slower and somewhat less precise. Base the mixture on the following overall ratios:

Edinburgh Etch for Copper

1 Start with 4/5 saturated ferric chloride solution (40%).

2 Add 1/5 citric acid solution which consists of 3/4 tap water + 1/4 citric acid powder (anhydrous).

In actual quantities, this works out, for example, to:

A 6 Liters saturated ferric chloride solution (40%).

B + 1:2 liters of tap water.

C + 400ml citric acid powder (by volume). (This equals 400g powder.)

Fill a bucket with 1:2 Litres of hot water. Gradually add the citric acid powder content while stirring continually. Once this has fully dissolved, gradually pour this into the ferric solution and keep stirring until you have produced a uniform liquid.

Pour this into the etching tank or tray which is now ready for use.

Try to maintain a reasonable temperature in your etching facility for copper. Good results are ensured at 18 to 20°C, but higher temperatures of up to 30°C can further improve biting times as well as the overall responsiveness of the mordant. This solution is exceptionally long lasting; a tank filling used daily, occasionally topped up to compensate for loss, has been known to remain active for several years without a significant drop in its biting properties. When eventually the mordant acquires a deep olive color, it becomes

less active and is then ready for replacement, neutralization, and disposal.

Tip: Even during etching Edinburgh Etch trays or tanks should be covered with a lid to prevent evaporation. When not in use, etching solutions should be stored in clearly labeled containers, stating the composition of the solution and the kind of metal etched in it. Also, place safety notices such as 'corrosive – wear eye protection' on all containers and work areas.

Edinburgh Etch for Brass

Brass is a superbly suitable material for intaglio etching and printing. The metal has a golden, mirror-like finish, and usually lacks the more or less pronounced rolling texture known from other industrial sheet metals.

It is often supplied by the same sheet metal merchants that sell copper and is only marginally more expensive. The Edinburgh Etch approach now allows for this noble metal to be etched as easily as a sheet of copper. Arguably, brass surpasses any other metal in terms of its versatility of marks, its faithfulness to etched detail, and its overall aesthetic expressiveness.

Brass can be etched in similar conditions as given for the Edinburgh Etch for copper. The golden aesthetic of this very hard alloy of zinc and copper combines the delicacy of copper intaglio with the robustness of etched steel - like steel, its open surfaces display a self texturing effect and, due to their hardness, plates do not suffer from wear in large editions. Brass plates yield unique textured effects in conjunction with the various acrylic wash and open bite processes, for instance, when a combined Speedball Screen Filler and carborundum wash medium is used.

Saline Ferric Etch for Steel

Mild steel etches best in the following solution in a well-aerated dip-tank. This solution uses a small addition of cooking salt as a catalyst rather than citric acid. Tray etching of steel plates in the

New Etching Chemistry

By Friedhard Kiekeben

saline ferric etch is most satisfactory if the bath is kept warm and is frequently agitated. Preferably, an upright tank fitted with aquarium aeration tubes should be used. The etch brings out a typical self-texturing property in steel which causes open areas of the plate to acquire an aquatint-like roughness. Open bite, if etched for long enough, has the typical 'tooth' on the surface of the bitten area that is so desirable for dense intaglio printing. An increase in the solution temperature, up to 30 degrees Celsius, is hugely beneficial for a much faster and crisper steel etch. Ensure that your etching area is in a warm location. Etching trays can also be placed on a darkroom tray heater or inside a warm water bath. Some etchers even construct a second 'radiator' tank around their dip tank which can be circulated with hot water for heating up the Edinburgh Etch solution in the inner tank.

Edinburgh Etch for Steel

1 8 liters of saturated ferric chloride solution (40%).

2 + 3 liters of tap water.

3 + 700ml table salt (by volume).

Mix the ingredients as described for Edinburgh Etch for copper.

Backing the Plate

Before a metal plate can be etched, the back of the plate has to be covered with an acid resist. Plates etched without this protection erode from the back, and the grounds applied to the front may lift off. A very quick and reliable way to cover the back of an etching plate is by applying sheets of self-adhesive film or strips of parcel tape to it.

The plate is now ready for etching if horizontal trays are used. If the plate is to be etched in an vertical dip-tank, a plastic packing tape handle has to be attached for lowering the plate into the bath (see page 140). The handling strip should be longer than the depth of the tank. Before etching, inspect the surface of the plate for any greasy deposits and clean if necessary.

Etching Safely

Etching should take place in a separate area of the etching workshop which may be combined with a stripping facility in an overall 'corrosive area'. It is important to keep this space separate from other workshop activities because the handling of acidic and alkaline substances requires extra caution, and a number of safety measures should be observed by users at all times. Artists become very absorbed by their work and are, at times, less aware of the safety aspects involved in their activity; however, in a corrosive work area, adequate protection in the form of acid resistant gloves and goggles or a visor should always be worn. Also make sure there is clean running water or an emergency eye wash station within reach. Mop up any ferric chloride (or copper sulphate) spills with sodium carbonate and water.

Etching in Vertical Dip Tanks

For most acrylic grounds, an aerated compartment of a vertical dip tank can be used; this gives a significantly faster etch than a still compartment. Fine aquatints can also be etched in a compartment of the vertical tank with reduced or no aeration or in a tray to ensure that the small acrylic granules are not damaged by the flow of the Edinburgh Etch.

The plate is held by the top end of the handling strip and gently lowered into the etching solution. The back of the plate should touch the wall of the tank so that the plate surface is facing the corrosive bath. It is advisable to suspend the plate in the solution rather than let it sink right down to the bottom of the tank. A good way of suspending plates is by clipping the acetate strip onto a tank divider with a plastic peg. In an aerated tank compartment, the plate should be placed about an inch away from the rising bubbles produced by the air pump. If several small plates are being etched, these can also be stacked above each

New Etching Chemistry

By Friedhard Kiekeben

other on one handling strip to create more space in the tank. However, it is crucial that plates do not have contact and are never sandwiched together.

Keep a record of the time when etching commenced. During biting, the depth of bite should be checked at regular intervals. For test purposes, the plate is lifted out of the tank allowing excess mordant to drip back into the bath before the plate is carefully rinsed. Most etchers develop their own preferred method of assessing the depth of bitten intaglio, bearing in mind its ultimate effect on the printed etching.

A pocket microscope gives a magnified view of the indentations being eroded into the surface and reveals to what extent etching really is a sculptural process. Bitten areas can also be carefully probed with a drypoint needle. Slightly damaged areas of the ground can be quickly mended by touching up with a soft wax crayon before further biting. Acrylic hard ground plates are so durable that test printing is possible without having to remove the ground. After proofing, the plate can be gently de-greased and etched further.

When the plate is satisfactorily etched, it is rinsed thoroughly under a running tap or hose. Copper and brass plates should also be de-oxidized with a solution of salt and vinegar in water before reapplication of acrylics. Oxidation is also minimized by blotting and speed-drying plates in hot air. If a plate has reached the reclaiming stage, it can be transferred into the stripping solution straight after rinsing to take the acrylic ground off. Any backing should be removed prior to printing.

Safety Note: All metal salt solutions in dip tanks and etching trays should be covered up or poured into sealed containers when not in use. This reduces cross-contamination between different solutions as well as evaporation, thus extending their useable life.

Neutralization and Disposal

An Edinburgh Etch solution for copper can be active for two to three years. The citric acid component in the tank allows for, literally, dozens of kilograms of metal to be dissolved without causing any precipitation. Once the solution becomes oily in consistency and of a black olive color, its ability to etch suddenly drops; and it is time for a replacement. A simple gravity-fed siphon pump is ideal for transferring the solution from the tank into plastic storage containers.

The best way to dispose of spent etching solutions is to take them to a chemical disposal company. Local authorities may also permit the disposal of ferric / Edinburgh Etch solutions down the drain if they have been properly neutralized, and highly diluted.

To neutralize an Edinburgh Etch or ferric chloride solution, add to it a strong sodium carbonate solution gradually you may also use a used stripping solution as the neutralizing agent. In a harmless fizzing reaction, carbon dioxide is produced. Allow this to settle before adding more sodium carbonate. Once the solution no longer fizzes when soda ash is added, neutralization is complete. This can be confirmed by a pH test showing a pH value of seven. After that, dilute with plenty of running water and discard.

The innovative design of integrating a 'corrosive area' with a ferric-based etching area and an alkaline stripping unit has the added advantage of being self-neutralizing during operation. As plates are etched and stripped, both acidic and alkaline residues are flushed into the drainage system, thus leading to a natural neutralization.

New Etching Chemistry

By Friedhard Kiekeben

Saline Sulphate Etch for Zinc

The saline sulphate etch for zinc is ideal for those etchers to whom the creative possibilities of the fairly inexpensive yet versatile and malleable metal zinc are indispensable. Intaglio text books often list the relative softness of zinc and its slight effect on some color etching inks (especially yellow) as a drawback; but, in practice, this is outweighed by the many unique pictorial possibilities of this silvery metal. Many printmaking suppliers stock the printing industry grade zinc which has a backing and is harder, but the cheaper titanium roofing zinc is also a popular choice.

This Saline Sulphate Etch for zinc works very well for straight tray etching and does not require additional measures such as heating or aeration. A copper sulphate solution(the Bordeaux Etch) as a safe mordant for zinc was (to my knowledge) first suggested by Cedric Green in response to a number of safety concerns about the use of nitric or ferric as a mordant for zinc. During three years of comparative trials, I found that a copper sulphate based etchant for the zinc etch is indeed superior to any other solution, both in terms of its safety and its creative possibilities within acrylic resist etching.

A straight copper sulphate solution does make a good mordant for zinc, but etching is somewhat slow and the solution becomes exhausted quickly. Similar to my thinking behind the Edinburgh Etch, I looked into ways in which the pseudo-electrolytic eroding potential of copper sulphate could be fully harnessed. I reasoned that, as with ferric, quite possibly the chemical 'hydrolysis bond' formed between the metal salt and water might account for a loss of reactivity.

I found this confirmed in recent tests. These showed that a solution made up from equal parts of copper sulphate and sodium chloride (i.e., cooking salt) activates the etch by diminishing the hydrolysis bond. This 'Saline Sulphate Etch' for zinc is three times more active than a straight

copper sulphate solution (Bordeaux Etch), while producing a very crisp etch without the denser sedimentation and surface roughness of the Bordeaux Etch. During biting a coppery sediment of metal hydroxides and oxides continually floats to the surface, thus keeping the bitten work from clogging up. Etching can also be aided by occasionally brushing the plate surface with a soft brush. Delicate marks, such as a spray aquatint or soft-ground, should, however, be etched without brushing. The solution works more effectively if floating solids are regularly skimmed off with a brush or a strainer and removed from the bath - this keeps the solution from turning alkaline and extends its useable life.

Making up the Saline Sulphate Etch for Zinc

The solution is made up from copper sulphate and cooking salt crystals which readily dissolve in water. This process works at its best if quantities and ratios given below are adhered to fairly accurately. It is recommended to use 'anhydrous copper sulphate' supplied reasonably priced in larger quantities by a chemical wholesale dealer. Do not use agricultural supplies, as these often contain impurities. As with most etching chemicals, specifically ask for 'production' or 'industrial grade' copper sulphate rather than 'laboratory grade', since the latter is a lot more expensive.

Wear gloves, dust mask, and goggles when handling the crystals to avoid touch or inhalation of dust particles. Once the solution is made up, it is quite safe to use with the customary etching precautions.

Saline Sulphate Etch for Zinc

1. 75 gms copper sulphate.

2. +50 – 75 gms sodium chloride (salt).

3. + 1 litre water.

(multiply these quantities by the same factor to make up larger amounts).

New Etching Chemistry

By Friedhard Kiekeben

Saline Sulphate Etch for Aluminum

Due to its softness and its coarse atomic structure, aluminum is somewhat less suited for intaglio printing than other kinds of metal. However, since aluminum plates are cheaply available from sheet metal merchants, many printmakers use them for straight drypoint work or as a substrate for ImagOn but, formally, the lightweight metal was rarely used for etched intaglio.

Using the following Saline Sulphate Etch solution, however, does provide benefits and features that are unique to aluminum etching. With the exception of copper, all metals build up a certain surface roughness during etching, which translates into more or less printable tones. Usually, aquatint has to be used in order to fill open areas on the plate with durable tones or a black. The Saline Sulphate Etch for aluminum is fundamentally different. During etching, a very distinctive surface roughness occurs in the open areas of the plate which can be compared to a hand-made mezzotint. This crystalline texture can produce a beautiful black on the print all by itself. As a consequence, there is no such thing as 'open bite' in this process since all bitten areas become carriers for etching ink, thus enhancing the graphic potential of the process.

Unusually, neither of the basic components of this Saline Sulphate etch, i.e. copper sulphate and salt, have any corrosive effect on the metal by themselves. But etching becomes possible in a combined solution containing, at least, double the amount of sodium chloride than the amount of copper sulphate. While all other metals easily erode as long as they are grease free, the surface of aluminum plates also needs to be evenly abraded with fine steel wool to create an etchable surface. This should be done before any acrylic grounds are applied to the plate.

As with the zinc process, the Saline Sulphate Etch for aluminum involves the production of a very loose coppery sediment which floats to the surface and should be removed regularly. However, the continuous rising of a minute quantity of hydrogen bubbles also indicates that etching is in progress. For disposal, proceed as with the Saline Sulphate Etch for zinc.

Saline Sulphate Etch for Aluminum

| 1 | 70gms copper sulphate.
| 2 | + 140gms sodium chloride (salt).
| 3 | + 1 litre water.

(Multiply these quantities by the same factor to make up larger amounts.)

TIP: When stripping acrylics off an etched aluminum plate, ensure that plates are not left in the soda ash stripping solution too long as this would result in further corrosion.

Disposal or Recycling of a Saline Sulphate Solution

The liquid component of a spent solution can be neutralized with sodium carbonate, diluted with plenty of water and then discarded. The surplus crystalline residues will remain at the bottom of the tray when the liquid is carefully decanted into another vessel. These can then be collected and kept in a sealed container. Once a container is filled with solid metal compounds it should be disposed off as chemical waste.

A different kind of saline sulphate etch for zinc and aluminum was outlined by Semenoff and Bader in the journal LEONARDO, Vol. 31, in 1998. This solution has a small salt content and is acidified with sodium bisulphate. In the same article, the authors suggest that a spent copper sulphate based etching solution such as the Saline Sulphate Etch can be reactivated by mixing it with sodium bisulfate which has a low hazard rating. Over a few days, the bath - which should be occasionally stirred - undergoes a reversed chemical reaction during which a fresh supply of copper sulphate solution is produced. This blue green liquid can then be decanted and reused for etching.

New Etching Chemistry

By Friedhard Kiekeben

By Dr, Paul Craig, PhD & Dr. Paul Rosenberg, PhD.

Corrosive Painting: Spit-Bite

There is an etching technique that does not involve the immersion of the plate in an etching bath. In 'spit biting', which is more precisely described as a 'creeping bite', an aquatint grain is etched directly into the plate by painting the mordant onto it. In traditional printmaking, this exposed the etcher to extremely volatile fumes. However, using a strong Edinburgh Etch or Saline Sulphate etch solution makes the process safe and controllable as no fumes are produced. Unique flowing, continuous forms, and tones resembling watercolor washes can be conjured up in this way.

Initially, an even layer of acrylic spray aquatint is applied to the plate. Areas not meant to etch should be stopped out or masked out with strips of adhesive tape. According to the kind of metal used, a jar filled with a strong solution of the appropriate metal salt solution should be at hand, i.e. Edinburgh Etch for copper or brass, or the Saline Sulphate Etch for Zinc. Also needed, are a jug of water and an assortment of soft brushes. This technique should be executed in the allocated etching area, and gloves and goggles must be worn.

The plate is placed in a tray and, gradually, marks are made by painting directly on the aquatinted surface with the salt solution. The longer the full-strength solution remains in one place, the darker the etched tone will be. Sharp edges can be avoided by brushing water around the etched areas; the dilution creates tonal blends. To control the depth of bite, the plate can be intermittently rinsed and inspected before more solution is brushed on. If the etched marks are meant to be more defined, a drop of detergent can be added. A spit bite usually etches quite quickly and dark tones can result from this fine but shallow etch within minutes. In order to make up a spit bite that produces no washes but only sharply defined brush marks, the metal salt solution needs to be thickened, for instance, by blending it with cellulose wall paper paste.

Art meets Science at R.I.T.

Recently the metal salt etching processes developed by Friedhard Kiekeben have been thoroughly tested by scientists. Dr Paul Craig and Dr Paul Rosenberg, both professors of chemistry at R.I.T., collaboratively wrote the following recommendation and safety assessment for the Edinburgh Etch and The Saline Sulphate Etch:

The Chemistry of Etching without Acid

In the past, metal etching for the purpose of printing or art was typically done with nitric acid, which has harmful vapors and is extremely caustic. In this chemistry lab nitric acid baths are always maintained in enclosed fume hoods with separate ventilation and filtering. Such hoods are often not available in print or art studios. The Edinburgh Etch uses a mixture of ferric chloride and citrate, which circumvents the safety hazards associated with nitric acid baths. The etching of copper with ferric chloride has been well-known for a number of years. However, etching is slow and results in precipitation on the surface of the copper, probably due to the accumulation of insoluble copper salts (perhaps copper hydroxide) on the surface of the copper. If these accumulate, they interfere with the normal oxidation-reduction reaction between the Ferric (Fe^{3+}) and the metallic copper (Cu^0). In the equations shown below for this reaction in water, a positive voltage indicates an energetically favorable reaction.

$$2Fe^{3+} + 2e^- \rightarrow 2Fe^{2+} \qquad E_o^! = +0.771V$$
$$Cu^0 \rightarrow Cu^{2+} + e^- \qquad E_o^! = -0.339V$$
$$2Fe^{3+} + Cu^0 \rightarrow 2Fe^{2+} + Cu^{2+} \quad \Delta E_o^! = +0.432V$$

The Edinburgh Etch adds one new ingredient to the ferric chloride etching bath: citric acid. Etching in this bath is much more rapid and reproducible than the original ferric chloride etch. This can be attributed to two causes:

1. The citric acid will lower the pH of the bath slightly (making it more acidic). Under these conditions, the Cu^{2+} is unlikely to form an insoluble salt (such as copper hydroxide – $Cu(OH)_2$) and thus will be more soluble.

New Etching Chemistry

By Dr, Paul Craig, PhD & Dr. Paul Rosenberg, PhD.

2. The Cu2+ will have a tendency to form a complex with citric acid as it is released from the surface of the metal, also increasing its solubility. The hazards associated with the Edinburgh etch are dramatically less than those associated with nitric acid. The solution is mildly caustic to the touch and does not emit noxious gases. In fact, the Edinburgh etch could safely be used in an open studio or laboratory, whereas the nitric acid etch can only be safely used with a fume hood. A small amount of hydrochloric acid may be released as the copper complexes with the citric acid. This is highly soluble in water and should not pose any serious risk of acid fumes in the lab. Nonetheless, when the Edinburgh etch is exhausted, it is still recommended that the solution and solids be disposed as chemical waste, rather than washing down the drain into the sanitary sewer system. High concentrations of iron and copper in the sewer system may interfere with normal bacterial recovery of materials in the sewer system.

The Edinburgh etch reacts very rapidly with the copper. In our studio, we etched a clean sheet of copper (20.35 cm x 12.85 cm, 0.5 mm thick, 127.56 grams, including an acrylic backing) until only the backing remained (10.50 g) in 13 hours. This was not a new etching bath – it had been in use for several months.

The Saline Sulphate Etch

The saline sulphate etch is recommended for etching aluminum or zinc. Use of the Edinburgh etch with these metals may result in the release of heat, flammable hydrogen gas, and acid fumes. The reaction is comparable to the thermite reaction which is used in munitions. The reaction between iron and aluminum (or iron and zinc) is a very high energy reaction (as indicated by the much higher voltage) and should be avoided.

$$3Fe^3 + 3e^- \rightarrow 3Fe^{2+} \qquad E_o^' = +0.771V$$
$$Al^0 \rightarrow Al^{3+} + 3e^- \qquad E_o^' = +1.677V$$
$$2Fe^3 + Al^0 \rightarrow 2Fe^{2+} + Al^{3+} \qquad \Delta E_o^' = +2.448V$$

$$2Fe^3 + 2e^- \rightarrow 2Fe^{2+} \qquad E_o^' = +0.771V$$
$$Zn^0 \rightarrow Zn^{2+} + 2e^- \qquad E_o^' = +0.762V$$
$$2Fe^3 + Zn^0 \rightarrow 2Fe^{2+} + Zn^{2+} \qquad \Delta E_o^' = +1.533V$$

The Saline Sulphate Etch uses the reaction between copper and aluminum, which is quite a bit milder than the reaction between iron and aluminum, as indicated by the lower voltage. The comparable reaction for copper and zinc is also shown.

$$3Cu^{2+} + 3e^- \rightarrow 3Cu^+ \qquad E_o^' = -0.339V$$
$$Al^0 \rightarrow Al^{3+} + 3e^- \qquad E_o^' = +1.677V$$
$$3Cu^{2+} + Al^0 \rightarrow 3Cu^+ + Al^{3+} \qquad \Delta E_o^' = +1.338V$$

$$2Cu^{2+} + 2e^- \rightarrow 2Cu^+ \qquad E_o^' = +0.161V$$
$$Zn^0 \rightarrow Zn^{2+} + 2e^- \qquad E_o^' = +0.762V$$
$$2Cu^{2+} + Zn^0 \rightarrow 2Cu^+ + Zn^{2+} \qquad \Delta E_o^' = +0.923V$$

In the absence of sodium chloride, a copper etch of aluminum or zinc is characterized by high levels of insoluble copper hydroxides in the solution, which may clog the etching process, for reasons like those proposed previously for the Edinburgh etch. The chloride in the saline sulphate etch is thought to partially prevent formation of copper hydroxide by competing with the hydroxide ion for binding to the copper. Copper chloride is much more soluble than copper hydroxide.

For the printer or artist, both these systems are mild and much safer than the traditional nitric acid bath for etching of metals, especially if proper precautions are taken when designing the reactions (e.g., no etching of aluminum with ferric chloride) and when exhausted materials are disposed of properly. To the chemist, these are very nice systems, which are highly complex. In the chemistry lab, we usually deal with much more dilute solutions of metal ions and salts than are described here. All would bear some study from the chemistry perspective. The real issues here are competitive equilibria. Chloro and citrate complexes of these metals are playing a major role in these systems. There is not much published information on these systems. There does not appear to be any significant or major chemical hazards associated with the chemical processes employed here, although a reaction between aluminum and iron could get lead to explosive results.

Standard reduction potentials were obtained from Harris, D.C. Quantitative Chemical Analysis, 6th edition, W.H. Freeman and Company, New York, 2003.

Eileen Feeney Bushnell, **Untitled**, 2003, Acrylic Resist Etching using acrylic soft and hard-ground with acrylic aquatint, 5" x 8".

Acrylic Soft - Ground

QUICK LOOK

1. Roll up etching plate with soft-ground.

1

3. Draw-release technique.

2

2. Lay soft texture imparting materials onto plate, cover with non-stick plastic, and run through the press.

3

4

4. Etch the plate; remove soft-ground and proof.

Soft - Ground

A

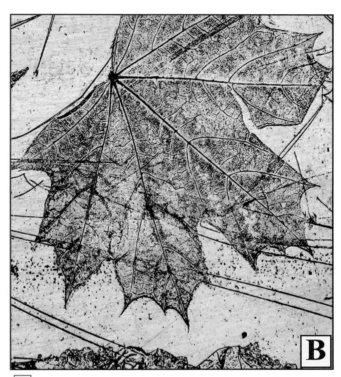

B

A Lifting a leaf, with the aide of a snap-off cutter, from a Orono soft-ground covered copper plate. Notice the texture or impression left by the leaf on the red colored Orono soft-ground.

Introduction

A soft-ground is an etch technique where a metal plate is covered with a modified ink-ground,them textures are pressed into this wet ink surface. The ink-ground is then dried, etched, and printed.

I first documented the use of the Graphic Chemical #1659 water-based relief ink soft-ground in my 1998 publication *Non-Toxic Intaglio Printmaking* and this technique remains as viable now as it was then. Most of the etch techniques that I have developed were designed to work on copper plates with the use of ferric chloride as the etchant. Other printmakers prefer zinc, brass, aluminum, and steel plates. These metals require different grounds and different mordants. To my knowledge, the most important developments made in advancing the technologies of acrylic resist grounds and mordants have been made by Friedhard Kiekeben, Susan Gross, and Cedric Green.

B Resulting soft-ground print made from a similar leaf shown in illustration A, left.

Cedric Green has developed an entire system of galvanic etching where plates are suspended in an electrolyte solution and etched in what can be described as a reverse electro-plating process using a 12V battery charger. There is not enough room in this publication to elaborate on this technique, but Cedric has a very informative web site where this information is freely available. **http://perso.club-internet.fr/gravert/galvetch/**

Friedhard Kiekeben, in collaboration with Susan Groce, developed the Orono-Ground which is a fortified and fast drying ink-ground made by adding special acrylics to the Graphic Chemical water soluble relief ink. Although the Orono-Ground requires more preparation, it yields a soft-ground with finer detail and greater ground strength and durability. It also is a more versatile ground which can be applied to copper, zinc, steel, and aluminum plates. *As it dries quickly, it also make a superb hard-ground.*

Acrylic Soft - Ground

As both the Graphic Chemical 1659 relief ink-ground and the Orono-Ground have virtually the same methodology, I will describe just one soft-ground method. It is understood that either the Graphic Chemical 1659 black relief ink or the Orono-Ground can be interchangeable.

The Orono-Ground
The following text, in italics, was contributed by Friedhard Kiekeben.

*The Orono soft ground consists of **two main components**:*

*The FIRST component is **Graphic Chemical water-based block printing ink**, such as the Peacock Blue (or Crimson red) which ensures good rollability of the Orono Ground.*

*The SECOND of these two components is the soft-ground **binder mix,** which needs to be made up from four ingredients and can then be stored in sealed containers.*

Ingredients:
*FIRST. **Graphic Chemical water based block printing ink** (as a stiff rolling base) For best visibility on the plate, I prefer using Peacock Blue ink, but other varieties, such as the 1659 Black, also work.*

*SECOND: **Binder Mix***
1. Golden Acrylics Medium GAC 200, or Lascaux clear gloss varnish 2060.

2. Lascaux Acrylic paint, 972, oxide black, or Golden acrylic black.

3. Golden additives, retarder 3580-7, or Lascaux retarder.

4. Golden, liquid thickener (long rheology), 98510, or Lascaux thickener.

*The **Soft Ground Binder Mix** is made in the following way:*

$\boxed{1}$ *Make up a **thickener solution** by adding 50% water (preferably de-ionized) very gradually to 50% Golden 98510 thickener; the alternative Lascaux thickener comes ready-mixed.*

$\boxed{2}$ *Mix one drop **thickening solution** per one milliliter GAC 200 or Lascaux 2060 varnish (i.e. 200 drops thickener per 200ml varnish).*

It is crucial to add the thickener in very small quantities while stirring continually. The mixing and stirring process can take up to ten minutes to create a good emulsion; the resulting mix should have a doughy consistency which makes a smacking sound when stirred.

$\boxed{3}$ *Now, add 10% retarder; add more retarder in hot conditions or if a soft-ground working time, in excess of 20 minutes, is required.*

$\boxed{4}$ *Add 1/5th Lascaux acrylic paint 972 or a similar product, such as Golden's acrylic black, and give a final stir.*

The soft-ground binder is now ready for use, and can be stored in a sealed container. A simpler, yet equally effective binder mix can be obtained by mixing 50% Lascaux varnish 2060 with 50% water based screen printing medium.

Making up the Orono soft-ground
The soft-ground should be mixed from the two base components prior to use; once mixed, it should be used within the next half hour or so. In its mixed state, it does not keep well, so do store the components in separate containers.

The mixing method is similar to the mixing of printing inks. Mixing takes place on a clean slab with a palette knife. First spread out a good amount of the Graphic Chemical block printing ink on the slab. Add an equal amount of the soft-ground base, and thoroughly work the two components into one another until a good blend has been achieved.

Acrylic Soft - Ground

The soft ground is now ready for rolling onto a degreased plate which can also be slightly sanded with 600 grit wet-and-dry sandpaper (wet method). A thinner layer will ensure the register of even the finest imprinted detail; but a thicker layer which also has good detail reproduction, ensures maximum acid resistance and is best for a deeper etch.

Refer to Keith Howard's explanation of soft-ground drawing and impressions. These methods are also suitable for application using the Orono-ground.

Tip: An ink roller used for the Orono-ground should be soaked in detergent solution immediately after use to prevent hardening of its delicate surface.

Soft-Ground Materials

1. Graphic Chemical water-soluble black relief ink #1659 or the Orono-ground.

Tip: Do not use the Graphic Chemical 1650 black relief ink as it dries too quickly for the soft-ground application.

2. Good medium density brayer. The better the quality of the brayer, the better the results.

3. Palette knife and inking slab.

4. Cleaned copper plate polished with wet sanding using 600 grit wet-and-dry sandpaper.

5. Variety of suitable textured material to impart textures onto the soft-ground Illustration 5, shows lace which imparts good textures

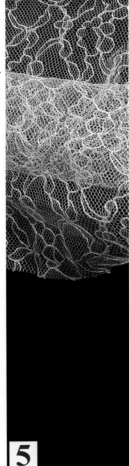

to the Graphic Chemical 1659 black ink soft-ground plate.

6. Ferric chloride or the Edinburgh Etch.

Tip: When using the Graphic Chemical 1659 ink soft-ground in a vertical etching tank, do not use the aerator. The aerator action can cause open-biting on the Graphic Chemical 1659 ink-ground.

7. Plastic packing tape or plastic shelf liner to apply to the back of the plate.

8. An inking hot-plate is a useful piece of equipment when it comes to drying the soft-ground ink.

Soft-Ground Step-by-Step

I often tell my students that they need the observation skills of an anthropologist to be a good printmaker. If, for instance, you become keenly aware of how the etching plate feels as you pull the wheel of the etching press, you will be alerted to any change in the press pressure. This observation is more appropriate in printmaking studios where more than one person uses the press; however, a tactile observation skill, such as this, may save your print or even prevent blanket and press damage.

The soft-ground technique epitomizes the use of keen observation skills as it is just as important to note how the ink-ground sounds when it is being inked-up as how it looks on the inking slab. Adequately describing the sound the brayer makes during inking is impossible. Suffice it to say that it sounds "sticky". If you tried to roll-up screen filler, there would be hardly any sound. With highly viscous ink, there is a distinctly unique sound. If there is too much ink on the brayer or roller, the sound is exaggerated. If there is not enough ink, the sound is softer. These are all observable clues to becoming an excellent printmaker. The key to a good soft-ground is to have a small amount of ink on the roller and plate.

Acrylic Soft - Ground

1 Lay down a thin bead of the Graphic Chemical 1659 ink or Orono-ground (illustrated) onto an inking slab.

2 Roll-up an ink slab by passing the brayer over the bead of ink and allowing it to spin for at least a couple of rotations. Lay down a section of ink about the same width as the brayer. If this first layer of ink on the inking slab has too much ink, repeat this inking method on a clean section of the inking slab without recharging the brayer with ink

3a, Lay a fine layer of soft-ground ink or Orono-ground onto the prepared metal plate. It is best to lay down multiple thin layers of the ink-ground rather than a few thicker layers. 3b, Lay down thin layers of soft-ground in multiple directions until the plate is completely and evenly covered.

3a b Work the brayer or roller in multiple directions to gain good coverage.

4 **Soft-ground density test**.
Using an HB pencil, draw a small line on the top side of a piece of bond paper at the corner of the soft-ground plate. This should be done immediately after the ink-ground has been applied to the plate. Once this is done, lift the paper from the plate.

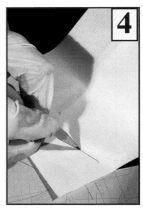

The pencil line should be clearly visible on the wet ink-ground plate. If done correctly, the actual metal of the plate can be seen. If there is absolutely no metal showing through the pencil line, it is an indication that too much ink-ground has been laid onto the metal plate. If this is the case wash the ink-ground completely off the plate, dry it, and repeat the ground application with less ink.

Drawing on top of bond paper will familiarize you with the drawing transfer soft-ground technique where "soft-ground" lines can be applied to any part of the plate.

5a,b After the plate has been completely inked up, it can be worked on with direct mark making

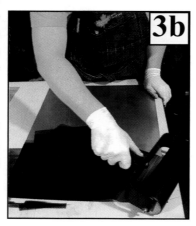

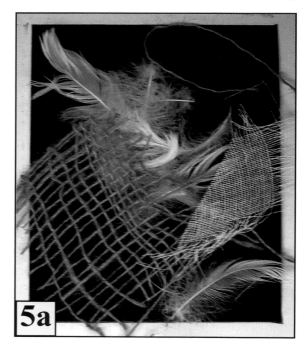

Acrylic Soft - Ground

5b

TIP: The etching press pressure may need to be released a little depending on how thick the texture imparting material may be.

6 Soft texture-imparting material are laid onto the soft-ground plate as shown in illustration 6.

6

BIG TIP: Do not use texture-making material, such as coins or any sharp or thick objects that can damage the press or blankets. Keep the thickness of any texture transfer objects to the thickness of the soft-ground plate or less.

7 After texture imparting materials have been laid onto the plate, cover the plate with anti-stick plastic. Make anti-stick plastic by using either the peel-back layer from a piece of ImagOn film or Glad® (Cling-wrap®) plastic food wrap. To give it an anti-stick property, spray the contact side of the plastic with spray cooking oil and rub it evenly over this contact area. Run the plate through the press.

techniques, such as wiping the plate with a rag or mark-making with a bamboo pen. Textures can be pushed into the wet ink-ground with fabric or sponges or many other similar materials. A brush charged with water can also be used to make wash-like marks, These are similar techniques that can also be done to an acrylic hard-ground plate.

The soft-ground technique is especially known for its ability to reproduce faithfully fine textures from soft organic and inorganic material, as demonstrated above in illustration 5a & b.

Pressing Textures into a Soft-Ground Plate

Within the soft-ground technique, there is a method whereby textures are pressed into the soft-ground plate via the etching press. After the ink soft-ground plate is prepared by rolling-up, it is placed onto the etching press bed.

7

8 Remove the anti-stick plastic and gently lift the soft-ground texture materials from the plate. It may be helpful to use the tip of a snap-off cutter to lift some organic materials which have been embedded into the plate by the pressure of the press. Notice the accidental lines pressed into the ink-ground, around the leaves, from wrinkling the anti-stick plastic.

Acrylic Soft - Ground

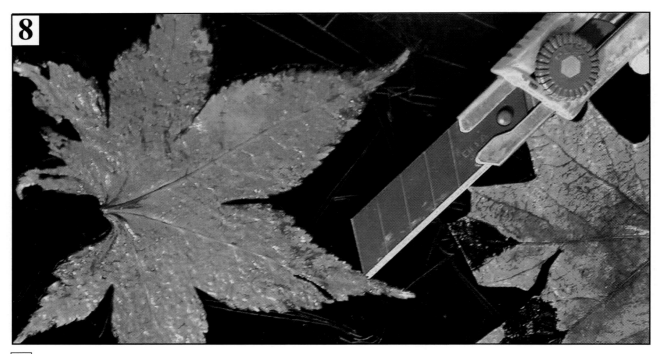

9 The plate is dried with a hair-dryer or, preferably, on an inking hot-plate. The Graphic Chemical 1659 ink-ground needs about an hour of drying time at about 100°F. The Orono-ground, generally, dries quicker depending on how much retarder is in the Orono-ground mixture.

TIP: This heating procedure is an important step in strengthening the ground.

10 Once the plate is completely dry, back the plate with plastic shelf-liner or brown plastic packing tape.

TIP: Do not use clear plastic packing tape as it is more difficult to remove from the plate.

11a, b The plate is now ready for etching in either the Edinburgh Etch or Ferric Chloride. Lower the etching plate into the Ferric Chloride tank.

Notice the packing tape handles. These handles are attached to the top of the etching tank with clothespins.

TIP: Mark your name and entry time on the tail end of the tape hangers.

12 Do not use the tank aerator. Etch the plate for 30 minutes in Ferric Chloride or 20 minutes in Edinburgh Etch. Take it out of the etch and, very gently, wash the plate with cold water. This rinse will open the plate by washing a thin veil of ink residue into the textured areas and allowing more detail to etch.

TIP: Use safety goggles when rinsing.

13 While rinsing the plate, in step 12, notice how much metal plate is revealed by this washing process. It is possible to over wash the plate and remove too much soft-ground. So, be careful.

Acrylic Soft - Ground

14 In this second etch cycle, the plate is returned to the etching bath for a final etch. If placed in ferric chloride, an additional hour is required; for the Edinburgh Etch, an additional 40 minutes is necessary. These etching times are based on fresh mixtures of mordants. Etching times for older mordants need to be increased proportionately with age. Also, etching times can be shortened for lighter results or lengthened for darker results.

15 After the two etching cycles have been completed, the ink-ground is washed off the plate with a sponge and Ajax or Comet powder and water.

16 The plastic backing tape is removed with the aid of a hair dryer or hot water directed towards the area of the tapes removal.

17 The plate is dried, and then printed.

Troubleshooting

Problem 1: Too much ink has been put on the palette. *Solution: Scrape the ink back with a palette knife or move the brayer to a clean inking spot and re-lay another inking pad.*

Problem 2. Lines and textures are transferred from the inking pad. *Solution: Replace inking slab with an unmarked one. If this problem has occurred it may alert you to the potential of transferring textures from other surfaces to the etching plate. If, for instance, you want the texture of a fly screen mesh, you can ink up this mesh with ink-ground and transfer it to the plate via a clean brayer. After the fly screen mesh has been inked up, pass a clean brayer over it, thus transferring the texture to the clean brayer. This, then, can be rolled out onto the clean copper plate (or even onto printing paper). This texture can be rolled out several times to create repeated motifs.*

Problem 3: Too much ink put on the plate, results in a loss of detail in the final print. *Solution: After the plate has been etched, you can remake the soft-ground plate. The following question then remains: how to integrate the marks from the partially etched plate to the new soft-ground application on top of these marks. Intriguing options are to rework the plate with the Construction, Wrinkled or Direct Intaglio-Type methods. This type of thinking opens up an entire world of new creative plate reworking possibilities.*

Problem 4: The Graphic Chemical 1659 ink-ground dissolves in the etching solutions causing unwanted open-bite type marks. *Solution: This may occur if the etching tank aerator has been left on during the etch cycles. This aerator should be off as the 1659 ink-ground is fragile. Also, if the washing process after the first etch cycle is too severe, it can cause unwanted areas of the ink-ground to lift. Cooking or baking the ink-ground onto the plate with a professional inking hot-plate at $100°F$ for 1 hour strengthens this ground considerably. If the problem persists, discontinue the wash after the first etch cycle.*

Problem 5: The Orono-ground dries too quickly. *Solution: Add more retarder to the Orono-ground mix.*

Problem 7: Fine pin-hole marks appear in what should have been the white areas of the print. *Solution: This is caused when not enough ink-ground has been applied to the plate. As a precautionary measure prior to etching any soft-ground plate, any intended white areas on the plate should be blocked-out. This is done by painting Future or Golden's Block-out solution onto the ink-ground plate in the intended white areas. Do this after the ink-ground has dried.*

Etching times given are meant for good standard results when plates are etched in fresh mordants. Etching times can be varied according to desired results. Deeper etched plates will require more time than recommended here. Because the desired results determine the etch length, knowing how long to etch a plate will be a matter of experience.

Scratching lines into a Orono hard-ground plate with an etching needle.

QUICK LOOK

1. Pour Future or Klear onto the etching plate. When dry, paint on black ink.

1

2

2. Or roll on Orono-ground; work either wet or dry.

3. Draw lines through hard-ground to expose the metal plate. Back the plate to ready it for etching.

3

4

4. Etch the plate, remove the hard-ground, and proof.

Acrylic Hard - Ground

Introduction

The acrylic hard-ground is an etch technique in which a metal plate is covered with either Future (Klear) acrylic floor finish or a modified ink-ground (Orono-ground). After the ground has dried, lines or wash-like marks are drawn through the hard-ground to revel the metal plate below. The plate is then backed with plastic packing tape, etched, and printed.

There are two basic methods of coating the metal etching plate. The first is *flow coating* and the second is *roll-on coating*.

Materials

1. Use Future® or Klear® acrylic floor finish and water soluble black India ink or fountain pen ink. Water soluble gouache can also be substituted for the India ink.

2. Use Orono-ground materials (See previous chapter) or Graphic Chemical 1659 black, water-soluble, relief ink.

3. Photo developing tray larger in width than the copper plate to be coated.

4. Good quality brayer and inking slab.

5. Clean rags and rubbing alcohol.

6. Medium tooth metal file.

7. 600 grit wet-and-dry sandpaper and palm sander.

8. Hairdryer or professional inking hot-plate.

9. Plastic backing tape or shelf-liner.

10. Edinburgh Etch or Ferric Chloride.

Flow Coating Step-by-Step

Although any popular etching metal can be used, I recommend roofing copper.

1 Prepare the copper plate by sanding it with 600 grit wet-and-dry sandpaper. Use the wet method and endeavor to polish the plate as close to a mirror-finish as possible.

TIP: If the copper plate has scratches it may be necessary to burnish and scrape them out ; otherwise they may show up as ink lines on the final print.

2 Roofing copper generally has sharp corners. Sometimes, blunt metal shears create a sharp, raised edge on the plate. To avoid injury, these sharp edges and corners should be filed down.

3 Directly after sanding and edge filing, use a clean cloth and a little rubbing alcohol to remove completely all copper sanding residue from the copper plate.

4a,b & c Position the copper plate vertically in a photo developing tray. While supporting the back of the plate with one hand, pour the Future over the plate with the other hand. Start pouring at the top of the plate allowing the cascading Future to flow down the surface of the copper plate into the photo tray.

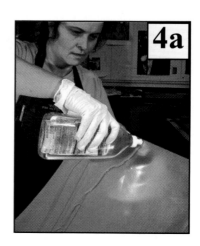

Acrylic Hard - Ground

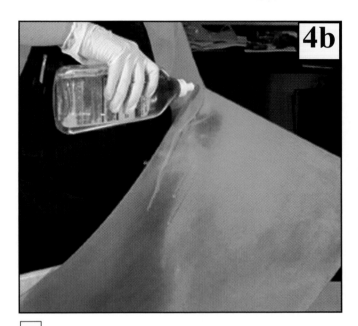

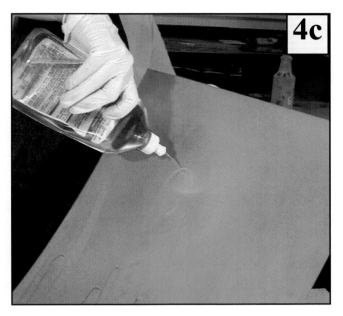

5 After the plate has been completely coated with Future, prop it vertically up onto a clean absorbent cloth. The cloth absorbs the run-off of the Future, preventing a thick residue at the bottom of the plate. Allow the plate to air dry.

6 Once the Future has dried, the copper plate will have a hard mordant resistant coating, which is the hard-ground. Anything that can scratch through or dissolve this hard-ground will open the copper plate up to the mordant.

The Future hard-ground is a transparent ground. This is advantageous when re-working the plate after the first or second etch.

This transparent ground can also be left on the plate through to the final editioning stage. It provides a glass-like surface on the plate, making it easy to wipe and will appeal to those printmakers who do not want plate-tone.

If, however, plate-tone is desired, provided the ground is not older than one week, it can be removed with ImagOn developing solution. After this week or so period, the acrylic polymers in the Future mature and removing the ground will require plate submersion in the strong soda ash stripping tank.

If the transparent Future hard-ground is not as desirable as the black conventional type of hard-ground, paint a thin layer of water soluble India ink or fountain pen ink (or black gouache) onto the dried Future hard-ground. You can easily scratch through both the Future and the India ink layer. Once the hard-ground drawing has been completed, wash this India ink off the plate before the etching process.

7 Once the hard-ground has dried, it can be worked with any tool that can break through the hard-ground surface. (A wire brush is used to create multiple lines through the hard-ground plate.)

Acrylic Hard - Ground

Roll-Coating Step-by-Step

The best roll-on hard-ground is the Orono-ground. The application of the Orono-ground is identical to that of the Orono soft-ground technique described in the previous chapter. The steps involved are summarized as follows:

1 a , b Lay out a palette of Orono-ground and apply a thin layer to the clean polished copper plate.

2a b & c The Orono-ground can be worked on when it is wet or dry. Below, a dry rag creates interesting open-bite and streaky areas on the wet Orono-ground.

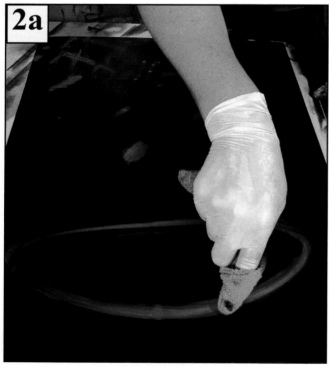

2 b Shows a brush charged with water creating wash-like effects on the wet Orono-ground.

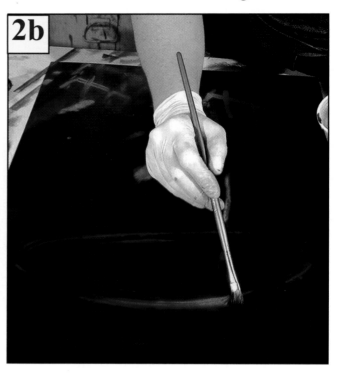

2 c After the Orono-ground has dried, it can be worked on by any tool that will break the ground surface such as a star-wheel as in illustration 2c. This tool was designed for the fabric industry and can create stippled lines and tones.

TIP: An Aquatint effect can be created on a hard-ground by running the dried hard-ground plate through the etching press in contact with dry sandpaper. Various grit sandpaper give varied results. You can also repeat this process to obtain a greater density of sandpaper textured areas.

Acrylic Hard - Ground

3 Once the etching has been completed, the hard-ground plate is be backed with plastic packing tape or shelf-liner.

4 The plate is etched in either the Edinburgh Etch 40 minutes or ferric chloride for one hour.

5 Once the etching cycle has been completed, the Orono-ground is easily removed by placing the plate first into the soda ash stripping tank for 15 minutes and then washing it with warm water and a sponge.

TIP: Wear eye protection and suitable gloves during this entire procedure.

Progressive etch

With almost any etch technique, the plate can be progressively etched. This is done in two distinctly different ways. In the first instance, the image to be scratched into the hard-ground is progressively created on the plate. In this way, the blackest areas of the image are scratched on the plate first. Then the plate is etched for 10 minutes, taken from the etchant, washed, dried, and re-worked by adding more lines to the image. It is, again etched for another 10 minutes. This cycle can be repeated as many times as necessary to complete the image.

TIP: The etching times suggested are only starting points and can be varied to accommodate individual image needs and printmaking styles.

In the second instance, the entire drawing is scratched into the hard-ground plate. The plate then goes through an etch and stop-out cycle until fully etched. In other words, the plate is taken from the etching bath at ten minute intervals, stopped out, dried, and returned to the etching bath as many times as needed.

TIP: The best stop-out to use is Golden's acrylic stop-out varnish for printmakers. Alternatively, Future, Klear, or Speedball Screen Filler can be used.

Reworking the Etched Plate

If the copper plate needs to be recoated with Future or Klear acrylic or the Orono-ground, is necessary to **deoxidize the plate before recoating**. This is also the case for Soft-ground techniques.

Once the copper plate has etched, it undergoes a rapid kind of tarnishing process which leaves an oxide on the surface of the copper plate. This oxide creates a barrier to acrylic hard-grounds that can cause the ground to fall off the plate at the slightest touch.

An easy way to make a de-oxidization liquid is to purchase a 4.5 liter container of white vinegar and add 1 cup of table salt. Shake the vinegar until most of the salt has dissolved, and place this liquid into a photo developing tray. Submerge the copper plate into this deoxidizing liquid for about 1 minute, remove, rinse with water, and dry.

TIP: Soy-sauce also makes a good de-oxidization liquid.

Reworking the Hard-Ground Plate with other Techniques

It should be noted that all techniques have the potential to be reworked with a variety of other techniques. For instance, most etch techniques can be combined with non-etch Intaglio-Type techniques. This allows for a greater diversity of mark making possibility.

One of the easiest ways to rework any plate is to paint directly onto the surface of the plate with Hunt Speedball screen filler. This produces a very painterly effect and when painted on thinly, the existing marks on the plate show through. If 320 grit carborundum is mixed with the screen filler, making an oil paint-like consistency, and is painted onto the plate, rich black marks result in the final print. The screen filler, laden with grit, simulates an aquatint which is why I call this concoction the liquid aquatint.

Acrylic Hard - Ground

Troubleshooting

Problem 1: Some areas of the copper plate, especially around the edges, resist the Future or Klear acrylic hard-ground application. ***Solution:*** *Generally, greasy marks, especially around the edges of the plate, are the result of finger prints. Use rubbing alcohol and a clean rag to remove these greasy marks.*

Problem 2: When applying the Orono-ground, the edges are difficult to roll-up equally with the rest of the plate. ***Solution:*** *This edge roll-up problem is caused by blunt metal cutting shears which bend the plate edge as well as cut them. A practical solution is to have the blades on the metal shears sharpened and properly aligned. It may be possible to completely correct this problem by aligning the blades of the metal shears so that they have the possibility to cut tissue paper. Alternately use a tool called Easy Bevel, available from Daniel Smith Art Materials and other printmaking suppliers, that manually removes the edge of metal plates. This tool is like a potato peeler; only it shaves off a thin strip of metal from the edge of the plate. If done repeatedly it will bevel the plate edge.*

BIG TIP: Restrict your metal shears to cutting only brass, copper, zinc, and aluminum plates. Do not use them to cut matteboard or anything else. Frequently, cutting paper products will blunt the cutting blade more than the listed etching metals. If nails or screws are cut in these type of cutters, they can chip the blade which translates into an irregular edge on your copper plate.

Problem 3: The hard-ground will not stay on the plate after the plate has been repeatedly etched. ***Solution:*** *Deoxidize the plate as on the previous page. There is a point, after about the second or third reworking of the plate, where Future will not stay on the plate due to this oxidization problem. If this problem persists use the Orono-ground which is far more resistant to this problem. For deeply etched plates that need reworking: first card the Orono-ground into the plate, followed by*

the recommended roller/brayer application demonstrated in the soft-ground chapter.

Problem 4: The hard-ground dissolves off the plate after the first etch. ***Solution:*** *This problem is generally related to the hard-ground failing to be completely dry before the plate is etched. If any etching plate has a polymer or acrylic ground, heating it at about 100°F for about 1 hour will strengthen the acrylic or polymer surface of the ground. The best way to do this is on a professional inking hot-plate.*

Sven Wohlgemuth (Germany), **No Result**, 2002, Intaglio-Type reworked with screen filler, 12" x 9". See also his German Web site:
<http://www.intaglio-type.de/home.html>

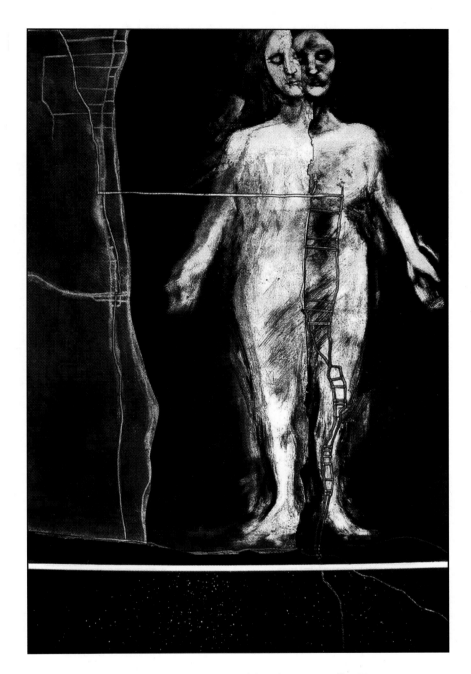

Erin Holscher, 2003, **Train**, Combination Intaglio-Type.
(Pastel Intaglio-Type, pages 87-88, with Construction Intaglio-
Type), 18" x 28".

Acrylic Aquatint

QUICK LOOK

1. Mix Speedball Screen Filler with 1/3 water and then prepare to test the spray. **1**

2 **3. Spray evenly the 60% spray onto the entire plate.**

3. Back the plate, etch it for 2 mins., remove it from etchant, wash it, and apply stop-out. Repeat until the image is done. **3**

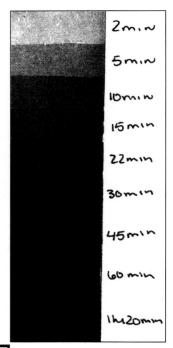

4 **4. When the etch cycles are completed, remove the Screen Filler, and proof the plate.**

Acrylic Aquatint

What is an Aquatint?

Aquatint is from the Latin word *aquafortis*, which means strong water and refers to an acid etchant; and *tinto* is the Italian word for tone.

An aquatint technique allows a printmaker to develop an image with tonality rather than line. In line etching, the plate is covered completely with hard-ground, and the surface is scratched by an engraving needle to uncover the metal plate. The aquatint is also a type of ground, but it only partially covers the metal plate.

The traditional aquatint technique involves dusting an acid-resistant substance, such as rosin or asphaltum powder onto the surface of a metal plate. The dust particles are adhered to the plate with heat. This aquatint procedure arranges thousands of particles in a congested, uniform, and/or random manner. However, these particles do not totally cover the plate; some metal is left exposed. When the plate is etched, each particle of rosin or asphaltum acts as an acid-resist. The longer the metal plate is left in the acid, the deeper the bite and the greater the amount of ink held by the plate. Those areas of the plate that receive the least amount of etching time represent the lightest tones within an image. Consequently, a tonal range could be created by varying the length of time the metal plate remains in the acid bath.

To create these tonal variations, an etcher would periodically pull the plate from the etching bath, stop it out with an acid-resistant varnish, dry the varnish, and return the plate to the acid for further etching. This process was repeated until the complete tonal range of the image was finished. After the plate was proofed, this entire process might be repeated again until the aesthetic demands of the final print were met. With traditional aquatints, it was sometimes necessary to re-aquatint and etch the darkest areas of the image several times to make them blacker.

Even for the experienced etcher, this process was difficult and time consuming. Learning to judge the depth of the bite is an art rather than an exact science.

This traditional approach to the aquatint technique, already arduous, becomes even more difficult when toxic effects of the acid bath, acid-resistant block-out varnishes and hydrocarbon-based solvents are factored in.

The Acrylic Aquatint

The first acrylic aquatint techniques were documented in my 1991 publication, *Safe Photo Etching for Photographers and Artists*. The concept behind the acrylic aquatint is to airbrush a liquid acrylic directly onto a copper etching plate to simulate a traditional aquatint. Each particle of the acrylic spray on the surface of the copper plate acts as a resist to the Edinburgh Etch or ferric chloride etchant.

By comparison to the traditional aquatint method, the technical simplicity of using an airbrush to make an aquatint is appealing. As an airbrush is used in this process, the actual size of the aquatint particle can vary throughout the image. Thus, it is feasible to virtually airbrush your image as you would airbrush a painting. (Most art material stores sell books on airbrush painting.) Complete tonal variations are possible within just one etch. This would be totally impossible with traditional toxic aquatint techniques.

As with any new printmaking technique, there is a learning curve that must be worked through to attain the optimal results. There is also the mechanical aspect of working with an air compressor and airbrush. The very mention of airbrushes sends some artists reeling off anecdotal stories of constant technical problems associated with this type of equipment. I must admit that initially, I was a little intimidated with the concept of using an airbrush, as my limited knowledge of

Acrylic Aquatint

this device was as a piece of equipment that was always clogging up and causing endless frustration.

However, once I glimpsed the image-making potential of the airbrush, I tried to develop a user-friendly system for the printmaker that reduces this frustration factor. To do this, I first identified the various types of airbrushes and determined which one would be the least problematic for airbrushing acrylics onto an etching plate. I approached the Badger AirBrush Company to help me with the research needed to perfect the acrylic aquatint technique outlined in this publication.

Airbrush Equipment
Airbrush Compressor
The better the quality of the airbrush compressor, the better the quality of the results.

TIP: Resist purchasing a cheap silent compressor with a low recovery rate. A poor recovery rate means that the air pressure can not keep up with the rate at which the acrylic aquatint is being sprayed onto the copper plate. You should start your airbrushing and finish the job without needing to stop periodically for the airbrush to recover its air pressure.

Badger offers a range of airbrush compressors with a variety of prices. For example, the Badger 180-11 air compressor yields excellent results and is also inexpensive.

An Airbrush
2a For general airbrush aquatint techniques, I recommend the Badger Model 350 seen in the illustration below, a bottom fed, single action, external mix model. The Model 350 allows for a great range of aquatint sprays - such

as interesting splatter marks and 'crackled' effects, while also spraying a fine, overall aquatint. This airbrush can be adapted with three different fluid assembly and air-tip nozzles for fine, medium, and heavy work. The width of the opening of this nozzle controls the ability to spray a thicker viscosity liquid and to spray a larger dot. As you develop a working familiarity with the airbrush aquatint, you will begin to appreciate the flexibility afforded by the use of these various sized nozzles. The Model 350 has only one drawback. It takes slightly longer to spray larger plates (18" x 24" and up) than other models. The Model 350, simple to use and clean, is a good choice for a busy, student-oriented environment.

2b For airbrush techniques that require a lot of fine detail and the ultimate in control of subtle gradations of tone, I recommend the Badger Crescendo Model 175, shown in illustration 2b below. This is a bottom fed,

dual action, internal mix model, with its needle extending in a shaft through the airbrush. The Crescendo can do detailed work not possible with any other model. It is ideal for working with thinner viscosity liquids on tight, controlled work. It can also rapidly spray a fine aquatint ground over a large plate.

When using the Crescendo Model 175 and thicker viscosity liquids, the needle must be retracted into the body of the airbrush so that the spray opening is widened to accommodate the thicker liquid. It is not possible to achieve fine detail with these thicker liquids.

The Crescendo Model 175 must be well cleaned with the Badger airbrush cleaning fluid after each use. It is best suited to a professional studio where printmakers are very conscientious about the maintenance of equipment.

Acrylic Aquatint

2c The Anthem Model 155, shown here, offers great flexibility.

The Anthem 155 is a bottom fed, dual action, internal mix model with its needle extending in a shaft through the airbrush. A great design feature is having the needle and chuck easily accessible through the body, while still fitting comfortably in your hand. The Anthem can spray most thicker liquids, as the Model 350 does, while still having the ability to spray detail almost like the Crescendo Model 175. It can quickly spray a large plate. It is fairly simple to clean. The Anthem Model 155 offers great flexibility for a busy professional or private studio.

For printmakers who routinely work on plates larger than 18" x 24", I recommend the Badger Model 400 Detail/Touch-Up Gun. It looks like the type of spray gun used by auto body shops for painting cars. This is a bottom fed, light weight spray gun, with an overhead convertible trigger for either right or left-handed individuals. This spray gun can be fitted with three interchangeable paint tips - fine, medium, and heavy. You have no control over detail with the Model 400, and it should be used only for speedy coverage of large plates.

The Original Acrylic Aquatint
The first liquid acrylic solution that I worked with was the Hunt Speedball Water Soluble Screen Filler. In a liquid state, this product is soluble in water, and when dry, it is waterproof. This product proved to be a unique aquatint solution because of the manner in which it etches. This particular variety of Screen Filler, when diluted and sprayed onto a copper plate and subsequently etched in ferric chloride, has the potential to produce a rich mezzotint-like black in only one etch. In fact, a 3 hour etch can be so 'extreme' that the tarlatan or

scrim will shred during the normal wiping process. The etched plate can have a surface like coarse sand-paper. This is due to the symbiotic relationship between the Screen Filler and the ferric chloride during the etching process and is why this particular aquatint technique is so extraordinary.

In traditional aquatint processes, the rosin, asphaltum, or spray lacquer yields a non-soluble particle on the surface of the etching plate which provides an impenetrable barrier to the etchant. Although undercutting can eventually remove this particle from the plate, it does not go through any particular structural breakdown. In contrast, the particles of Speedball Screen Filler undergo a structural breakdown. It breaks down in such a way as to produce a fine aquatint within itself.

The Limitations of Screen Filler
Up until the Autumn of 1996, I was using the combination of a simple, siphon fed, single action craft airbrush and Speedball Screen Filler, diluted with water, to produce an acrylic aquatint. While this was successful for most applications, it did present drawbacks, although manageable ones. First, the Speedball Screen Filler is earth red in color, and when sprayed onto a copper plate, it is extremely hard to see. After working with this screen filler for some time, printmakers learn to judge the spray coverage by the matte surface of the copper plate. Using a 30-power pocket microscope makes it easier to examine the dot structure through periodic interruptions of the spraying process to check the build-up.

TIP: Some printmakers add a bottle of India Ink to the Screen Filler solution to make it more visible.

The second problem is the natural thickness of the Screen Filler. Even after dilution with water, the Screen Filler remains quite thick. This high viscosity means that only a large nozzle can be used on the airbrush to prevent clogging which prohibits spraying fine detail. This thick liquid prohibited me from spraying the fine gradations of

Acrylic Aquatint

tone that airbrushes are designed to produce. Many printmakers may be satisfied with a medium to coarse aquatint, but I needed a finer aquatint. With this aim in mind, in October, 1996, Elizabeth Dove and myself began researching the Badger product line to develop a fine spray acrylic aquatint technique.

The New Acrylic Aquatint

Along with the Speedball Screen Filler, I recommend the Badger Acrylic Aquatint Solution for Printmakers. This product is now packaged especially for printmakers by the Badger AirBrush Company and sold through leading printmaking suppliers. When this liquid acrylic is diluted 50% with water, it sprays a very fine aquatint. The actual acrylic that makes up this solution is so strong that it will stand up to the longest etches, even 3-4 hours. The Badger Acrylic Aquatint is black and, therefore, easily visible during spraying. Observing the build-up is now a simple matter. The aquatint dot is remarkably small. The quality of the very fine etch is superior to the Screen Filler.

The new standard combination I recommend is the Badger Anthem Model 155 and the Badger Acrylic Aquatint, diluted 1:1 with water. This solution and airbrush produce a very fine dot, a seamless spray, and a rapid coverage time. For an aquatint, try to spray an even, overall, fine dot coverage of about 60%. With this black color, it is easy to see the density of spray. When working on small to mid-size plates, spray with the airbrush needle pushed almost all the way out and a slow, side to side, horizontal movement. For larger plates, fractionally retract the needle into the body of the airbrush. This speeds the coverage over a larger area and removes some of the possible tedium of the application process.

BIG TIP: The dilution of 1:1 with water is very important. Using the pure, undiluted Badger Acrylic Aquatint Solution involves a much longer spray application time and is very difficult to remove. Never use this solution as a block-out as it is extremely difficult to remove from the plate.

For a busy, student-oriented environment, I recommend using the Badger Model 350 because of its simple design and ease-to-clean feature. For the finest detailed sprays, I recommend the Crescendo Model 175.

Aquatint Materials

1. Badger Acrylic Aquatint Solution.

2. Speedball Screen Filler.

3. Small bucket of water with small quantity of household ammonia.

4. Stencil material such as bond paper a the Badger low-tac stencil material.

5. Masking tape.

Setting Up

An aquatint station consists of a spray booth with an exhaust system, an airbrush compressor, airbrushes, stencil material, a mild ammonia and water solution for cleaning up, and acrylic aquatint solutions.

The Badger airbrushes I use include two different reservoir bottles that each attach to the airbrush. These bottles are useful for preparing aquatints on large plates. Although both the Badger Acrylic Aquatint and the Speedball Screen Filler are certified as being non-toxic by the Art and Craft Materials Institute, *avoid inhaling any spray produced by the aquatinting process.* Basic health and safety precautions should be followed. If an over-spray has the potential of being inhaled, it is essential to work with a respirator that will adequately filter this spray. If you work within a spray booth with an efficient exhaust system for removing the over-spray you can eliminate the respirator as long as there is no possibility of inhaling the over-spray.

Acrylic Aquatint

Acrylic Aquatint Variables

There are 5 'main' variables which work in combination with this process. They must all be negotiated to utilize the full creative potential of this acrylic aquatint technique. These variables are as follows:

1. The viscosity/dilution of the Badger Acrylic Aquatint or Screen Filler solution.

2. The air pressure of the compressor.

3. The distance from your airbrush to the plate during the aquatinting process.

4. Type of airbrush and nozzle used.

5. Duration of the spray, including, repetition and continuous spraying in one spot.

These variables account for many different aquatint effects, all of which could be considered 'good aquatints'. As with airbrush painting, the airbrush can spray a variety of densities of pigment onto the surface of the copper. This allows for a variety of tonalities within a single etched aquatint. Consequently, a plate can be etched *only once* to produce a full tonal range from the richest blacks to the softest grays. This is virtually impossible with any conventional aquatint method. Mastering this technique is based on experience. After gaining this experience, you can expect a new level of predictability and time economy in the aquatint process.

There is not enough room in this text to fully describe the creative possibilities of varying the density of the spray and the actual nature of the dot sprayed. Many types of spray will etch well from fine sprays used to simulate traditional aquatint purposes to splatter sprays for interesting textures to intentional over-sprays where the built-up aquatint solution begins to crackle and create abstract patterning.

One thing to avoid is unintentionally over-spraying and covering too much of the plate. Over-spraying blocks out the copper plate and prevents the etchant from working unless your intention is to produce some totally white areas in the finished print.

Acrylic Aquatint Step-by-Step

1 Copper tarnishes which creates an oxide film on the surface of the plate. The best plate preparation is to sand/polish the plate with 600 grit wet-and-dry sandpaper. Alternatively, the copper plate can be polished with Comet and a pot scourer.

2 Tape a clean piece of newsprint inside the back of the spray booth. The newsprint will help you ascertain the density of the spray on the plate. By spraying slightly past the edges of the plate, you can observe the over-spray as it builds up on the sheet of newsprint. Prop up the copper plate vertically against the newsprint.

3 Place two parts of the Speedball Screen Filler into the airbrush reservoir and add one part water.

TIP: Make sure the screen filler is thoroughly mixed before adding the water. The consistency of the Speedball screen filler sometimes varies so it may be necessary to add a little less or more water.

4 Set the airbrush compressor to about 30 P.S.I. (pounds per square inch). Remember this air pressure can be varied to more or less pressure for varied results.

Acrylic Aquatint

5 Hold the airbrush off to one side of the copper plate and start the flow of the acrylic solution through the airbrush onto the newsprint. Adjust the spray by adjusting the needle position until it has an even spray consistency.

6 Keep the airbrush about 18" - 24" from the plate and start moving the airbrush parallel to the plate in even horizontal side to side strokes. This airbrushing technique is made with the whole arm and not just a wrist movement. The aim is to lay several thin layers of acrylic aquatint down evenly over the entire plate.

Each stroke lays down only a small strip of aquatint spray onto the plate. Continue seamlessly from one stroke to the other; do not stop spraying in the middle. Develop a rhythm. Keep your finger consistently pressed on the airbrush fluid control valve.

TIP: Do not repeatedly push up and down on this control trigger as this will cause the spray to splatter uncontrollably.

Although this does require some practice, it is easily mastered. Stop periodically to check the total dot coverage on the plate. If you wish to lay down a traditional type of aquatint layer, you must try to obtain a 60% coverage of spray on the plate.

7 Periodically, check the spray coverage by lifting the plate away from the backing paper. There should be a very distinct over-spray pattern created by the plate. Once the spray is dry, the dot structure can be checked with a 30-power pocket microscope.

8 Thoroughly dry the acrylic aquatint, and back the plate with plastic shelf liner or packing tape.

9 Use your first acrylic aquatint plate to make a step test to determine what kind of tonal range will be expected with your etchant.

10 Paint on Golden's Acrylic Stop-out varnish, or the Speedball Screen Filler to stop-out your aquatinted plate. Divide the length of your aquatinted plate into 9 equal segments in minutes as follows; 0, 2, 3, 5, 10, 15, 20, 30, and an additional 30. Block-out the 0 minute segment. Now, etch the plate for 2 minutes.

11 Take the plate from the etchant and wash off the etchant.

Acrylic Aquatint

12 The copper plate oxidizes after the first etch. It is necessary to drop the plate into a deoxidation vinegar/salt solution between each etching cycle. (Deoxidation solution is made by adding 1 cup of table salt to a 4.5 liter of white vinegar. Leave the plate in this solution for about 30 seconds.)

TIP: The deoxidation process is absolutely necessary for good results.

13 This etch-wash-deoxidize-dry-block-out sequence is repeated until the plate has gone through a 9 cycle etch. After the 9 step-test etch sequence has been etched, the plate can be stripped easily in the soda ash stripping solution. Alternatively, it can be scrubbed with Comet a nylon pot-scrubber, and warm water.

BIG TIP: *Between each airbrush cycle, run water through the airbrush by submerging it in a small bucket of water and pressing the action lever of the airbrush. Leave the airbrush in the water until the next airbrushing cycle.*

14 Remove the backing tape, dry, and proof the plate.

TIP: If you do not remove the plastic backing tape, ferric chloride may be trapped in the tape seams and squeeze out onto the print during the printing process.

How Long to Etch an Aquatint?
Knowing how long to etch an aquatint is the age old question. It relates more to a printmaker's experience than to anything else. Even an etch for a few seconds will register as a faint tone in the final print. Some printmakers want deep etches resulting from plates etched for 3-9 hours. It really is a matter for each printmaker to develop a familiarity of the aquatint technique, thus learning how it can best suite his or her image making demands.

It is best to do a step-test to determine etching time with your particular etchant or mordant. Conducting this test, in your own ferric or Edinburgh Etch solution, provides the best answer to the question of how long to etch an aquatint. The age, temperature, strength of the etchant, and whether or not it is agitated or not contribute to additional etching variables.

New Dimensions of the Acrylic Aquatint
It is entirely possible to airbrush a complete tonal range onto a copper plate, then etch the plate only once to end up with a full tonal range in the final print. This presents a wonderful technical challenge, but it is a difficult skill to learn.

Airbrushing tonal areas that are gradated from dark to light is less difficult.
Areas of the plate can easily be masked out with bond paper or low tac Badger airbrush masking film. In this way *airbrush aquatinting* the image can be an integral part of the aquatinting process.

Alternative Aquatint Sprays
A Splatter sprays are composed of small and large dots of the acrylic aquatint clustered together. This splatter spray works best with a lower PSI of about 15-20 PSI rather than 30 PSI. Work 8" - 10" from the plate to splatter the spray. To obtain the largest dots, abruptly start and stop the air pressure, periodically, throughout the spray.

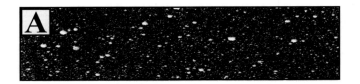

Acrylic Aquatint

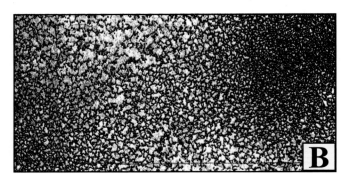

B To create this splatter spray with the Crescendo Model 175 or the Anthem 155, retract the needle ALL the way into the body of the airbrush. With the Model 350, use the heavy tip and nozzle and twist the nozzle all the way forward for the best results. The Badger Hobby Abrasive Gun 260-1 will give a natural and consistent splatter. Unfortunately, as it is designed to be such on dry abrasive material, this is all that it is can do.

Unusual textures can be created by 'over-spraying' the aquatint on the plate. The etched pattern resembles a variegated crackle; for this reason I refer to this over-spray as a 'crackle' spray. Speedball Screen Filler, diluted 2:3 with water, is the best choice to create this crackle spray.

TIP: The Badger Acrylic Aquatint Solution and water does not produce crackle results as well as the Screen Filler and water.

As you spray the diluted screen filler solution, it builds up on the surface and begins to create dozens of small pools. A pattern of cracked lines forms between these pools, and these lines will etch in the ferric chloride. When over-spraying the plate to create this crackled pattern, lay the plate flat down in the aquatint spray booth. If you attempt to over-spray the plate while it is positioned upright, the acrylic will just run down the plate and never form the crackled pattern. Allow the Screen Filler to dry before moving the plate. The Anthem 155, Crescendo 175, and the Model 350 all produce interesting, crackled sprays.

Stencils and the Airbrush

C Simple paper stencils can be used in conjunction with the airbrush aquatint, adding a new creative dimension to the aquatint process. The wet or dry acrylic aquatint can be manipulated with water, or redissolved with a mild water and ammonia solution, to create unique wash-like marks within an aquatinted area. (Please refer to the chapter on the Water Resist/Aquatint Stencils.) Both the Speedball Screen Filler and the Badger Acrylic Aquatint Solution can also be used with other techniques. (See the chapters on The Destruction Ground and The Reverse Mezzotint.)

New Approach and New Thinking

Printmakers have a problem with this 'new' aquatint technique in carrying over the perceptual and technical limitations from conventional aquatint techniques. Simply to view this acrylic aquatint technique as a substitute for the old is, conceptually, to shackle it. This method offers new potential which I invite you to explore.

Troubleshooting

There is potential technical trouble at almost every turn with airbrush aquatints. **By far, the greatest problem is airbrush clogging**. To avert problems you must first, understand the nature of the airbrush and how it works. Second, establish a strict working routine in which the airbrush is never left for longer than 30 seconds, without submerging it in a small tub of water. This practice, alone can prevent the airbrush from clogging.

How the airbrush works?

The mechanics of an airbrush are relatively simple. The airbrush acrylic is siphoned up

Acrylic Aquatint

through a plastic reservoir tube into the front part of the airbrush. This part of the airbrush has a tapered needle inside, which when pushed all the way forward, almost completely blocks this chamber. Thus, the needle allows us to control the flow of acrylic through this chamber and directly out the end of the airbrush onto the plate.

Learn how to disassemble your airbrush and clean each part separately. The Badger 350 is by far the easiest to take apart. (See the instructions that come with your airbrush kit.)

How to Stop Your Airbrush from Clogging Up
Airbrushes have an inherent tendency to clog. This tendency can be reduced by doing the following:
1. Never just leave the airbrush after applying the aquatint spray. **Even a few seconds will eventually result in clogging.**

2. When you have finished the spray aquatint, immediately rinse the nozzle and reservoir out by airbrushing water through the unit until only water is spraying out. Make sure there is no residue of the acrylic left in the airbrush or the reservoir. If you leave a plastic pail of water in the airbrush booth, washing out the airbrush with water is a simple matter and can be done completely submerged.

3. Badger also have an airbrush cleaning liquid in which disassembled airbrushes can be soaked overnight. This, however, is a last resort for hopelessly clogged airbrushes.

4. An area of the airbrush that needs regular cleaning and is often overlooked is the breather hole at the top of the airbrush glass liquid holding reservoir. This reservoir normally has a metal screw-top lid which, also, has a small hole in the top. It needs to be regularly cleaned. If it blocks up, the airbrush liquid acrylic will not be allowed to siphon up into the airbrush chamber. This results in great frustration as it is a place where we least expect problems.

Other Problems:
Problem 1: The spray from the airbrush spits and creates an uneven spray pattern. ***Solution:*** *This problem is generally related to;*
1. Air compressor pressure.

2. Dried particles in the airbrush liquid acrylic.

3. Unclean airbrush.

4. Improper use of the airbrush.

First, try changing the air pressure gauge on your compressor, providing you have one. Some models do not have air pressure gauges. Although the optimum air pressure is about 30 P.S.I., increasing the air pressure may open up an insecure blockage in the airbrush.

Dried particles of acrylic can pollute the screen filler, in which case it must be replaced. The airbrush will, also, most likely, need to be disassembled and cleaned.

Irregular splattering also results from the manner in which the airbrush is used. If you continuously depress and release the airbrush action trigger you will create this type of splattering. Instead, once you have a good spray started, leave your finger pressed down on this action trigger for the duration of the spray aquatint.

Problem 2: **T**he acrylic stop-out falls off the plate after etching as demonstrated below in the step-test plate. ***Solution:*** *This is the classic result from not deoxidizing the plate between etching segments. The acrylic stop-out will not stay on a plate that has not been properly deoxidized with the vinegar salt solution. Mix one cup of table salt to 1 gallon of white vinegar to make the deoxidation solution.*

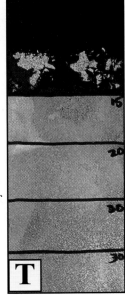

Aquatint Stencils - Liquid Resists
QUICK LOOK

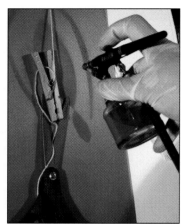

1. Airbrush a 50% acrylic aquatint onto the plate. Place stencils on top and airbrush more acrylic.

 1

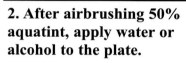

 2

2. After airbrushing 50% aquatint, apply water or alcohol to the plate.

4

4. Etch the plate from 1 to 3 1/2 hours in etchant.

3. Use hand-cut stencils or hand painted Lanolin marks to create the image on plate.

 3

5

5. Clean the acrylic aquatint from the plate and print it.

Anne Jones, close-up acrylic aquatint, 1997.

Aquatint Stencils - Liquid Resists

Introduction

While giving a workshop in 1994 at the Dublin Institute of Technology, I was approached by a printmaker who had used the destruction ground technique and wanted to spray to selectively aquatint certain areas of her plate. She wanted to airbrush an aquatint in some areas and leave the plate unaffected in others. In this way, more than one technique could be combined at once. How could this be done easily? The quickest block-out technique that I could think of was to brush water over those areas of the plate that were to be protected from the spray aquatint. Then, with the plate lying flat, I airbrushed the entire plate with the Speedball Screen filler aquatint solution. Once the screen filler aquatint had dried, which was only a couple of minutes, I wiped the water from the plate revealing the unaffected destruction ground technique under the water.

This idea lead to a series of "What if's" which evolved into an entirely new way of plate-making revolving around several key concepts, which were:

FIRST: Creating marks, with liquids or solid objects, directly onto a degreased metal plate and applying an airbrush acrylic aquatint on and around these marks/objects.

Illustration ☐1 is an intaglio print created from a plate where an was object used as an aquatint resist. In this example, a copper plate was first given an overall acrylic aquatint spray. Clothes pegs were laid onto the plate and more acrylic aquatint was sprayed around them. This second spray aquatint acted as a partial block-out around the clothes pegs, allowing the shapes of the pegs

to be revealed in the final print. The plate was then backed with plastic tape, etched, and printed.

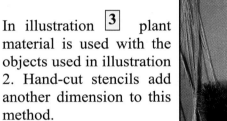

Illustration ☐2 shows scissors, string, and a clothes peg used as an aquatint stencil. This idea, of using such objects and hand-made paper stencils, evolved into the **Stencil Aquatint Technique**.

In illustration ☐3 plant material is used with the objects used in illustration 2. Hand-cut stencils add another dimension to this method.

Illustration ☐4 shows a simple hand-cut Bond paper stencil which was adhered to the plate with masking tape turned back on itself. This type of stencil produces a unique airbrush edge on the cut paper stencil because the paper stencil is not firmly adhered to the plate. This allows a small amount of the acrylic aquatint spray to "flutter" under the paper stencil edge. If a sharply defined edge is desired, use either low-tac airbrush stencil film or some other easily removable liquid, such as hand cream or Lanolin®, as

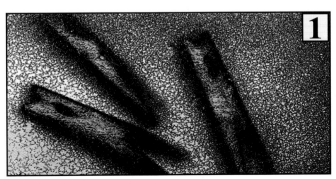

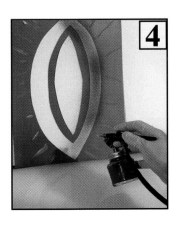

Aquatint Stencils - Liquid Resists

shown in illustration ⑤. The Lanolin or hand cream simply stops the acrylic aquatint spray from adhering to the plate. Thus, an image can be created by using a combination of acrylic aquatint spray and Lanolin stencils. Once one layer of acrylic spray has dried, wipe the Lanolin from the plate with a clean rag. Lanolin provides a quick stencil solution that is not required to dry before continuing.

If you want a liquid stencil block-out that will dry, use the Speedball Drawing Fluid®, available at most art material stores. It is blue in color and, although designed for screen-printing, works extremely well as an airbrush stencil liquid.

Liquid Stencil with Aquatint

① One logical way to work, in building up a series of tones in an image, is to start by airbrushing a good overall 50% coverage of acrylic aquatint spray onto the entire copper plate. Use either Speedball Screen filler or Badger Acrylic Aquatint Solution for Printmakers.

TIP: When using this drawing fluid, it is not necessary to wait for the drawing fluid to dry before continuing with the airbrushing.

② Wait until the acrylic aquatint spray has dried. Then, block out the areas of the plate that will eventually be the white areas of the print with the drawing fluid.

③ The next applications of acrylic aquatint spray onto the plate will establish the tonal range of an image.

It is at this particular point that the technique enters into a new realm of difficulty, as the tonal range is established by the degree to which the rest of the plate is blocked-out with the acrylic aquatint spray. Remember that the plate is already covered with an initial 50% spray aquatint. This leaves only 50% of the plate open for additional aquatint spray coverage. The more this 50% potential coverage is broken down into divisible segments, the more tonal variety will exist in the final print.

Ⓐ pocket microscope is invaluable in visually monitoring the spray coverage on the plate. Knowing how long to spray the acrylic aquatint solution onto a plate, to create a full tonal range, is equally as complicated as the toxic traditional method of progressively etching a rosin aquatinted plate in nitric acid. Both methods demand experience in mastering the technique.

④ After all layers of acrylic aquatint have been applied to the plate, make sure that they are completely dry. Place the plate into a tray of room temperature water, and remove the blue Speedball Drawing Fluid with a soft sponge.

⑤ Dry, and back the plate with plastic tape.

⑥ Etch the copper plate in fresh Ferric Chloride for 1 hour 15 minutes or 40 minutes in the Edinburgh Etch. If using older etchants, lengthen the etching times.

⑦ After the plate has fully etched, remove the acrylic aquatint spray from the plate. Either leave it in the soda ash stripping tank for 20 minutes (or until it has dissolved) or use Ajax or Comet Cleanser, with a nylon pot-scrubber and warm water, to remove the acrylic.

Aquatint Stencils - Liquid Resists

8 Remove the backing, dry, and proof the plate. Here was another example of the creative possibilities of which I was becoming increasingly aware.

When using the water painted onto the copper plate as a spray aquatint resist, I noticed that the water collected the screen filler in an unusual way. If the water stencil with the spray acrylic aquatint solution was allowed to dry, it created unusual patterns on the plate.

Illustration **6** is a print of a typical mark created when a water resist stencil is allowed to dry, is etched and printed.

A variation of the above can be created immediately after the screen filler is spray aquatinted onto a clean copper plate; while this screen filler is still wet, run water down the plate. Illustration **7** shows water running through the wet screen filler aquatint solution. This technique can be used as an airbrush water resist stencil or as a mark-making method by itself. As a water resist, the water prevents the airbrush acrylic aquatint from landing on selected areas of the plate. As a mark making technique, the acrylic aquatint is allowed to sit on top of the water which is drying. The water and the acrylic particles blend, making a thin wash-type mark. The plate is then etched in ferric chloride or the Edinburgh Etch for periods of time up to 3 1/2 hours, depending on the desired results.

Once this concept is grasped, all kinds of liquids can be applied to the plate, not only as an aquatint stencil, but also, as a kind of Destruction Ground.

One of my graduate students, Nancy Flemm, used witch hazel, which gave an unusual effect similar to that from alcohol. Another graduate student, Meg Zylwitis, substituted the water with 91% rubbing alcohol, which gave consistently unique "clam-shell"-like marks. Also, you can substitute tap water with soapy water, which does not bead and has more controllable brush marks.

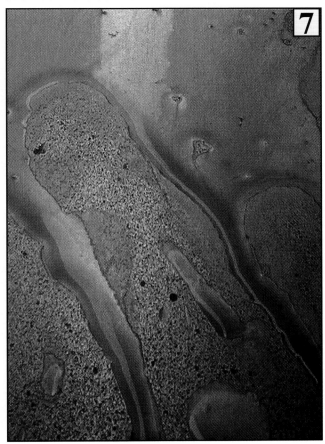

Aquatint Stencils - Liquid Resists

Water/Alcohol Resist Step-by-Step

1 A copper etching plate is degreased by wet sanding, with 600 grit wet and dry sandpaper, polished to a mirror finish.

2 After the plate is dry, it is placed flat in the aquatint spray booth. Water is then brushed onto it in the desired design or shape. The water cannot be controlled precisely, as it will bead. To prevent this beading, add a few drops of dishwashing detergent.

3 Prepare the airbrush with an acrylic aquatint solution. Hover the airbrush above and slightly away from the plate. Apply a layer of aquatint

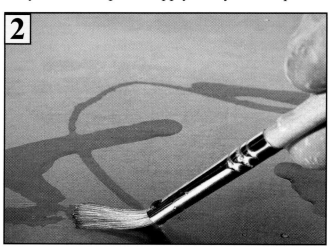

spray over the entire plate, the same amount as would be required for a good aquatint. Spray from about 2-3 feet above the plate and use an air pressure of about 30 P.S.I. The acrylic spray lands on both the dry and wet surfaces of the plate. Where it lands on the water, the acrylic floats on the surface. Because of the curved shape of each area of water, a percentage of this acrylic spray migrates to the outside edge of the water. This principle applies equally when alcohol is added to the plate in the next step.

As the water evaporates, this migration forms a very delicate acrylic build-up around each water resist shape, (as seen in illustration 6). Consequently, the plate is protected from the etchant in these areas and produces white edges in the finished print.

4 Rubbing alcohol can also be applied to the plate in a similar manner to the water. It however dries very quickly and requires a quicker airbrush application.

TIP: Prick a small hole in the cap of the rubbing alcohol bottle for a more controllable application.

5 Illustration 5 shows a typical plate after it has dried. It is best to allow the plate to air dry.

6 After the plate has completely dry back it with either plastic, brown, packing tape or shelf liner.

7 Etch the plate in a either ferric chloride or the Edinburgh Etch, without the aerator. The optimum etching time, in ferric chloride ranges between 1.5 - 3 hours. Reduce the time by about 1/3 for the Edinburgh Etch. This etch time is largely determined by the acrylic aquatint spray

Aquatint Stencils - Liquid Resists

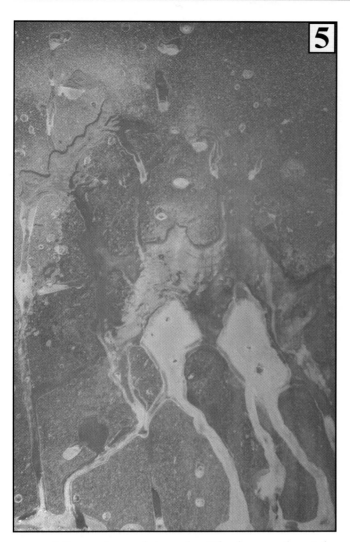

5

Other Aquatint Stencils

Once you understand how the water, alcohol, Lanolin was used as a block-out for the acrylic aquatint spray, it does not take too much creative thinking to come up with alternative block-out substitutes such as the following:

1. Create a very coarse aquatint by sprinkling sugar over portions of the plate. The sugar acts as a temporary block-out when applying the acrylic aquatint spray from above.

2. Stencils can be cut from paper, cardboard, or stencil material such as Badger's low-tack airbrush stencil film. These cut stencils can be used either to control and shape an aquatint spray, or they can be repositioned and sprayed several times.

TIP: Use masking tape. doubled back on itself, to create a double sided tape. Use small pieces of this tape to hold the paper stencils in place.

4. Once the spray aquatint screen filler has dried, back the plate with plastic packing tape or shelf liner.

5. Etch the plate in ferric chloride or the Edinburgh Etch for periods of 1.5 - 3 hours.

Once the principle behind this simple aquatint block-out technique is understood, all kinds of three-dimensional objects can be utilized for direct image making.

around the water resist marks. The longer the etch, the darker will be the spray aquatinted areas of the image.

8 After the etching cycle has been completed the acrylic aquatint can be washed off the plate a soft sponge and a little Ajax. It can also be placed into the strong soda ash stripping solution for about 20 minutes, then washed and dried.

9 It is also advisable to place this plate in a deoxidation solution before step10.

10 Remove the backing tape. The plate is ready to be proofed.

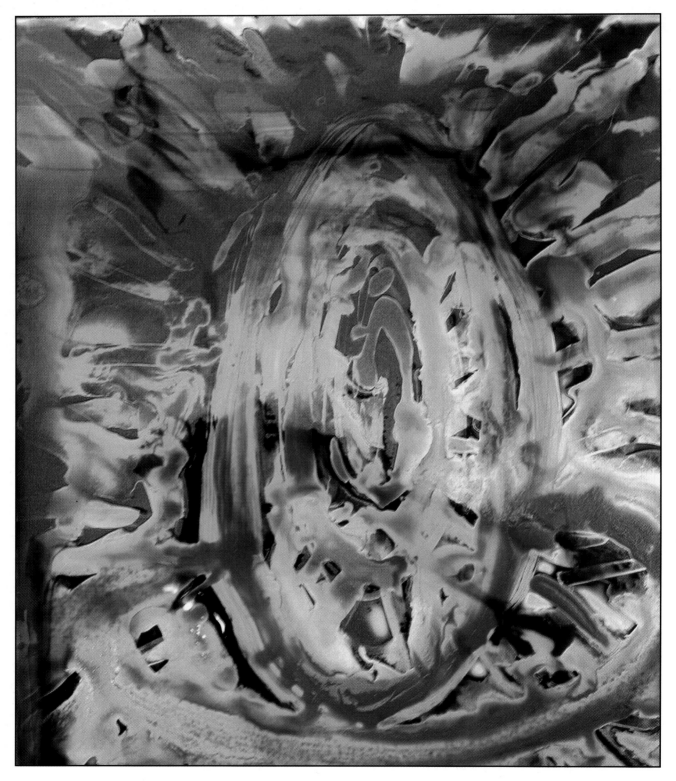

Above: Washing the ferric chloride off the Destruction-Ground plate directly after a 3 hour etch.

Destruction Ground

QUICK LOOK

1. Dilute the Speedball Screen Filler with water and paint it directly onto the cleaned copper plate. **1**

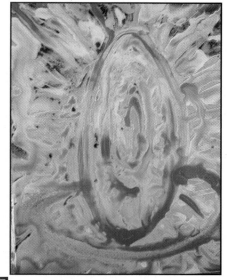

2 3. Etch the plate from 1 to 3 hours. Then, wash and clean it.

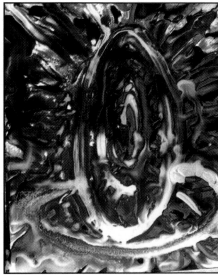

3. Print the plate. Where screen filler was thickest on the plate resulted in lighter areas in the print. **3**

Destruction Ground

What is Destruction Ground?
A copper plate is covered with washes made from Speedball Screen Filler, Badger Acrylic Aquatint Solution or some type of acrylic. Water is added to these solutions which is then painted directly onto the plate. The plate is then etched for periods up to 3 hours. The thicker the wash solution is on the plate, the whiter will be the corresponding area in the print. The etchant dissolves the washes slowly during the etching process. Hence, the name of the technique is Destruction Ground.

Destruction Ground Step-by-Step
1 Prepare the copper plate by wet sanding with 600 grit wet and dry sandpaper to a polished finish.

2 Paint diluted Speedball Screen Filler directly onto the prepared copper plate. The degree of dilution will correspond to the tonal scale desired in the finished print. The more dilute the screen filler, the darker will be be the corresponding tone in the final print.

3 Back the plate with plastic packing tape.

4 With the aerator turned off, place the Destruction Ground copper plate into the ferric chloride tank and etch for periods from 1-3 hours.

As with many hand etching techniques, it will be necessary to make a few test plates to familiarize yourself with degrees of dilution of the acrylic washes on the plate and also the strength of the ferric chloride. This technique also works with the Edinburgh Etch with shorter etching times.

5 After the Destruction Ground plate has etched for about 1 hour, gently take it from the etching bath and examine the surface to see if the Screen Filler is breaking down in the etchant. There should be a milky film appearing in the thinnest washes on the plate. DO NOT WASH THE PLATE, gently return it to the etching tank and complete the full etching cycle.

6 After the etching cycle has been completed, remove the plate from the etching tank and wash.

7 Remove the Destruction Ground by placing the plate into the soda ash stripping tank for about 15 minutes or scrub the plate with warm water, Comet cleanser, and a nylon pot scrubber.

8 Once the plate is dry, print it.

Aquatint Destruction Ground
Another variation is to pre-aquatint the plate with an airbrush application of the Speedball Screen Filler. After this screen filler aquatint is dry, dilute the same screen filler and apply to the plate, in various dilutions, and allow it to dry. When the plate is etched, both screen filler applications go through different levels of destruction. There is a kind of symbiotic relationship between the ferric chloride and the screen filler.

As the Badger Acrylic Aquatint Solution or the screen filler is diluted with water, its color changes, much as watercolors and other wash-drawing media do. The darker and thicker these solutions are painted onto the plate, the lighter will be the corresponding area of the print. In essence you are making a negative reading plate which will have a "positive" reading print. This is the key to understanding this particular process. Once the plate has been painted and dried, it is etched for times ranging from 1 - 3 hours.

Knowing how long to etch these plates is learned through working experience. The best results seem to occur after the plate has been in the ferric

Destruction Ground

chloride etchant for well over 1 hour and when the Baume of the ferric chloride is around 42. If the Baume of the ferric chloride measures higher than 42 during etching, this technique will not work. It should be between 38-42.

Troubleshooting

Problem 1: Too much screen filler is left on the plate after the 3 hour etching time had elapsed. *Solution: There are two main reasons why this problem occurs. First, the screen filler was not diluted enough. Try adding more water to the screen filler and re-painting it onto the plate. Secondly, test the specific gravity of the ferric chloride solution with a heavy liquid hydrometer. This technique works best with the ferric chloride at around 38-40 Baume.*

Most scientific material companies sell a heavy liquid hydrometer with a Baume scale which measures Ferric chloride density. It looks like a long thin test tube with an internal set of numbers (the Baume scale). The hydrometer floats in the ferric chloride bath where the number at the floatation level reads the Baume of the Ferric. If the Hydrometer is placed into water, the hydrometer should read "0".

Problem 2: After the plate has etched for 1 hour and been visually inspected, it is obvious that the screen filler has not broken down in the Ferric *Solution: If there is a great deal of screen filler on the plate after it has been in the etchant for 1 hour, it can be washed with water. Washing will sometimes open the plate. If the plate remains "blocked out", place it in the stripping solution for a brief time from 10 seconds to 1 minute. Wash it and place it back into the etchant. If too much of the plate opens up, deoxidize the plate, dry, and add more screen Filler to the open areas of the plate. Then re-etch the plate.*

Keith Howard, **Boat**, 2002, Stencil Intaglio-Type, 3"x 7".

Health & Safety

By Monona Rossol

Introduction to Monona Rossol

When it came to adding a chapter to this book on Health and Safety I looked towards one of the most respected and published authors in this field, Monona Rossol. She not only graciously wrote the following chapter but also gave me "much needed" advice to applying many health and safety issues throughout this book.

The information supplied here is but a beginning. I would further encourage every reader to THOROUGHLY investigate and take responsibility for every issue pertaining to health and safety in your printmaking studio. Keith Howard, April 2003.

Health & Safety for Printmakers
By Monona Rossol

No matter how hard we try, printmaking always will involve some chemicals that are toxic. Even so-called "non-toxic" substances are hazardous when exposure is excessive. For example, if you drink 10 times the amount of water that you need, you can die! Using safer materials is only one part of the "non-toxic" printmaking process. Another part is educating ourselves about the products we use. Actually, formal training about hazardous products is required by law if you are employed to teach or to make prints. Canadian Occupational Safety and Health Administration (OHSA) and the U.S. Occupational Safety and Health Administration (OSHA) laws require training of all workers, including teachers, who use toxic products.

If you are an artist working alone, you do not come under these laws. However, these laws provide a common sense structure around which you can organize your safety efforts.

Printmaking and the "Right to Know".
Canada's Workplace Hazardous Materials Information System (WHMIS) or Right to Know law applies to all workers who use potentially toxic chemicals. A very similar law exists in the U.S. called the Hazard Communication (HAZCOM) Standard.

The three most important requirements of WHMIS and HAZCOM are:

1 Labeling on the containers must include the name of the chemical, hazard warnings, precautionary measures, and the manufacturer's name and address. In other words, all the information needed in an emergency must be on every container for everyone to read.

2 Material safety data sheets (MSDSs), which are technical information forms from manufacturers, must be on file and readily available to employees during all working hours. These sheets should be obtained with each purchase of supplies.

3 Worker education and training programs must be developed. For example, it is useless to provide MSDSs if the workers haven't been taught to interpret them.

There are other requirements which affect employers and school administrators such as keeping certain records, developing written programs, and enforcing the rules.

The Right to Know and Students
While occupational health and safety laws protect teachers, they usually do not apply to students. For example, if teachers are injured on the job, they are covered by Worker's Compensation. If students are injured or made ill by classroom activities, their remedy may be to hold the school and/teacher legally liable. The liability of schools and teachers can best be protected by extending to students the same rights accorded to workers. In some Provinces and States, this is required. But since students are younger and less educated than the teachers, they need even better training than the law requires for workers.

Personal Protective Equipment
OHSA and OSHA regulations require training for workers who wear personal protective equipment such as face shields, hard hats, special shoes,

Health & Safety

By Monona Rossol

hearing protection, goggles and gloves. This training, of course, should be extended to students.

Eye Wear

Workers and students must be taught how to take care of the eye wear, how to identify defective and worn out equipment, how to don and doff them, and the use and limits of the eye wear. For example, students given eye wear for protection against chemical splash must be warned that this eye wear will not protect them from impact when using grinding equipment or from ultraviolet radiation from light sources.

Gloves and Aprons

Gloves, aprons, and other protective clothing should be chosen to resist the chemicals used. Many chemicals can penetrate thick plastic or rubber gloves without changing their appearance. Glove manufacturers provide charts which list the penetration times for hundreds of chemicals. Printmaking studios should use these charts to select gloves. No single glove, no matter how thick or expensive, is impervious to all liquids. Rubber latex medical gloves are easily penetrated by most solvents and should only be used with solvent free products and dry materials. Wearers also should be warned about the severe allergies associated with natural rubber.

Respirators

Proper use of masks and respirators requires; training of workers about procedures for cleaning, disinfecting, storing, inspection, and repair; formal fit testing to assure that contaminated air will not leak into the face piece; and medical screening.It is important to understand that the breathing stress caused by wearing a respirator can worsen certain heart, lung and other physical conditions.

In the U.S., it is a violation of OSHA regulations to allow workers to wear respirators unless they have been medically certified by a health professional.This makes respirators a very expensive option.

Ventilation

Adequate ventilation, not respirators, should be the primary means of controlling airborne toxic substances. Two types of ventilation should be considered for printmaking studios

Dilution Ventilation

These systems usually consist of an exhaust fan combined with a source of fresh or conditioned air to replace the exhausted air. Dilution systems are appropriate for removal of small amounts of moderately toxic airborne gases or vapors.Examples include using small amounts of petroleum distillate solvents, solvent-containing products, or photo developers.

Local Ventilation

These systems are designed to capture contaminants before they get into the general room air. Examples are spray booths, flexible duct exhausts, or chemistry fume cabinets. These are used primarily for processes that emit large amounts of solvent vapors, acid gases, mists, or dusts into the air. Examples include spray painting, airbrushing, sanding, and mixing powdered materials.

Children & Special Students

Students in grade 6 and under should not work with substances for which ventilation and training are required. These students cannot be expected to understand the hazards of toxic substances or to carry out precautions effectively or consistently. Their art rooms must be "child proofed" to prevent even unintentional access to toxic materials or dangerous machinery. Adult printmaking students also must not bring their children to class.

Special training is required for adult students who are illiterate, who do not speak English (or French in Canada), have learning disabilities, or for any other reason cannot readily comprehend written materials or follow directions. These students must demonstrate comprehension orally, in another language, or some other way or else

Health & Safety

By Monona Rossol

liability for accidents falls on the teacher or the institution that provided access to the toxic materials or dangerous machinery. Toxic material must never be given to students of any age who have serious neurological or psychological impairments which make them unable to appreciate the hazards or perform precautions consistently.

Safety Rules

All precautions for printmaking can't be covered in a single chapter. However some basic rules include:

1 Do not eat, smoke, or drink in studios.

2 Wear special work clothes and remove them after work.

3 Wash hands carefully after work, before eating, using the bathroom, and applying make-up.

4 Provide an eye wash station which can deliver 15 minutes of continuous washing and be turned on in one second if chemicals which can harm the eyes are used. If gallon quantities of such chemicals are used, you may need an emergency shower.

5 Store reactive chemicals separately.Consult each product's Material Safety Data Sheet and other technical sources for advice. Storage of flammable chemicals should conform to all state/provincial fire regulations.

6 Prepare for spills by having on hand commercial absorbents or kitty litter and hazardous waste containers. Dispose of waste or unwanted materials safely in compliance with federal and local environmental protection regulations.

7 Prepare for fire and health emergencies by having each student instructed in the school's emergency plan.This plan includes posting emergency numbers near telephones, discussing

procedures in advance, and training in use of any equipment present such as first aid kits and fire extinguishers.

Health and Safety Programs

To set up coherent occupational health and safety programs for your school or studios, obtain copies of all the occupational laws and regulations.

In Canada, contact your Provincial Department of Labor.

In the U.S., contact your state or federal OSHA. These agencies will have free publications and compliance material to guide you.

Another source of help for schools and artists is Arts, Crafts and Theater Safety. ACTS provides; training and educational materials; publishes a monthly newsletter; maintains a worldwide free information service by phone, letter, and e-mail; provides speakers for lectures, workshops, and courses; conducts US and Canadian OSHA compliance training and inspections. Services are either free or below-market value. ACTS takes no advertising or donations from art material manufacturers or businesses.

Contact:
Arts, Craft and Theater Safety (ACTS)
181 Thompson S., #23
New York,
NY10012-2586

(212) 777-0062

eMail: ACTSNYC@cs.com

< h t t p : w w w . c a s e w e b . c o m / A C T S >

Contemporary Printmaking at R.I.T.

R.I.T. and Rochester, New York

The Rochester Institute of Technology is home to approximately 12,100 full-time and part-time undergraduate students, and 2,400 graduate students. Enrolled students represent all 50 states and more than 80 foreign countries. Deaf students number approximately 1,150. R.I.T. occupies about 1,300 acres in Rochester, New York and is about 6.5 driving hours from Boston and New York City, but with inexpensive flights offered through JetBlue <www.jetblue.com> and the nearby Rochester International Airport, these cities are about 1.5 hours away by air travel. Directly to the north of the city is Lake Ontario. The area is about a 3 1/2 hour drive from the thriving city of Toronto, Canada, and en route to Toronto is Niagara Falls. To the south of Rochester is the famed Finger Lakes region.

Contemporary Printmaking at R.I.T.

The Contemporary Printmaking Program at R.I.T. was initiated to expand the offerings of the School of Art to include the latest innovations in the fine art field of printmaking. We view the Contemporary Printmaking program as an important component and complement to the other fine art disciplines that rank R.I.T.'s School of Art as one of the top in the country.

Contemporary (non-toxic) Printmaking at R.I.T. can become a major area of study within the M.S.T (Masters in the Science of Teaching) and M.F.A. (Masters in Fine Art) programs.

The printmaking studios utilize the newest technologies from etching presses to computer equipment. The program is infused with a continual stream of visiting artists while students have the opportunity to take many course offerings outside the major area of study.

Graduate Certificate for MFA Graduates and Teaching Professionals

To meet the demand of in-service or re-training of printmaking professionals, R.I.T. has initiated an intensive 12 credit Graduate Certificate in Contemporary Intaglio Printmaking. This Graduate Certificate has been designed so that printmaking professionals can make the transition from traditional toxic intaglio printmaking media to the safer contemporary ones. The Graduate Certificate would allow practicing professionals to upgrade their qualifications in contemporary printmaking without giving up full time careers.

Those Graduate Certificate students who have access to alternate printmaking facilities may work independently with faculty in a mentoring relationship depending on professional background. These applicants should have time, material resources, self-discipline, and motivation to dedicate to this kind of learning option. Studio workbooks and portfolio reviews are major elements related to course completion. In cases where applicants have already attained a Masters of Fine Art degree or have teaching experience, transfer credits may apply.

Printmakers Wanted

If your educational institution is looking for highly trained **Printmaking Faculty,** we at R.I.T. encourage you to contact us for your job placement. Our graduate students are some of the finest talent I have seen. Please feel free to call or eMail Keith Howard about your new faculty appointment, sabbatical replacement, visiting artist or part-time staff appointments.

Contact: Keith Howard at R.I.T. for further information. eMail howard@mail.rit.edu

<www.rit.edu>

<www.democratandchronicle.com>

Amy Williams, **Untitled**, 2003, Pastel Intaglio-Type, 8" x 11".

Printmaking Summer Workshops

Introduction

For well over a decade I have been traveling the world offering Contemporary (Non-Toxic) Printmaking courses. The aim of the information herein is to provide those printmakers with the knowledge of where these workshops will be. I welcome inquiries from people who are interested in bringing me to their country to give workshops. Please eMail:

KeithHoward@KeithHoward.org

I also have ongoing national and international Contemporary (non-toxic) Printmaking Workshops which are listed on the following internet sites:

www.KeithHoward.org

www.waterbasedinks.com

http://www.mtsu.edu/~art/printmaking/

In the past several years I have given repeat summer workshops in both the United States and Scotland. The following is the contact information for these workshops:

College of Santa Fe, USA
http://www.printmakingcenter.com/

Printmaking Center
1600 St. Michael's Drive,
Santa Fe
NM 87505
1-800-456-2673, x6564
1-505-473-6564
Contact Don Messec <dmessec@csf.edu>
or tpc@csf.edu

Keith Howard at the College of Santa Fe, USA

These workshops offer a hands-on exploration of the new creative dimensions of ImagOn ULTRA photopolymer intaglio film. The courses are suitable for printmaking professionals and other artists .

2003 COST: $499/five day workshop
June 8-13, 2003.
Each participant is responsible for their travel and accommodation.

Keith Howard & Friedhard Kiekeben at the Gracefield Arts Centre, Scotland

28 Edinburgh Road,
Dumfries DG1 1NW
Scotland
UK
http://www.web-link.co.uk/gracefield.html
To receive further information and/or to make a booking please contact:
Lesley Tait + 44 01387 262084: + 44 01387 255173 Email: LesleyT@dumgal.gov.uk

Keith Howard & Friedhard Kiekeben at the Gracefield Arts Centre, Scotland

This is a unique opportunity to learn innovative acrylic resist etching methods directly from, Keith Howard and Friedhard Kiekeben, in the welcoming environment of The Gracefield Arts Centre.

Gracefield Art Centre, located in the Scottish historic town of Dumfries, will once again be hosting two five-day workshops in non-toxic intaglio printmaking at its recently established open access printmaking studio. Fees include tuition, materials, lunch, and accommodation. Participants will have the opportunity to work side by side with top printmakers from around the world. The courses are suitable for printmaking professionals and other artists.

Friedhard Kiekeben, artist and lecturer at Chester College, UK, has invented the 'Edinburgh Etch' process and his etched sculptures, prints, and installations are shown internationally.

The intaglio methods presented during the workshops vastly expand the vocabulary of fine art print processes whilst eliminating the health hazards of traditional printmaking.
2003 - COST: £ 500.- (appr. $780) includes accommodation, lunch time catering, refreshments, and materials. The costs listed above are only for 2003. Costs can be expected to change from year to year. Please check the internet sites listed for the latest information.

Sources of Supply

Due to limited space I am only able to list those suppliers that have had specific dealings with the kinds of specialized products and equipment related to this text. A great place to look on the Internet for over 120 printmaking resources is on Christie Nuell's Printmaking Links web: **http://www.mtsu.edu/~art/printmaking/** There is also a Printmakers Forum, at the above web site, which allows printmakers to have an ongoing dialogue about printmaking..

IMAGON ULTRA SUPPLIERS QUICK REFERENCE
If you are unable to contact one of the distributors listed, send an email to; **imagon@comcast.net** or call, 1-877-332-6832.

1 Daniel Smith, 800-426-6740, USA.

2 Graphic Chemical, 800-465-7382, USA.

3 Takach Press Corp., 1-800248 3460, USA.

4 Renaissance Graphic Arts, 1-888-833-3398, USA.

5 Praga Industries, 1-800-844-9421, Canada.

6 Polymetaal, +31 (0) 71-5222681, Holland.

7 Oktogon, +49 (0) 4779-921550, Germany

8 Intaglio Printmaker, +44 (0) 171-928-2633, England.

9 Art Book Press, 1-206- 285-2665, Seattle WA. USA

10 Melbourne Etching, +61(0)3-9419-5559, VIC. Australia.

11 Jacksons Drawing Supplies, +61 (0) 8-9381-2488, Aust.

11 National Art Supplies, +64(0)9-634 0325 New Zealand.

IMAGON ULTRA AND PRINTMAKING SUPPLIERS

1 **DANIEL SMITH SALES**
4150 First Ave. S.
Seattle
WA 98124
USA
Phone: 1-800-426-6740
Customer Service, customer.service@danielsmith.com
USA and Canada: 1-800-426-7923; FAX: 1-800-238-4065
International: 206-223-9599: FAX 206 224-0404
eMail: sales@danielsmith.com
www.danielsmith.com

2 **GRAPHIC CHEMICAL & INK CO.,**
728 North Yale Avenue
Box 7027, Villa Park,
IL 60181
USA
Phone: 1-800-465-7382; Fax: 630-832-6064
eMail: sales@graphicchemical.net
www.graphicchemical.com

For Etching Presses contact the
Printmakers Machine Company:
724 North Yale Avenue,
Box 7191, Villa Park,
IL 60181 USA
Toll free: 1-800-992-5970 Local 630-832-4888
or eMail; **sales@printmakersmachine.com**
www.printmakersmachine.com

3 **TAKACH PRESS CORP.**
3207 Morningside N.E.
Albuquerque, New Mexico
87110 U.S.A.
Toll Free 800-248-3460
Fax 505-242-7674
eMail: info@takachpress.com
eMail: takachcorp@aol.com
www.takachpress.com

4 **RENAISSANCE GRAPHIC ARTS, INC.**
69 Steamwhistle Drive
Ivyland, PA 18974 USA
Phone -1-888-833-3398; Fax 1-215-357-5258
pat@printmaking-materials.com
www.printmaking-materials.com

5 **PRAGA INDUSTRIES**
510 Coronation Drive, Unit 17
Toronto, Ontario
M1E 4X6 Canada
Phone: 416-281-0511
Fax: 416-281-0056
Toll Free: 1-800-844-9421
Toll Free: U.K. 0-800-328-9971
E-mail: praga@praga.com
www.praga.com

6 **POLYMETAAL GRAPHIC ARTS EQUIPMENT**
Evertsenstraat 69 C,
Leiden, 2315 SK,
P.O. Box 694 Leiden,
2300 AR.the Netherlands,
Phone: +31 71.5222681;
Fax.: +31.71.5214244
eMail: info@polymetaal.nl
www.polymetaal.nl

7 **OKTOGON- Intaglio-Academy,**
Rita Helmholtz,
Osterende 21,
21734 Oederquart, Germany (Supplier to German speaking areas)
Phone: ++49 (0)4779-921550, Fax: ++49 (0)4779-921520
eMail: RHelmholtz@aol.com
www.oktogon-intaglio.de

8 **INTAGLIO PRINTMAKER**
62 Southwark Bridge Rd.
London SW1 OAS
England
Phone: +44 (0) 207-928-2633; Fax: 207 928 2711
www.intaglioprintmaker.com

9 **ART BOOK PRESS**
Beth Dunn
4703 Ballard Ave.
Seattle, WA 98119
Phone: 206-285-2665
book@speakeasy.org

Sources of Supply

10 MELBOURNE ETCHING SUPPLIES
33A St David St,
Fitzroy,
Victoria 3065,
Australia
Phone (03) 9419-5666; Fax (03) 9419-6292
eMail: etch@mes.net.au
www.mes.net.au

11 JACKSONS DRAWING SUPPLIES
HEAD OFFICE:
103 Rokeby Road
Subiaco
Western Australia
Australia
Phone:+61 (0)8-9381-2488,
Fax: (08) 9382 4252
eMail: sales@jacksons.com.au
www.jacksonsdrawingsupplies.com.au

12 NATIONAL ART SUPPLIES
P. O Box 29-130
41 Neilson Street
Onehunga,
Auckland, New Zealand
Phone: + 64 9 634 0325; Fax: + 64 9 634 0912
eMail: natart@ihug.co.nz

ETCHING PRESSES & GENERAL INTAGLIO SUPPLIES
Contact the above companies for more details about their presses and ask for copies of their product catalogs: See also:

REMBRANDT GRAPHIC ARTS
P.O. Box 130,
Rosemont,
New Jersey 08556 USA
Phone: 1-800-622-1887 (IN US)
1-609-397-0068 (International Callers) Fax: 609 397 0666
eMail: SALES@REMBRANDTGRAPHICARTS.COM
www.rembrandtgraphicarts.com

T N Lawrence & Son Ltd
208 Portland Road
Hove BN3 5QT
UK
Tel +44 1273 260260
Fax +44 1273 260270
www.lawrence.co.uk

Cornish shop:
T N Lawrence & Son Ltd
38 Barncoose Industrial Estate
Pool
Redruth TR15 3RQ
Tel +44 1209 313181
Email artbox@lawrence.co.uk

The Golden Acrylic Stop-Out Varnish for Intaglio Printmaking. Ask your favorite printmaking supplier to stock this item.

Graphic Chemical & Daniel Smith Fine Art Materials.
See the Golden Web page for more information:
http://www.goldenpaints.com/index.htm
http://www.goldenpaints.com/stpoutvn.htm

PRO-VERTICAL ETCHING TANK
These tanks should be available through your favorite printmaking supply store. To locate a sales distribution point in your country and area, or for more information please contact;
Marmit Plastics
Box 366 Grande Prairie
Alberta T8V 3A5
Canada
780 532-0366 Fax: 780 532 0540
eMail: garth@marmitplastics.com
mloos1@telusplanet.net
www.marmitplastics.com

TANK AERATOR
Any aquarium store sells the aerator pump, the 1/4 air hose which connects to it and the air hose control valve.

FERRIC CHLORIDE AND CITRIC ACID
http://www.artmondo.net/printworks/articles/ferric.htm
Available from most printmaking supply houses.

GRAM SCALES
Best ordered from the Internet from the following web sites:
http://www.myweigh.com/onlinestores_usa.html
http://www.wolverinesports.com/scales.html

PAPER
Hahnemühle papers have been exclusively recommended through this text. For more information on these papers and to locate a supplier near your location contact:
Atlantic Papers
1800 Mearns Rd, Suite P,
Ivyland
PA 18974
U.S.A.
Phone 1-800-367-8547
Fax 800-367-1016
http://www.atlanticpapers.com/
info@atlanticpapers.com
(int'l 215-773-9758)

AKUA INTAGLIO INK.
Rostow & Jung Akua Water-based Inks
219 East 4th Street
New York, New York 10009, USA
Toll Free Calls; 1-888-473 4670,
International and Local Calls; 1-212-473 4670
email: wb-inks@att.net
website: www.waterbasedinks.com
Visit the Akua web site for updated information about their educational video series and publications on printing Monotypes and Color Intaglio-Type plates.

SODA ASH FOR MAKING IMAGON DEVELOPER
Most ImagOn suppliers also sell Soda Ash or sodium carbonate (chemical name of soda ash), which is also commonly available at swimming pool suppliers. Check your phone book for a local supplier.

Sources of Supply

DRAFTING MYLAR is a plastic tracing film, not tracing paper, which is commonly used by architects. This is available from most drafting supply stores and also Daniel Smith Fine Art Materials.

Also available in Canada from Nordraft Art and Drafting check out the following web page:
http://www.artistsupplies.com/catalog14.htm

The Intaglio-Type **AQUATINT SCREEN** is available through the same art materials stores that sell ImagOn. This aquatint screen is vital for those printmakers who wish to use drawn and painted imagery. Not all **Aquatint Screens** are created equally. Some are better than others. If you would like information specifically relating to the best Aquatint Screen for ImagOn go to the following web site: **www.elizabethdove.com**

True-grain Textured Drafting Film is a unique polyester film which holds tone. Developed in the UK by printmakers for printmakers this remarkable film allow all kinds of drawing an wash materials to be used with ImagOn without the intervention of the Aquatint Screen.

TRUE-GRAIN
John Purcell Paper
15 Rumsey Rd.
London SW9 0TR
England
Phone: 171-737 5199; Fax: 171-737 6765

ARTEX is a similar textured polyester film sold by **Takach Press Corp., 1-800248 3460, USA**

PHOTOCOPY TONER can be obtained or recycled at virtually no cost as most photcopiers have a toner exhaust bottle which collects exhausted toner. This is generally thrown away. If you can find someone who is throwing this toner away you may be able to have a free supply of toner. Otherwise toner bottles are available at most office/business suppliers.

The **SPEEDBALL SCREEN FILLER** is a fairly commonly found product. It is available at most art supply stores that sell Speedball Screen printing Inks.

GOLDEN ARTIST COLORS , Molding Paste, High Solid Gel, Medium Gloss and Pumice Gels.Golden make an astonishing variety of top quality acrylic paint for artists. They also make Acrylic Gels, Mediums which can be used in non-toxic intaglio printmaking. They have one of the most useful internet sites which is well worth a visit at ;
http://www.goldenpaints.com/

DREMEL TOOLS are sold by most large hardware stores.

The **30 POWER POCKET MICROSCOPe** is available at most Radio Shack stores in North America. To locate a Radio Shack store nearest to your location check the following internet site; http://www.radioshack.com/locator/

ACETATE OR POLYESTER CLEAR FILM available from Daniel Smith Fine Art Materials. They have a very special Grafix Prepared Acetate which has a unimolecular structure which allows this clear sheet to hold water media drawn on its surface.

P.E.T.G. AND PLEXIGLAS PLATES, DRAFTING MYLAR AND CLEAR INKJET FILMS. One of the biggest suppliers in North America is Laird Plastics. They have a very good web site with a locator map, to show you the closest store to your locality along with comprehensive price list. **www.lairdplastics.com**

EXPOSURE SYSTEMS FOR THE INTAGLIO-TYPE
Olec equipment is available worldwide. For a complete listing of sales offices check out the following web site:**www.olec.com**
Further sales inquiries can be directed to;
Olec Corporation
17112 Armstrong Ave.
Irving
California 92614 U.S.A.
Phone; (714) 930-2500; Fax (714) 930-2501
Toll free (800) US-4-OLEC

PORTABLE EXPOSURE UNIT
LSM LTD.
10910 - 97 Ave.
Grande Prairie
Alberta Canada T8S 4C4
www.golsm.com
e-mail: dale@golsm.com

AIRBRUSH COMPRESSOR
The Badger Airbrush Company products are widely available throughout the world. They have a great web site at the following URL; **http://www.badgerairbrush.com/**
Badger Air-Brush Co.
9128 W. Belmont Ave.
Franklin Park, IL 60131
Phone (800)AIR-BRUSH; Local (847) 678-3104
Fax (847)671-4352
eMail: info@badgerairbrush.com

The **BADGER ACRYLIC AQUATINT SOLUTION FOR PRINTMAKERS** is supplied by most printmaking suppliers. If not ask your favorite printmaking supplier to supply this product.

GRAPHIC CHEMICAL RELIEF INK 1659 can be purchased from Graphic Chemical & Ink Co.; Toll free 1- 800-465-7382 See comprehensive listing on page 231, bottom left.

HEALTH AND SAFETY FOR PRINTMAKERS
One of the best health and safety resources in the world is;
Contact:
Arts, Craft and Theater Safety (ACTS)
181 Thompson S.,
#23 New York,
NY10012-2586
Phone: (212) 777-0062
eMail: ACTSNYC@cs.com
http:www.caseweb.com/ACTS

Sources of Supply

Information on
Keith Howard's Intaglio Video

TITLE:
Keith Howard's
Non-Toxic Intaglio
Instructional Video
SERIES ONE:
Using Du Pont's 'NEW'
ImagOn™ ULTRA
photopolymer film.

LENGTH:
1 hour 20 minutes

FORMAT:
VHS and PAL

COST:
For 1 VHS tape Plus 24 page Companion
Manual, US$33.95 plus shipping costs
of $4.05 Total Cost for one tape $38

VIDEO CONTENT:
Introduction -
2. Making a film Dispenser
3. Materials for Laminating ImagOn ULTRA to
   a Copper Plate.
4. Laminating a Copper Plate
5. Laminating a Small Copper Plate
6. Mixing ImagOn Ultra Film Developer
7. Toner Tusche Wash
8. Developing the Toner Tusche Plate
9. Printing the Toner Tusche Plate
10. Etched Intaglio-Type
11. Step Test for Etched Intaglio-Type.
12. Exposing Etched and Non-Etched Intaglio-
    Type Plates
13. Developing Etched Intaglio-Type Plates
14. Mezzo Intaglio-Type
15. Spit-Bite Intaglio-Type
16. Layered Intaglio-Type
17. Wrinkled Intaglio-Type
18. Clean-Up
19. Conclusion
20. Credits
Finish

ORDERING INFORMATION:

Send US$38 (make checks payable to Write-
Cross Press, with return address too:

Write-Cross Press
27 Lansdale St.
Rochester
NY 14620
USA

See Video Information at:

<WWW.KeithHoward.ORG>
or
<www.waterbasedinks.com>

Sources of Supply

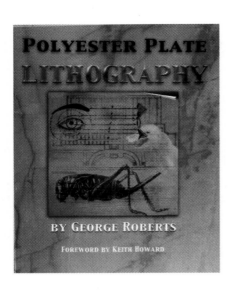

Polyester Plate Lithography
By George F. Roberts

ISBN 1-931041-41-5

More Information at:
www.nontoxic-printmaking.com

TRIBUTE TO THE LATE GEORGE F. ROBERTS

George Roberts was the pioneer of Polyester Plate Lithography. The above book describes fully his method in a sixty-three page text covering the following information:
Chapter
1. Introduction
2. Photolithography
3. Toner
3. Drawing Techniques
5. Wash Drawing Techniques
6. Resists
7. Printing
8. Color Printing
9. Clean Up
10. Polyester Plate Litho Materials
11. Trouble Shooting

This book is highly recommended by Keith Howard.

Available from:

1. Daniel Smith, 800-426-6740, USA.
2. Graphic Chemical, 800-465-7382, USA.
3. Takach Press Corp., 1-800248 3460, USA.
4. Renaissance Graphic Arts, 1-888-833-3398, USA.
5. Praga Industries, 1-800-844-9421, Canada.

Tribute Travelling Exhibition to George Roberts - Re: Imaging the Multiple

In 2001 George Roberts curated and organized a show of contemporary prints entitled, **Re:Imaging the Multiple,** which was first viewed at Boise State University. Since that time it has travelled to galleries in Utah, New York, Scotland and Spain. Re:Imaging the Multiple has now become a Travelling Tribute Exhibition to George Roberts and it will continue to travel the world for many decades.

This is a Dynamic and Incredible show comprising of 83 works of art. Every printmaker in the world would be interested in this exhibition. If you want to bring this exhibition of to your part of the world contact:
Keith Howard at kjhfaa@mail.rit.edu

Bibliography

PRINTMAKING JOURNALS IN ENGLISH

Printmaking Today
Chello Press Limited
Office 10-Spinners Court
55 West End, Witney
Oxon OX28 1NH United Kingdom
Phone:+ 44 -20 7739 8645; Fax: + 44 -19 9370 1992
eMail: mail@pt.cellopress.co.uk
www.printmakingtoday.co.uk
NB: I personally recommend Printmaking Today as a vital part of being 'Contemporary' as a Printmaker. It is one of the few magazines in the world that offers printmakers technical innovation and knowledge that can be applied to printmaking. Its the best. What else can I say! Its a great magazine and Great for Printmaking.

The **American Print Alliance** is a nonprofit consortium of printmakers' councils which publishes Contemporary Impressions, the international journal about prints, paper-works and book arts.
American Print Alliance
302 Larkspur Turn
Peachtree City, GA
30269-2210
U.S.A.
eMail: printalliance@mindspring.com
www.printalliance.org

ART ON PAPER -- MAGAZINE
Art on Paper
39 East 78th Street, Suite 501
New York, NY 10021
Phone: (800) 685-9777; Fax: (212) 988-6107
E-mail: info@artonpaper.com
www.artonpaper.com

PRINT WORKS ON-LINE PRINTMAKING MAGAZINE.
http://www.artmondo.net/printworks/index.html
Wonderful on-line resource for printmakers.

THE AUSTRALIAN PRINT COUNCIL published a high quality journal called **IMPRINT**; Subscription inquiries can be made by contacting;
The Print Council of Australia Inc.
The Meat Market
42 Courtney Street
Melbourne
VIC 3004 Australia
Phone: + 61 3 9328 8991; Fax: + 61 3 9328 8993

Email printcouncil@netspace.net.au
http://www.printcouncil.org.au/

GENERAL PRINTMAKING REFERENCE
The Complete Guide to Prints and Printmaking, Edited by John Dawson. New York: Excalibur Books, 1981.

Screenprinting: Water-Based Techniques, Henning Roni, New York: Watson-Guptill Publications 1991.

The Complete Printmaker, John Ross and Clare Romano. New York: The Free Press, 1972.

Innovative Printmaking, Thelma R. Newman. New York: Crown Publishers, Inc., 1977.

Intaglio Simultaneous Color Printmaking, N. Krishna Reddy. Albany, New York: State University of New York Press, 1988.

Photographic Printmaking Techniques, Deli Sacilotto. New York: Watson-Guptill Publications, 1982.

Printmaking: History and Process, Donald Saff and Deli Sacilotto. New York: Holt, Rinehart, Winston, 1978.

The Art of the Print, Eichenberg, Fritz, NY: Abrams 1976.

New Ways of Gravure, Hayter, Stanley William, London: Oxford University Press, 1966.

Prints and Visual Communication, Ivins, William M., London: M.I.T Press 5th Printing, May 1982.

Safe Photo Etching for Photographers and Artists, Howard, Keith John, Canada: Wynne Resources, 1991.

Mezzotint: History and Process, Wax, Carol, New York: Abrams.

Non-Toxic Intaglio Printmaking, Keith Howard, Printmaking Resources, Canada, 1998. (Out of Print)

Monotype: Mediums and Methods for Painterly Prints, Julia Ayres, 1991.

Printmaking in the Sun, Dan Weldon & Pauline Muir, 2001.

Silicone Intaglio Workbook, Nathan Kanofsky and Heather Arak-Kanofsky (spiral-bound, 88 pages, 1999).

Water-Based Inks: A Screen Printing Manual, Lois M. Johnson and Hester Stinnett (paperback, 38 pages, 1990)

Water-Based Screen Printing, Lynwood Kreneck (spiral-bound, 56 pages, 1988).

Wood Engraving Techniques on New Polymers, Richard J. Woodman (paperback, 25 pages, 1991).

Complete Etchings of Rembrandt, edited by Gary Schwartz.

Curatorial Care of Works of Art on Paper, Anne F. Clapp (paperback, 260 pages, 1996).

Handbook of Non-Toxic Intaglio Acrylic Resists Photopolymer film & Solar Plates by Henrik Boegh, 2003, web-site: www.grafiskeksperimentarium.dk

Keith Howard's Collectors Circle

Become part of an exclusive group of 50 Private Collectors world-wide who belong to the Keith Howard *Private Collectors Circle.* **All dealings within this Collectors Circle are directly with Keith Howard. There are no intermediaries. Private collectors get first choice on buying new art works.**

Keith Howard rarely produces editions larger than 50 prints with many edition sizes running between 2 and 20 prints depending on the nature of the plate and size of the image. Collectors discounted price will range from the least expensive works at $200 to the most expensive of $8000 as of 2003 pricing. Arts works are not limited to print and may include other media.

Members of the Keith Howard's Private Collectors Circle **will have first option to purchase his work at a 60% discount from the retail price.**

Collectors will have exclusive access to his *Private Collectors Circle* web page *where they can view recent works and other works for sale.* **This site will be password protected** and all collectors will be notified by eMail once a new edition of prints have been posted on this web site. Collectors then have the option to purchase the new work of art at the 60% discount rate. This will be done on a first come basis. Once all art works have been sold a 'sold out' a notice will be posted on the art work.

Shipping Works

Works purchased by Private Collectors will be immediately shipped to them through FedX. A shipping and handling charge of $25 per shipment will be charged. Where more than one work is shipped to the Collector there will be no additional charges. Collectors have two weeks to decide that they want the work. At any time during that 2 week period they wish to return the work they can, without question, with a handling charge of $50. Once the work has been returned a refund of the purchase price, less $50, will be sent to the Collector.

Eligibility to become a Collector

Anyone is eligible to become part of the Keith Howard's *Private Collectors Circle;* it is on a first come basis. Each collector will be assigned a number from 1-50. Once 50 collectors have been established then the *Private Collectors Circle* will be completed. No new members will be accepted until a member drops out of the circle, either by notification, or by lack of purchasing activity. If a work of art is not purchased within 11 months then that collector will be notified by email. If a work is not purchased during the 12th month then that collector will be dropped from the circle and the first name on the waiting list will be notified. It does not matter how many works a Collector has purchased in one year, lack of purchasing activity in any consecutive 12 month period will mean a drop from the Collectors Circle.

Become a Member of the Keith Howard's *Private Collectors Circle*

To become a *Private Collector* you must purchase one work from the available selection (minimum of 10 new editions will be created each year) with the promise to purchase one additional work every 12 months. As of 2003 *Private Collectors* have a choice of prices on art works from $200 - $8000. There is no written contact. There is no limit to the number of works that can be purchased. There are no additional discounts for bulk purchase of editions.

Contact Keith Howard by eMail and request a temporary password to access the *Private Collectors* web page.
   KeithHoward@KeithHoward.org
Once the 50 member *Private Collectors Circle* has been reached no outside access will be allowed to the Private Collectors Circle web page.

Once a prospective member has gained access to the web page they have a period of 2 weeks in which they can choose to become a member. Their membership is secured once a work of art is purchased and they are assigned a membership number.